The
Northampto
Village B

THE VILLAGES OF BRITAIN SERIES

Other counties in this series include

Avon*
Bedfordshire*
Berkshire*
Buckinghamshire*
Cambridgeshire*
Dorset
Essex*
Gloucestershire*
Hampshire
Herefordshire*
Hertfordshire*
Kent
Leicestershire
  and Rutland*
Middlesex*

Nottinghamshire*
Oxfordshire
Powys Montgomery*
Shropshire*
Somerset*
Staffordshire*
Suffolk
Surrey
East Sussex
West Sussex
Warwickshire*
West Midlands*
Wiltshire
Worcestershire*

*Published in conjunction with County
Federations of Women's Institutes

The Northamptonshire Village Book

Compiled by the Northamptonshire
Federation of Women's Institutes from notes
and illustrations sent by Institutes in the County

Published jointly by
Countryside Books, Newbury
and the NFWI, Northampton

ISBN 185306 0550
Cover Photograph of Mears Ashby
taken by Norma Pearson

Produced through MRM Associates, Reading
Typeset by Acorn Bookwork, Salisbury
Printed in England by J. W. Arrowsmith Ltd., Bristol

Foreword

Northamptonshire is often described as the County of spires, squires and forests, and this beautiful English shire of 998 square miles with mellow stone houses is steeped in history. Great historical events took place here, notably the Battle of Naseby. It is not difficult to imagine the Cavaliers charging recklessly over this terrain. Rockingham Castle was used as a hunting lodge for King John, and in the Civil War Rockingham received a heavy bombardment from the artillery of Fairfax.

The traveller will delight in visiting such houses as Althorp, set in a large estate and owned by Earl Spencer; also Castle Ashby, Deene, Boughton House, and Easton Neston which lies not far from the Grand Union Canal. On the Canal and well worth a visit is the Blisworth tunnel which runs for 2,900 yards underground. Squire Sir Henry Dryden, resided at the House of Canons Ashby, while the 16th century Manor at Sulgrave was the early home of the ancestors of George Washington. It was sold by Henry VIII in 1539 to Lawrence Washington, who built the present Manor House. The Saxon Churches of Brixworth, Earls Barton and Brigstock are famous.

The wealth contained in the fertile soil and the underlying stone makes the County a desirable place for landowners. The sand and gravel deposits in the valley of the River Nene have been removed in large quantities to help in the building of the thousands of houses in the huge expansion of Northampton over the past decade. In the past the County's main industry was the manufacture of boots and shoes but this has been hard hit in recent years. However, Northamptonshire is considered to still produce the best footwear in the country. The facts mentioned in this book, along with many other local memories and tales, will be an indispensable guide to our County life. We hope all who read our book will share a rich reward and gain enjoyment from it.

Caroline Raven
Federation Chairman

Acknowledgements

The Northamptonshire Federation wishes to thank all the Institutes whose members have worked so hard, with others, to provide information about their villages.

Our thanks also to Alan Powell, a Braunston member's husband, for the series of drawings. Finally, we extend a special thank-you to Sue Bird, the co-ordinator of the project.

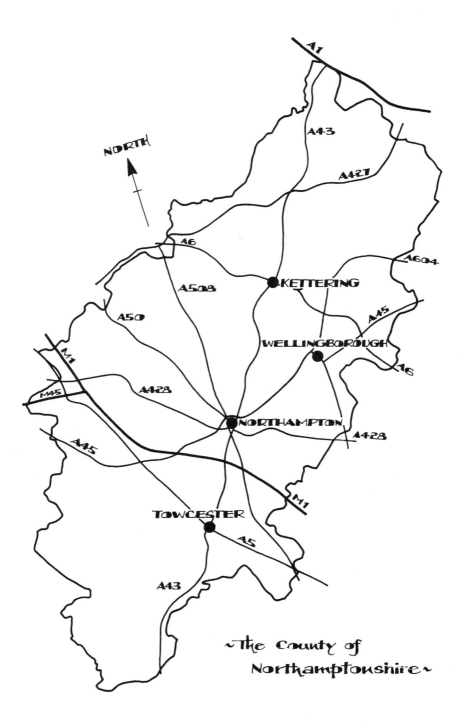

Blisworth village

Abthorpe

The village of Abthorpe stands three miles south-west of Towcester and, until the early 1920s, most of it was owned by the Duke of Grafton.

The links with the Grafton family were strong: the Grafton Hunt met on the village green and in 1871, the Duke contributed much of the £2,500 required for the rebuilding of St John the Baptist church. The church is a modern adaptation of Early English and Decorated styles. Abthorpe was originally a chapelry dependent on the vicarage of Towcester, from which it was separated in 1736 by Act of Parliament and constituted a distinct parish.

The village at one time supported two pubs, two shops, a blacksmith and a wheelwright. Of them all, just one pub – The New Inn – now remains.

Village employment centred around two businesses – making pillow lace for a Leicestershire buyer and doing 'outwork' for the local shoe factory. The factory building is still in business use, but now the products are not shoes but radiators for vintage motor cars.

Many orphans will have fond memories of Abthorpe. A headmaster resident in the village was a keen supporter of Dr Barnardo and encouraged his neighbours to take in children from Dr Barnardo's Homes.

The generosity of a 17th century benefactress is still remembered today, as villagers gather in the village hall on social occasions. In 1646, Mrs Jane Leeson bequeathed to the poor in her will certain property in Abthorpe and other villages, which produced £31 annually. She also built the school in Abthorpe and endowed it with £8 a year. The school closed in 1959, but is now used as a village hall.

The Abthorpe Feast Day – the second Sunday in July – was always a time for great merrymaking on the village green. Children took eggs and flowers to church and chapel and these were then donated to Northampton hospital. The village green is still the setting for Feast Day celebrations, although the day has now been brought forward two weeks, in accordance with the new Church calendar.

Aldwincle

Aldwincle, mentioned in the Domesday Book as Eldwincle, was probably so named from the Saxon word 'wincel', meaning bend or corner. The river Nene has a great double bend between Thorpe Waterville and Wadenhoe and it is here Aldwincle is situated.

Gathering to itself the calm and beauty of the valley, stands All Saints' church, now redundant. There is a brass to William Aldewynkle, dated 1463, in the chancel floor. Its 15th century tower has carved heads and figures, while its 13th century interior has fine proportions of space and arch, emphasised by the lack of furniture, making it a perfect setting for exhibitions, fund raising and plays.

The houses in Aldwincle are varied in style, with grey stone and red brick predominating. Here and there are cottages handsomely thatched by the local thatcher, who lives in the village. Others are slated or pantiled. Many are graced with climbing roses, wisteria, clematis and forsythia.

Watching over it all is St Peter's church, dating from the 12th century and with many interesting features. It is reputed to have one of the best broach spires in the county, topped by a gleaming weathercock.

The Baptist church, opened in 1823, offers a warm welcome and, combined with church, school, shop and societies, seeks to make the village a friendly place in which to live.

Twelve red may trees and most of the village seats were provided by the Spendlove family. Old villagers remember the 'Tommy loaf' and the coal charities. Twelve loaves for widows were baked in the bakehouse, which still exists as a building. The loaf and coal charities, because of shortages during the Second World War, were incorporated as money in the Green charity which exists today, giving money each year to those who apply and are considered suitable recipients. The money originally came from rent for land near the village but eventually the land was sold and the money invested to continue the charity for the 'poor, needy and thrifty'.

John Dryden, the poet and playwright, was born at the rectory opposite All Saints' church in 1631 and was christened there. Thomas Fuller, divine and historian, was born in the rectory of St Peter's in 1608. The rectory was pulled down circa 1790, but it stood in today's Rectory Field. When Fuller was curate at St Benet's Cambridge, he buried Thomas Hobson, the carrier, who used to hire out horses. Anyone hiring a horse could not choose their animal but had to have the horse nearest the stable door! The term 'Hobson's choice' exists today, meaning no choice at all!

Apethorpe

The village of Apethorpe, which lies on the road between King's Cliffe and Woodnewton, is mentioned in the Domesday Book, and the famous Hall was built by Sir Walter Mildmay in the 16th century, when he was lord of the manor. It is now in private ownership and is not open to the public, but the attractive facade can be seen from the road between Apethorpe and Woodnewton.

The village was originally all part of the manorial estate – the present lord of the manor being Lord Brassey. Some of the houses are now in freehold ownership, but the names of houses such as 'Dairy Cottage', 'The Keeper's House', 'Laundry Cottage' and 'The Old Post Office', all give an idea of the original village. There has been some modern building and conversion of old farm buildings into dwelling houses, but they are designed to blend with the old – of local stone, built at various times between the 16th century and the present day, with roofs of thatch or Collyweston slate.

The stream which flows through the village, the Willow Brook (called by locals, 'The Willy Brook'), is a tributary of the river Nene, and passes under a picturesque hump-back bridge, flanked by thatched cottages which lead towards the church.

There is evidence of a church building dating back to the 12th century, but the present church of St Leonard celebrated its 500th anniversary in the 1980s. To mark the occasion, the ladies of the village made needle-work hassocks, which can be seen in the church. Although the adult population numbers no more than 120, there are more than 60 hassocks, every one different.

The Mildmay Chapel was built on to the church in 1621 as a memorial to Sir Anthony Mildmay and his wife, Lady Grace, whose effigies lie on the sarcophagus. The stained glass window in the chapel is of very fine workmanship.

Opposite the church are the original stocks and whipping post used to chastise offenders!

There is a village school which has been in continuous use since 1846 and provides education for four to nine year olds. The inhabitants of the village gather in the school for fund-raising events, and many of them help the children with cooking, sewing etc, to maintain the true village atmosphere of education within the community.

The only pub, The King's Head, was built at the turn of the 20th century, when an older one was demolished, but has been refurbished.

Surrounded by arable farmland, this small village is a haven of peaceful, rural England.

Arthingworth

Arthingworth is located a mile and a half off the A508 Northampton – Market Harborough road; with Kelmarsh to the west and Harrington to the east. Approaching the village along the winding lane from Kelmarsh, Arthingworth Lodge stands on the left, one of the five farms in the parish.

The oldest building is St Andrew's church, dating from the 12th century. The rectory was sold some years ago and since then there has not been a resident rector. There has long been a manor house and the present manor would appear to be the fourth building on the site. The first was moated, and part of the moat, by the present Lodge House, is still apparent. There were three farmhouses in the village itself, Glebe Farm (opposite the public house), Church Farm and Home Farm. These three houses, together with Bosworth House, The Old Rectory, Sunny

Bank, and a few other occupied dwellings are all that remain of pre-1940s Arthingworth.

The 1851 census indicates that 257 people lived here. As would be expected they were largely employed either in agriculture or in 'service', although there were 17 ladies employed in making lace. By 1861 the population had grown to 273 with the rector, Henry Rokeby, at the manor house and the recently installed Captain Charles Cust, JP at Arthingworth Hall. The lace-making trade had declined, employing only eight people, but the railway had arrived together with Mr James King and two railway labourers. The trains ceased to operate on this line after 123 years service, in August 1981.

From the few older dwellings still in use it would seem that the village was a poor place in which to live, lacking the substantial stone cottages which exist in surrounding villages. It is recorded that in the comparatively recent past a number of the cottages had mud walls and thatched roofs.

Pre-1940 housing was largely concentrated on Sunny Bank, in Kelmarsh Road, where in the early 1920s the rent of a cottage was one shilling per week, and in Long Row and Short Row, which were off the lower end of Oxendon Road. Much has been demolished since the Second World War. The new houses may not be as picturesque as the earlier cottages but they are infinitely more comfortable, with conditions and amenities that our predecessors could have barely imagined. The population seems to have declined over the past few years to an estimated figure of around 210.

One of Arthingworth's only claims to fame was the Waterloo Run, when in 1866 the Pytchley hounds ran from Arthingworth to Keythorpe (in Leicestershire), an 18 mile chase, lasting three hours and 45 minutes.

Ashby St Ledgers

The village is tucked into the north-western corner of the county, almost into Warwickshire. If you are arriving via the busy A5, signposts state that it is a 'gated road', but there are now no gates. It is as well to travel carefully though, to avoid the odd wandering pheasant or rabbit, and the roads are not always wide enough for vehicles to pass easily.

The Domesday Book entry gives the place name Ascebi (ash tree settlement). 'St Ledgers' is a corruption of the name of St Leodegarius, the patron saint of the church, which stands at the east end of the village beside the manor house. Both buildings are of ancient foundation.

The manor was gifted to Hugh de Grentemaisnil by William the Conqueror and passed to various other occupants until about 1375 when it became the principal residence of the Catesby family and remained so

The Gunpowder Plotter's Room, Ashby St Ledgers

for nearly 250 years. William Catesby was one of the favourites of Richard III. After the defeat of Richard by Henry Tudor at the battle of Bosworth in 1485, William was beheaded. A Robert Catesby later became one of the leading figures in the Gunpowder Plot, and the half-timbered gatehouse next to the church is reputed to be the meeting place used by the conspirators.

There are memorials to the Catesbys in the church, along with several other fine brasses and monuments. During the Reformation, unfortunately, the wall paintings here were defaced and the rood destroyed, but the remaining rood screen is still magnificent and some of the wall paintings have now been uncovered. There is a rare Jacobean three-decker pulpit.

Early this century the manor became the property of Ivor Churchill Guest, 1st Viscount Wimborne, Lord Lieutenant of Ireland, who employed the architect Sir Edwin Lutyens to remodel some of the manor house, and to design the row of thatched cottages which stand on the north side of the main street. Also on the north side stands what was an imposing gateway, now somewhat decrepit, giving a view through an avenue of trees, formerly a carriage drive to the manor house.

After these historic events, the village now presents a very peaceful and attractive appearance, especially in springtime when the wide verges are flowering with daffodils, almond and cherry blossom. On the south side of the main street near the A361 exit, stands The Coachhouse inn and post office. There is a recreation ground for the children of the village. The old schoolhouse still stands and has been converted into a dwelling, and the village hall is a thatched stone building, once a barn. In recent years some of the older buildings which had fallen into disuse have been restored and converted into dwellings, but care has been taken to conserve the rural atmosphere.

Ashley

The village of Ashley is situated on the border with Leicestershire, and settlement here probably dates back to Roman times, since many relics were discovered not far from the village during the construction of the railway in the 19th century. Ashley station and the railway line were closed in the 1950s.

The church of St Mary the Virgin occupies a prominent position on the north side of the village and is built of warm brown ironstone and silver grey limestone. The interior is a resplendent blaze of colour since it was restored by the Rev Pulteney who paid for all the alterations himself, under the direction of the architect Gilbert Scott. Not only was he vicar from 1853 to 1874 but he was also the village squire and the stained glass window was dedicated to his memory. He also installed the organ in 1868 and built the village school (opposite the church) in 1858. This was used by local children until 1966, when they transferred to Wilbarston primary school.

The rectory, now a private house, stands adjacent to the former school and the village does not have a resident vicar any more. Prior to 1919 the house known as Ashley Court, built in 1650, provided accommodation for the rector of Ashley.

The manor house situated to the north of the church, in Hall Lane, contains a room previously known as the Court Room, where the lord of the manor used to collect his dues at regular intervals during the year.

The Welland valley has always been mainly an agricultural area and it must have been thirsty work because at one time the village supported five inns! The George is now the only one that remains and can be found in the main street opposite to where the village blacksmith had his forge.

Fifty years ago Ashley was a very different place from today. The beer for The George was brought up from the cellar in jugs and 'Devil among the tailors' and table skittles were popular games, with darts just being introduced. There was a village cricket team that was very well known in the district and bread and cakes were baked by the village baker. Milk, creamy and thick, came straight from the farm. All this now no longer exists. The local bus service was very good and the railway enabled villagers to be mobile, but most of the youngsters cycled or walked. They attended the surrounding village dances where all the families knew each other, having lived in the same villages for generations. The Fat Stock Show at Market Harborough was one of the highlights of the year.

The village hall, built in the 1950s, provides a focus and venue for village events. Ashley villagers take a great pride in their community and have opened their gardens to the public on several occasions.

Aston-le-Walls & Appletree

Situated on the borders of Warwickshire and Oxfordshire, the village is unusual in having two churches, but no pub! The Protestant church of St Leonards was built in 1240 and the Catholic church in 1827. The font in St Leonards is Norman. The church was restored in 1875, when the south aisle porch was rebuilt and the chancel restored at a cost of £400. The Catholic church was built by the Plowden family who owned the Aston-le-Walls Estate up until 1920 except for the Rectory and Rectory Farm.

William Francis Plowden's estate consisted of four farms. When the estate was broken up in 1920 the tenant farmers were able to purchase their farms. The villagers bought their cottages, one little cottage only costing £50!

The whole area including Appletree is 1,270 acres. The population has doubled in the last century. In 1881 it was 101; today it is 244.

Right up until the 1960s water for the village was supplied to nearly all the houses from a spring on Hall Farm. The cottages paid 2/6 rent per annum, the school 10 shillings. When mains water was finally brought to Aston the village was not allowed to have the spring water any more.

The Welsh Lane runs from east to north at the bottom of the village. This lane was used in the past for the drovers to take their cattle to and from Wales, with lots of noted resting places on the way.

The village school was nearly closed just after the Second World War as there were not enough pupils. Today the authorities run a coach to pick up the children from surrounding villages, so they can keep their numbers up.

There is a charity in the village. The interest of a bequest of £75 is divided amongst the poor annually on Good Friday together with the proceeds of the two acres of land situated within the parish known as 'Nibble & Clink'.

Aynho

Aynho has a recorded existence back to the time of Edward the Confessor, although the spelling of the name has changed over the centuries. Nearly all the buildings in the old part of the village are of local limestone and most were originally thatched. Many have been reroofed in slate or tile and, slates needing a less steep pitch than thatch, it can be seen how the walls were raised to create extra room inside. The oldest cottages in the village, formerly known as Pintle Row, are on Blacksmiths Hill. One has a 60ft well in the front garden and is dated c1500.

The Cartwright Arms, an old coaching inn, was named after the family who were the squires of the village from 1616 to the 1950s. The original manor house was burnt down during the Civil War by Royalist troops retreating from the battle of Naseby. Charles II paid the family compensation after his restoration to the throne and Park House was restored in 1680. A tragic car accident in 1954 killed the squire and his son, and the estate has now been broken up and is in private hands.

The church of St Michael and All Angels is built of limestone and the tower is 14th century. Severe damage was caused to the church during the Civil War and the main body was demolished in 1723, then rebuilt in the Grecian style. Outside is the old preaching cross.

From the churchyard can be seen the old icehouse in the grounds of Aynho Park, which was used to store ice in the days before refrigeration. Lumps of ice cut from the canal would keep for up to two years when packed with straw in its depths.

The village hall was built in 1920 from stones taken from the ruined plaguehouse in Pesthouse Wood. Plague victims were once isolated there and villagers would leave them food every day at the boundary fence. There are many other interesting buildings in the village, including the Jacobean grammar school and the almshouses built in 1822 with a bequest from John Baker, an Oxford glazier.

There are still some examples to be seen of the famous apricot trees, grown against the side of cottages. They were traditionally on high rootstocks to prevent children from picking the apricots. It is thought that the fruit was given to the Park House as part payment of the rent for the cottage.

Badby & Fawsley

Badby and Fawsley are joined by woods and parkland and lie at the extreme end of the Cotswolds. They are situated four miles west of Weedon on the Daventry to Banbury road. Fawsley is renowned for its centuries-old connection with the Knightley family and Badby has been described as one of the prettiest villages in the county. Its 180 acre wood is well known for its bluebells but is even more notable for its carpets of wood anemones. The wood is now incorporated in the Park of Fawsley and is surrounded by rolling farmland, which has long been hunted over by the Pytchley and Grafton huntsmen.

One of the county's famous earthworks is Arbury Hill, half a mile north-west of the village and the highest point in the county. Standing on a 24 acre site at the top of this hill is the remains of a probable Roman settlement, as well as a Saxon camp. Though only a bare 735 ft high it nevertheless has wonderful views of the surrounding countryside. On a clear day the Malvern Hills are visible.

Badby has a long and varied history, first being mentioned in AD 833. The Abbot of Evesham had oversight of the populace until the Dissolution of the Monasteries, after which the manor passed to Sir Edmund Knightley. Thereafter much of the employment in the village was connected with the estate in one form or another. There were various gatehouses on the perimeter of the estate, and one of these, known as the Arch, was occupied until 1890. It is on Long Roods by the cricket and football pitches.

Both Fawsley and Badby have very distinctive medieval churches dedicated to the Virgin Mary. There are two shops (one of them the post office) and two public houses. Three new housing developments have been integrated into the existing village since the 1950s. Along with this infilling it is good to see several of the older properties being restored, with thatched roofs again. Fawsley has also seen development and revitalisation, and from being almost a 'lost' village is now a thriving community.

Badby seems to have been known as a friendly village for as long as anyone can remember. This perhaps is partly due to the fact that a lot of the villagers brought up children from Dr Barnardo's Homes. They grew up happily in their adoptive families, added a lot to the community and often married and settled down in the village. And, of course, during the Second World War Badby had its quota of evacuees, who were also made to feel welcome. Even today newcomers feel they have been here forever!

The village is lucky to have a very good Youth Hostel which is a splendid base from which to discover the footpaths and walks in the area. The Knightley Way from Badby to Greens Norton starts right opposite the church and many ramblers come to enjoy the delights of the countryside.

Barby

Barby lies between Rugby and Daventry on Northamptonshire's border with Warwickshire. It is on high ground, overlooking the Warwickshire plain to the north and west. Remains of a substantial medieval motte and

Cottages at Barby

bailey can still be seen at Castle Mound to the north of the village, but recent excavations have established it was originally a Roman site.

The church, dedicated to St Mary, dates from the 13th century, its earliest known rector being appointed in 1230. The tower, although not very high, can be seen from every approach to the village, and is decorated at the top with a row of carved heads which must surely portray past local worthies, they are so lifelike!

The Grand Union Canal skirts Barby's hill on its way from Braunston to Hillmorton, and the M45 motorway also passes through the parish, but both are well away from the village centre. The village is mentioned in *Tom Brown's Schooldays* of 1832 in connection with the Barby Run – 'everyone who comes in within a quarter of an hour of the hares'll be counted if he has been round Barby church' – and this event still takes place from Rugby School via Barby and back to Rugby, but no longer round the church!

A local ghost story relates how a Mrs Webb died in 1851 and left everything to her nephew, Mr Hart. He let her cottage to a family whose daughter was terrified several nights in a row by an old woman who came and stood by her bed pointing to the trapdoor into the roof. On being told of this, the nephew decided to investigate the loft, and discovered a bag of gold coins and papers relating to debts owed by his aunt. After the debts were settled, the apparition was seen no more.

In the past agriculture provided the main occupation although many men carried on other trades as well, weaving being particularly important in the 18th century. The population varied little between 1820 and 1920, averaging between 600 and 800 people, but by the 1950s it was declining as the young people left to seek work in the towns. However the motor car and the building boom of the 1960s revived the dwindling numbers, and in 1967 a new school was built at the southern end of the village.

In 1971 the new village hall was opened, built on to the old school. There are several shops, a garage, post office and garden centre, a public house – the Arnold Arms, – named after a former lord of the manor, also some light industry, some of which is home-based such as the pottery and a leather shop. Perhaps the most interesting development came in the 1960s from the owner of Arnold House, Mr Owen MacLaren, a retired engineer. He designed the original lightweight Baby Buggy folding push-chair, developing his business in the outbuildings at his house. In time the firm grew and moved to larger premises in Long Buckby, and today the MacLaren products are known world-wide.

Anyone visiting the village sees a variety of houses, a few dating from the 17th century, the most attractive being those built of cob or mellow Northamptonshire stone. Only two retain their thatched roofs. Some 19th century houses are of brick, no doubt produced from the local clay or transported by the canal, and at least two are built from the bricks made for the great railway tunnel at nearby Kilsby, which Robert Stephenson supervised during the construction of the railway to London.

Barnwell

For a village with a population of 350, Barnwell has a lot to offer. The oldest cottages are built of local stone, and many still have thatch or Collyweston roofs. Recent planning policy has tried to ensure that new houses blend with their surroundings, and the brook, with its wooden footbridges, that runs along the centre of the main street has attracted many painters and photographers. A colony of ducks inhabits the brook, and the mature lime trees along its banks are particularly lovely in autumn.

The manor house at the north end of the village is the country home of the Duke and Duchess of Gloucester, and its gardens are opened to the public two or three times a year. Within the gardens are the handsome ruins of a 13th century castle, built for Berengarius le Moine, and haunted, so some have claimed, by a monk brandishing a whip!

A pretty stone bridge opposite the side entrance to the manor leads to a beech-lined footpath to St Andrew's church, with its carefully tended graveyard. The church dates back to the late 13th century, and among the carved flowers and leaves that decorate the north doorway is a face with its tongue sticking out. This is a medieval 'Jack-in-the-green', relating to a May Day custom when young men camouflaged themselves in leaves before flirting with the girls.

The Reverend Nicholas Latham, who died in 1620, has an elaborate monument near the altar, and it was he who originally endowed the almshouses that are situated opposite the church, next to the school. Nicholas Latham also endowed the village's first school – now a private dwelling called Tudor House in the main street – and the present flourishing primary school contains a stone taken from it, with the inscription: 'Instruct Me O Lord That I May Kepe Thy Lawes'.

At the bottom of the hill past the church is the village green with its tall cluster of lime trees, and a stone bridge that leads over to the Montagu Arms. Part of the pub building dates back to the 18th century, and it is a properly traditional country inn.

A long time ago, Barnwell was divided into two parishes, St Andrew's and All Saints, and part of the church of All Saints, its chancel, stands on a rise beside the lower end of the main street. The rest of the church was demolished in 1825 after falling into a bad state of repair, but the chancel was saved because it housed the family vault of the Montagu family, Earls of Sandwich. It is still used for occasional worship, and has a very peaceful graveyard, with a lovely view – especially at sunset – over the fields behind. Near the entrance is an ancient gravestone carved in the image of a monk, and it is this monk who is said to haunt the All Saints end of Barnwell.

Barton Seagrave

Barton Seagrave has a charm of its own. Retaining an old world village atmosphere, it still enjoys the benefits of the town of Kettering barely two miles away.

In the 14th century there was a castle at Barton Seagrave ruled over by Lord Segrave (spelled without the 'a'), and he is the subject of a popular local ghost story. Segrave fell violently in love with the beautiful Lady Isabel, daughter of Lord Latimer of Burton Latimer. Alas, Isabel was already betrothed to Hugh Neville. Segrave ranted and raged and at last captured Isabel and imprisoned her in the rat-infested dungeons beneath the castle, but she still refused his advances.

Hugh Neville and her brother rescued her one night and had reached the ford of the Ise, when they heard Segrave galloping after them. They fought mid-stream in a terrific thunderstorm and Neville was killed and both Isabel and her brother were drowned. Isabel haunted Segrave to his death. The beautiful Lady Isabel still skims like a filmy white swan over the river Ise.

Barton Hall, now a home for the elderly, is reputed to have been built from stones from the castle in the reign of Queen Elizabeth I. In 1665 the house was given as a wedding present to his daughter by William Trumbell on her marriage to John Bridges. Their son, Northamptonshire's famous historian, was born at the Hall in 1666 – his memorial is displayed inside the church.

Polwell Lane was named after a communal well (with the pole now missing) which you can see in the post office garden. This used to be called Polewell Lane but now the 'e' has been taken off the signposts. Surely the old Bartonian Pole Well was more attractive than the bald Polwell!

The tithe barn next to the church was used for the storage of flax, crops, hops and saffron in the 17th century. It was dilapidated when the owners bought it in 1967 but now it is a most attractive home. Mullion dressed stone was found in the rebuilding, possibly from the castle.

Benefield ❧

The village lies between Oundle and Corby, about four miles each way. In Upper Benefield is the Wheatsheaf Inn and the village shop, while Lower Benefield has the post office and the church of St Mary.

One villager remembers life in Benefield at the beginning of the 20th century. 'The school was in the Lower and we walked the mile there and back – which meant four miles during the day. There were three teachers and about 50 pupils. May Day was always kept and we carried a garland of flowers round both villages singing the May songs, collecting money for a tea. What money was left over was divided between us, after which we danced with music provided by one of the villagers who played a fiddle.

'The next event was harvest holiday. After the corn was cut and stooked it was time for gleaning and picking up the loose grains, which were used for cattle food. The corn was threshed and ground into flour for the winter.

'During the First World War we had searchlights around the village, which we watched as we walked to school in the evenings for concert practices. The concerts raised money to make things from wool – socks and gloves – and were great fun to do. We did more during the Second World War when we had American airmen in camps around the village. The airmen were very good to the village and gave many parties and presents.'

The village has completely changed now. The volume of traffic has increased considerably, but the planes still fly over – now new fast fighters. On the agricultural scene, pastures have given way to cereal production, which has meant the demise of the associated flora and fauna.

On a mound surrounded by a moat near the west of the church is the site of Benefield Castle, and in the fields opposite are the 'swallow holes' through which, when the land floods, the water flows into the brook between the two Benefields. This can cause flooding to the lower part of the village and near here there was a pumping house which pumped drinking water into reservoirs and supplied the village. Houses have now been built on this site and on the site of the American base.

Blakesley cum Woodend

Blakesley is a picturesque village, situated roughly midway between Northampton and Banbury, five miles west of Towcester. The area of the combined parishes is 3,940 acres and the population at the 1981 census was 611. In Saxon times Blakesley was surrounded by Whittlebury Forest, hence Woodend.

The Hall, which stood on the south (Woodend) side of the brook, was formerly a hospice of the Knights of St John of Jerusalem. The last lord of the manor was Mr C. W. Bartholomew (1875–1919) who, during his residence was a generous benefactor to the village. After standing empty for several years the Hall was, sadly, demolished in 1957.

One of the many novel innovations brought to Blakesley by Mr Bartholomew was a 15″ gauge railway. The track, which ran between the Hall and the main-line station was laid down in 1903. Two American steam locomotives were used to pull the train of open carriages and in 1909 a petrol-driven locomotive, built by the well-known Northampton firm of Bassett-Lowke was added to the rolling stock and given the name Blacolvesley. In 1939/40 the whole outfit was taken to Yorkshire. Blacolvesley is still running and one of the American locomotives is in a Norfolk museum.

A grammar school for boys was endowed by William Foxley in 1669, but lost its grammar school status in 1850. In 1876 a girls school was built and in 1912 the boys school was enlarged to accommodate children of both sexes. In view of the generosity of the Squire, as Mr Bartholomew was known locally, by largely subscribing to the cost of the new school, the deeds of the now redundant girls school were made over to him, and he in turn presented the building to the village for use as a village hall.

In the early part of this century the village supported a resident doctor, a village policeman, a builder, two wheelwright/undertakers, two blacksmiths, four public houses and an outdoor beerhouse. All that remains today is one public house, the Bartholomew Arms, previously known as the Red Lion. There were also three or four cobblers.

Blakesley Show, inaugurated in about 1873, is renowned throughout the farming and hunting fraternity as one of the best village shows in the country.

In 1895, Mr Bartholomew encouraged the formation of a village band. A Mr Joseph Rogers of Northampton trained a group of local men and by the time Mr Frank Brown took over as conductor they were able to enter, at first local, and later national contests with considerable success. The band flourished until the outbreak of the Second World War in 1939 when it was disbanded and has never been re-formed.

Blisworth 🦢

Blisworth (or Blidesworde as it was recorded in the Domesday Book) lies snugly on the A43 between Towcester and Northampton, surrounded by pleasant open farmland.

It still retains much of its historical charm with many of the thatched cottages dating back to the 16th century. One house, at the bottom of Courteenhall Road has a room still known today as the 'Brethren Room', although it is now the main living room. On one of the walls is a fine example of early wall painting, a panel approximately 4ft by 2ft depicting the words of Psalm 143. Many of the houses are built of Blisworth ironstone together with Northampton sandstone, and the variation of light and dark materials is an interesting feature throughout the village. Blisworth ironstone was the first to be quarried in the county.

Blisworth is in the centre of the county and could have developed into a much larger community. In the 17th century it became the main stop-over for coaches from Cheltenham and Stratford, and the Grafton Arms, which today is a private house, standing opposite the mill, was a well known roadside inn. During the 18th century with the coming of the Grand Junction Canal, Blisworth again was the most convenient place for the loading and unloading of boats from London, Midlands and the North. However, Blisworth Hill was an obstacle for the canal engineers and whilst a tunnel was constructed to take the canal through the hill, the Blisworth Hill Railway was built to carry boats' cargoes *over* the hill.

The railway was opened in 1800 and ran until 1805 when the tunnel was opened – a tremendous feat of engineering. The contractor who excavated it was Barnes of Banbury, a man who could neither read nor write and who carried all his calculations and estimates in his head! Blisworth Tunnel is today the longest navigable canal tunnel in the country (3075 yds long) and it is a great challenge to today's holiday boaters, who of course use Blisworth as a convenient stop-over for shopping or for refreshment at the Royal Oak, now the only public house in the village. The once well known inn Sun, Moon & Stars, is today derelict.

After the canals came the railways and in 1838 another first for Blisworth when the London-Birmingham main line built a station here. With the coming of the railways the Blisworth Hotel was built and its Pleasure Gardens attracted many travellers with their new 'excursion tickets'. Entertainment was provided by hot air balloons rising from the gardens, and by famous music hall stars and actors and actresses from London theatres. Blisworth station was closed in the 1960s and today the hotel alone remains, the once Pleasure Gardens are now a mobile home park.

Today Blisworth has still just under 2,000 inhabitants, and the new-comers in their new houses live happily alongside the older families in their thatched cottages. The motor car has meant the loss of a local butcher, baker and cobbler, but there is still a post office and village shop, a thriving school, and many local associations make use of the village hall.

Boddington

The parish of Boddington is recorded in the Domesday Book as 'Botendon'.

The medieval church is mainly 15th century but has examples of 13th century work and some interesting external features. Its churchyard, while not exceptionally rich in wild flowers, is known for its 80 species of lichens including one county rarity. The church registers date from 1558, when the manor and estate came into the Spencer family, but much of the land had been sold when both Upper and Lower Boddington were enclosed 200 years later. A copy of the Enclosure Map of 1759, unfortunately for Upper Boddington only, has been found in the church.

Most of the parish is still the traditional 'patchwork' landscape. Hedgerows are therefore a significant feature, particularly in May when the cuckoos call and hawthorn is in blossom. The rarer midland thorn, a woodland species, grows in many of the pre-enclosure hedges as do those other indicators of ancient hedges: hazel, dogwood and field maple. Two especially rich hedgerows border the road east from Upper Boddington. At its junction with the Welsh Road, an old drove road for cattle from Wales going to market in London, sweets could once be bought from a woman reputed to live in a hollow tree called Nannie's Hole!

The villages themselves hold much of interest, with 29 listed buildings, the oldest thought to date from the 15th century. Since the 1960s the villages have altered greatly owing to infilling, building which still continues at an increasing rate.

Despite these changes, Boddington remains a peaceful yet lively community. Both villages have a pub with darts and skittles teams but unfortunately only the upper village has retained its post office and shop. The school, supported by a vigorous PTA, is bursting at the seams while both church and chapel maintain an active presence. There is a large village hall, much improved thanks to massive voluntary fundraising, and the Cowper Field which is used for sport and recreation. The Lapworth Charity provides coal for needy villagers from the rental of a field set aside for 'the poor' since the enclosures.

From 32 pre-war farms, all milking, the number has fallen to twelve with only two now producing milk, yet a significant proportion of the population of 640 still works in agriculture. Small businesses have replaced the many craftsmen of a hundred years ago. While these provide additional local employment, many people commute to towns such as Banbury which, although in Oxfordshire, remains the centre of influence.

Boughton 🖋️

Boughton is a tiny Cotswold-like village, three miles north of Northampton off the Harborough road.

The village was first situated on the edge of the triangular-shaped field known as Boughton Green, near the remains (still consecrated) of the old parish church of St John the Baptist. It is said that after the Black Death, the villagers moved to the present village site, then a hamlet built by the local landowner outside the gates of his manor.

The site of the old smithy was at the far end of the green in Butcher's Lane, and the recently closed post office and shop in Church Street was the old timberyard. There were two farms within the village, and others outlying the village.

The present place of worship was erected in 1545, with opposite, the rectory, still in its original form, built in the early 18th century.

Near the church, the thatched house now known as 'Merewater' was once 'Tudor Cottage', and was built in 1574 with alterations in 1639. It was at one time a pub, The Lion. Another hostelry, The Griffin, was part of the still-thatched block of cottages just outside the imposing gate to Boughton Hall, beside the tiny village green. In the house which was The Griffin, old beams revealed the hooks which held the hams for smoking over the fire, and at one re-thatching operation a Cavalier's sword was found among the reeds.

Farming was always the local occupation and Boughton's situation in the country led it to be a meeting place of one of the largest fairs. This was the annual three-day horse fair, held on Boughton Green for centuries. It was chartered in 1351 and continued until 1916. The first day was for the sale of agricultural and wooden goods; the second day, after a service in the church on the feast of St John the Baptist, was given over to merriment, with lace and ribbons and fripperies on sale. On the third day horses, cattle and property changed hands. Highwaymen were rife in the area at the time of the fair and the last to be caught – Captain Slash – was hanged at Whitehills on Gallows Hill in 1826.

In the mid 18th century the 2nd Earl of Stratford, the then lord of the manor, built the obelisk on the hill beyond the present spinney to the south, and dedicated it to the Duke of Devonshire. In 1776 he 'castellated' several of his barns, and built a 'Folly Arch' with side towers in Spectacles Lane off the road to Moulton. This is just below Holly Lodge, an Elizabethan house, which itself adopted the castellated style. Here you will also see more modern agricultural gates – made of working implements.

At this time also, the Earl built that unusual building known as the 'Hawking Tower', at what is now the main Harborough Road access to the Hall.

In the 1930s the village was allowed to expand, after the estate had sold off most of its property to individuals. Butcher's Lane, named after the old butcher's shop, by the smithy, was developed on one side almost to the 'watercress bridge'. Then further expansion in the 1960s and a new estate, brought the village to its present day composition. The Hall has now been divided into two dwellings, with the outhouses also being modernised to individual houses. Boughton, however, remains a pleasant village, and the centre is protected by a preservation order.

Bozeat ༔

Bozeat can claim to be an ancient village as remains have been found of a Saxon burial ground. The parish church of St Mary dates back to 1130 and was probably built on the site of an earlier church.

Fortunately the church survived the Great Fire of Bozeat in 1729. A villager, Widow Keech, living in a row of cottages by the churchyard, is said to have been responsible for starting the fire. Rumour has it that she left her baking unattended in the hearth to gossip with her neighbours. Within a few hours, helped by a strong wind, many houses, farm crops and buildings were burnt to the ground.

In the 15th century there was a thriving weaving industry in Bozeat and the Weavers' Guild gave rich and beautiful gifts to the church. There were also many pillow lace workshops in the village. One was in Easton Lane, kept by James Nichols, who died in 1884. These lace schools lasted until the machine lace of Nottingham ruined the village trade.

Later Bozeat was known for its boot and shoe factories. Many British soldiers marched to war in 1914 in boots made in Bozeat. In the heyday of the shoe industry Bozeat could boast four factories. The village revolved around the factories as these provided work for most of its inhabitants, the women having special working hours to enable them to provide meals for their children and menfolk. Shops, too, were either closed all day or open for limited hours when the shoe factories were shut for holidays. Until very recently, Bozeat was an incongruous mixture of factories and farming, there being twelve farms around the village, half of them with large milking herds. Today there are three farms with milking cows and only one small closing-room remains of the shoe industry.

Although not a 'son' of Bozeat, one young airman of the Second World War is remembered each year on Remembrance Sunday with great gratitude by the village. When his plane developed engine trouble, he instructed his crew to bale out. Then Lt John Ahern, aged 22 years, of the United States Air Force, crashed his plane beyond the village, in the fields of Red Gables farm. His life was lost, but lives and property in Bozeat were saved on that day.

Faces and cottage interiors, unknown to the outside world but well remembered by Bozeat's older generation, were made immortal in the paintings of Charles Spencelayh RA. For many years, Charles Spencelayh lived in a house in London Road, Bozeat. He painted many of the older folk and was well known in the village, where he helped many an aspiring artist.

During the 1960s Bozeat's population was almost doubled. Three new housing estates brought young families to rejuvenate village life. At first there was a feeling of 'us and them' but old Bozeat's strong village spirit prevailed and soon old and new merged to form to-day's lively and caring community.

But years before the new homes were built Bozeat was a divided village. The ever increasing volume of traffic on the A509 cut through the village bringing noise, unwanted fumes and damage to both property and humans. This hazardous division has taken villagers years to overcome. But 1989 sees the opening of the long awaited Bozeat by-pass and then those living on the east and west of the main road through the village will safely unite.

The Bramptons

The two villages of Church and Chapel Brampton are situated about four miles north-west of Northampton on the western side of the valley through which runs the river Nene. They were part of Earl Spencer's estates.

Chapel Brampton is on the old turnpike coaching route from London to Nottingham via Leicester, and had a coaching inn and an alehouse used by villagers called the Spencer Arms. The latter is still flourishing, although no longer as the 'village pub'. The other, the Old Posting House and stables, has been converted into several private homes.

Brampton House was demolished in 1967 to make way for the 30 odd houses of Cedar Hythe, which subsequently won a National Award for Architecture. The ancient tulip tree, which is recorded as having been planted in 1688, was retained and still blooms. The estate overlooks the redundant Northampton to Market Harborough railway line where steam railway enthusiasts are working diligently to repair carriages and engines, with the intention of opening the line and attracting tourists. The old railway station has been converted to a popular restaurant and bar.

The village is very picturesque with its lovely early 19th century sandstone houses. A policy of 'infilling' only has resulted in a considerable number of new houses which generally complement the old. Stones from the old toll house were used to build the bus shelters, which were paid for by the WI.

In earlier years the villagers boasted a baker, a blacksmith, a butcher, a shoemaker, and an undertaker and coffin maker. Today it is fortunate to have a village post office and shop which provides many of the essential services, in addition to being a social focus.

In Church Brampton stands the 14th century St Botolph's church, and until early this century there were few houses in the village, apart from some workers' cottages and almshouses, now converted to modern homes. It is noted for having one of the earliest county golf courses, and has developed largely into a dormitory village. There is also a large riding stables, for horse riding is a major leisure pursuit in the area.

Braunston

Braunston village, built on a hill, looks a little way down on the canal, which gently follows the contours of the land. Its wharf, locks and scattered cottages have a character of their own. There are still canal people here, who were brought up on working narrowboats.

At Little Braunston, at the blind end of Dark Lane, where the lane and canal run parallel for a stretch, stands an old public house, a bridge and a lock. It is perfect material for a picture postcard.

It is also the perfect setting for a ghost story. There is a blocked-up doorway in one wall of the old inn which seems to attract a ghostly visitor. Customers have seen a figure in black walk straight through the wall and pictures have fallen from their hooks. The landlord himself has had some odd experiences. He and his wife were sitting in the bar one night when the glasses suspended above the bar started to rattle, just as they might if a heavy vehicle had passed. Of course, there was no heavy vehicle. But strong wind whipping up the canal and in that old door might well have created enough draught to set glasses vibrating!

The village of Braunston

Braybrooke

Braybrooke is a small village three miles to the west of Desborough and three miles south-east of Market Harborough. The population is about 380, and the main London railway passes through the parish, which is situated in a valley bisected by the river Jordan.

The village is surrounded by fertile agricultural land, over 300 acres of which is glebe land bequeathed by Mrs Field, wife of the rector, in the early 19th century. The parish is farmed as a mixture of arable land, used for the growing of corn and rape, and pasture, used for the fattening of beef cattle and sheep.

In the late 18th century the main village industry was weaving, and the rush industry was also important. One small field is still called 'Osier Beds'. Rural weaving declined with the growth of the Northern mills.

The old heart of the village was the 13th century church, which was surrounded by cottages long since demolished. Their stones were removed to build other houses, and their cobbled pavements and streets are from time to time uncovered by ploughing. The church is in Early English style. Braybrooke's rare vamping horn, an ancient musical instrument once used in the church, is now on loan to the Market Harborough museum.

The main site of historical interest is the old castle site. This was originally the manor of Robert de Braybrooke, which was rebuilt in the reign of King John. The castle was demolished about 1633 and a farmhouse was built on the site. This too fell into decay in the early part of the 20th century, and was pulled down in 1960. All that remains is the old farm brewhouse and a series of mounds marking the fishponds.

The village was subject to flooding in times of storms and melting snow, and in 1986 a dam was built by Anglian Water across the river Jordan on the castle site to hold back surplus water and divert it into the fishponds.

The houses in the village are a mixture of old and new. The oldest houses date from the 16th century, with the 'Old Rectory' and 'Bleak House' being listed buildings, along with the Latymers' stone bridge built in 1402. The Swan Inn is 18th century and was originally called the Black Swan. The small Baptist chapel was rebuilt in 1815 and the children join with the children from the Anglican church to attend a Sunday school. There have been three schools in Braybrooke, and the first, an endowed National school built in 1836, has been converted into the village hall.

Brigstock

Brigstock's origins go back to the Iron Age but the Brigstock we know today began as a Saxon settlement in a clearing in Rockingham Forest. The church shows much evidence of its Saxon origins, especially in the tower which has excellent long and short work and one of the finest arches of this period in Europe. Until fairly recently the church bell was tolled three times a day to guide travellers lost in the woods between Brigstock and Weldon.

In the Middle Ages Brigstock developed into one of the largest villages in the Royal Forest and became a centre for administering the Forest Law. However, as early as the time of Elizabeth I the village had gained notoriety as the haunt of deer-stealers and by the time of Charles I it was common practice for villagers to defy the keepers and hunt at will.

The ill reputation the village acquired at this time was probably not helped by the high number of licensed premises which flourished in the 17th and 18th centuries. At least twelve buildings have been public houses at some time in their history. There are now only two – both still at the centre of village affairs as they have been since 1725.

Hunting has always been part of life in this area, wolves as well as foxes being hunted in the Middle Ages. In 1873 the Woodland Pytchley Hunt broke away from the North Pytchley Hunt and set up its kennels at Brigstock, where they remain. Lord Lonsdale came with his young wife to hunt from the Three Cocks and in 1881 took over the Mastership. He kept 72 chestnut horses stabled in the village and brought with him one of the finest packs of hounds of the day. The Ring and its stabling at the junction of Kennel Hill and Stable Hill was built by the Duke of Buccleuch in 1873. In the 1980s the land was sold and a small development of houses built there.

To counteract the multiplicity of pubs, Brigstock entered early into the field of education. The first school was endowed in 1620 by the Rev Nicholas Latham, parson of Barnwell, near Oundle. He was the son of the keeper of Brigstock Great Park. The actual building no longer exists but it is the site of the war memorial on Hall Hill.

The obvious and actual centre of the village is Hall Hill, with its circle of stone houses around the ancient market cross, where since 1466 the village women have sat and sold their produce. Edward IV granted a charter for a weekly market, but there were three days in the year when special markets or feasts were held. In the 1980s the WI resurrected the old custom of the street market.

There are many memories of Brigstock's more recent past told by our village elders. Between the two World Wars and for some years in the 1950s, Brigstock had a very good Silver Band. It also had a very small drummer and one day going down Church Street, the band turned right over the bridge towards Grafton, but the drummer, unable to see over the top of his drum, kept marching on to Thrapston!

The Bringtons

The Bringtons, namely Great Brington, Little Brington and the hamlet of Nobottle are in the west of the county.

In the 19th century much of Brington, in common with the neighbouring villages of Harlestone and the Bramptons, became part of the Althorp Estate, home of the Spencers, and comparatively little land was in other ownership. It is interesting to compare the 1880s with 1980s. A hundred years ago the Estate and its tenant farmers were the principal employers; the majority of the population dwelt under Estate roofs; the local blacksmith, whitesmith, shoemaker, tailor, carpenter, grocer and of course the licensed victualler provided for a self sufficient community of over 800. Children were taught in schools established by successive Earls (by the 1880s the main school was being visited by Her Majesty's Inspectors) and by the turn of the century Reading Rooms for adults had been established in both villages. Early in the next decade piped water was taken to all properties and a sewerage system installed, possibly prompted by a typhoid epidemic. As he was patron of the living, one could say that body, mind and spirit were cared for by the noble Earl.

How things have changed! Althorp House is open to the public – a demanding job for the Earl and Countess, which must put them high on the tourist trade productivity graph. The School is now owned by the County Council, but The Stores, the Post Office and the two pubs are still Estate property. In other ownership they could well not have survived the 1960s and 70s when the population dropped to 350 and supermarkets and motor cars revolutionised shopping. Redundant farm buildings, houses and surplus land have been sold: by letting former workers' cottages the Estate has helped to meet the demand for rented accommodation. Not every face in the street is familiar, some upwardly mobile families have passed through the village leaving scarcely a footprint, but the majority have put down roots. With a population heading for 500 modern Brington is a lively community.

Agriculture, the base line of the 19th century economy, is still a dominant feature of the environment. Each settlement in the parish is surrounded by farm land, much of it pasture. The difference between then and now is the increase in arable land: the seasons are reflected on a changing patchwork of bare ploughed soil, the green of new growth, the yellow slashes of flowering rape and then the warm tones of ripening grain. The first commuter, a Northampton shoe manufacturer, came to Brington before the First World War: commuting is no longer limited to nearby towns. That valley to the south, the communications artery, is traversed by the M1, Watling Street and the London to Glasgow railway. It also carries the Grand Union Canal, now devoted to leisure pursuits, but at times more quickly negotiated than the motorway!

There is a certain nostalgia: for the lost hedgerows and wild flowers; for the slower tempo of life when the bread, baked in the village, was delivered by horse and cart; for some of us, for the pure cold spring water from our own wells; for the brown long-eared bats, whose barn habitats are being developed for humans. Brington's other bat, the pipistrelle, more venturesome has migrated to modern houses.

Brixworth

The village of Brixworth today is an architectural hotch-potch of ancient stone buildings, Victorian houses, some very pleasing to the eye, and a sprawling mass of modern properties dominated by the now famous ancient church which has stood sentinel on the hill for well over a thousand years.

The remains of a large Roman villa found at Brixworth indicate that a Roman of some importance once lived here. Later the Saxons built a church and Roman tiles may be found incorporated into the fabric of the present building. A sacred relic, said to be part of the larynx of St Boniface, is kept in the church and pilgrims in past ages came to pay homage to the saint or to pray for a miracle. His day, 5th June, has been celebrated with feasts and fetes in the village for centuries, and still is today.

Brixworth Hall was built in Tudor times. The watercourse we know as 'Merry Tom', where once stood a mill, must have been more of a raging torrent then, unlike the gentle stream where today children paddle and fish for tadpoles. A stone archway and converted stable block are all that remain of the old Hall, built by the Saunders family who owned the mill.

Brixworth is the home of the famous Pytchley hunt, with grand kennels near the site of the former railway station.

Brixworth became an important coaching stage en route between London and the North. Such was the haste to change horses that at the entrance to one inn yard, with little room for manoeuvre, the stone wall was worn away on one side by the constant friction of passing horseflesh.

In 1851 the railway came to Brixworth, changing the lives of the people as never before. There was now an accelerated drift from the agricultural work that had been their mainstay for centuries. Soon after, iron ore was found and this was to change not only the village, but the contours of the surrounding countryside. There are still those who remember the stories of the hard and dangerous work, the low pay and the heavy drinking, for this was indeed thirsty work. Brick-built cottages sprang up to house the workers, and public houses sprang up to slake their thirst.

After the iron ore was worked out light industry began to take a hold. There is now an expanding industrial estate, built unobtrusively on the edge of the village.

In the centre of the village is an unusual and attractive stone building which is all that remains of the once notorious Brixworth Workhouse. It opened its doors in 1837 and was an unhappy place for the destitute of the parish and beyond. Conditions only began to improve when a farm labourer, not afraid to speak his mind about the unjust treatment, was elected to the Board which administered the workhouse.

The quarries now are gone and the grassy hills and hollows left where the ironstone was removed, echo to the shouts of children at play. One of the artificially created hills makes a wonderful toboggan run!

The conservation areas away from the main road are reminders of the Brixworth of many years ago. There is an ancient butter-cross on the green below the church, and the village stocks are now only used by visitors posing for a photograph. The old coaching inns remain, much rebuilt and refurbished. There is a restaurant, a library and a pottery, and a book shop in lovely old Pound House. And the church of All Saints, mangificent in its simplicity, continues to draw pilgrims and visitors from all over the world.

Brockhall 🦡

The hamlet (once a village) of Brockhall lies ten miles west of Northampton and five miles from Daventry adjacent to, but hidden from, the M1, the A5, and the Grand Union Canal, and a mile from the site of the medieval village of Muscott. It was recorded in the Domesday Book as Brocole.

The Eyton family were responsible for building the Hall and, c1617, the manor house, which are virtually as seen today. The Hall is built of Hornton stone, which is also used along with lighter limestone and some of the Northamptonshire ironstone/sandstone in the church.

In 1625 Lawrence Eyton sold the property to John Thornton. Thus began the long association with the Thornton family whose name in this part of the county appears alongside the Spencers of Althorp and the Knightleys of Fawsley. The last of the direct male line of the family, Colonel T. A. Thornton, died in 1978. Tragically, his elder son Major T. R. Thornton was killed in action in Italy in 1944 and younger son N. L. Thornton died in an accident in 1951. There are numerous memorials and a hatchment to the family in the church.

Brockhall is a pretty place, with its Hall, manor house, row of thatched cottages in Northamptonshire stone and its church. Fortunately the Hall is being well maintained by its present owner, but the small community is finding it hard work to fund the restoration needed by the church although some grant has been offered by English Heritage. Once upon a time the 'town' of Brockhall must have been relatively extensive, probably reaching up to the A5 and beyond the present settlement, where some mounds can be seen.

Broughton

Broughton is situated three miles to the south-west of Kettering and is the largest of the seven villages in the Borough of Kettering. The busy A43 has until recently passed through the middle of the village, though for part of its length both Cransley and Broughton parish boundaries met in the middle of this road. On 18th December 1984, after more than 40 years of campaigning, a by-pass was finally opened which now sweeps to the west of Broughton and the hamlet of Little Cransley.

There has been a settlement on the site of the village for hundreds of years and Broughton was mentioned in the Domesday Book of 1086, when it was known as Burtone.

In 1988 the population of Broughton was estimated to be about 1,790. With little employment locally most workers now travel to surrounding villages and towns to work. Traditionally, however, Broughton was a community of agricultural and shoe workers. In the early 19th century there were some lacemakers too, but when the ironworks opened in the area some deserted their former interests for the better wages offered in the iron and steel industry.

Broughton has one factory which makes shoe uppers, a post office, six shops, a blacksmith's, two public houses and a working men's club, a Baptist chapel and a church. Other amenities include a modern village hall with a large playing field and children's play area, a second horse chestnut-ringed recreation area and a recently constructed amenity woodland site.

The church, dedicated to St Andrew the Apostle, has a Norman doorway in the south porch and the fabric of the church also has 14th and 15th century work. In 1965 the clock was struck by lightning and the mechanism hurled across the clock gallery. The clock was subsequently repaired by the local blacksmith, Mr Frank James. The lightning strike also necessitated the reinforcement of the church tower.

Local ironstone was used in the construction of many older houses in the village. Two such buildings are The Gables in Church Street, dating back some 400 years, and The Yeoman House in High Street, designed by Inigo Jones.

Broughton is well known for its old custom of the Tin Can Band. Each year, on the first Sunday following 12th December, villagers assemble outside the church and at midnight set out around the streets banging a variety of tin cans and dustbin lids and blowing whistles and trumpets. Some say this tradition was to exorcise devils, some that it was to drive away gipsies. The band travels to the boundaries of the village, returning eventually to the church. Legend has it that if ever the event did not take place the practice would thereafter have to cease. During the First World War one local man beat the bounds on his own to keep the custom alive.

Bugbrooke ✎

Bugbrooke, named in the Domesday Book as Buchebroc, lies to the south-east of Northampton. The B4525, the road to Banbury, passes through the village, which is intersected by both the Grand Union Canal and the London North Western railway line. The river Nene skirts its northern boundaries and a brook, a tributary of this, meanders through the village.

Bugbrooke has changed greatly over the last century. A hundred years ago it was almost self-supporting and boasted the first soap factory in England, together with a brickyard, bakeries, mills and many other trades needed to maintain a thriving village. Now the only traditional industry remaining apart from farming is corn milling carried on at Heygate's Mill, a large concern which is situated by the side of the Nene and can be seen on the right when entering the village from Northampton.

The old part of the village is dominated by a fine 14th century church, set alongside the B4525 with parkland to the rear. It is a beautiful church with many interesting and historical features, the finest of which is the exquisite 15th century wood screen, one of the few remaining in the county. The other place of worship is the Baptist chapel, opened in 1808. This stands on the High Street and is now the meeting house for the Jesus Fellowship, a sect which owns a great deal of property in the area and has many followers. In the past, other denominations were active. A small Methodist chapel was built in 1847, but has since been demolished. Another and much older sect was that of the Quakers. Their meeting house was Quaker's Cottage, which is still standing just off the High Street.

Also along the High Street is the county primary school. This was built in 1874 as the Board School and the children of generations of villagers were educated here. Now there is also a secondary school on the road out to Northampton. This is the Campion School named after a local resident and farmer.

There are four general shops, a butcher, hairdresser, flower shop, post office, two public houses, two garages and several other thriving businesses.

Sports are very popular and team sports are well catered for. There is a large playing field on the edge of the village and football, hockey, cricket and rugby are keenly supported. In the centre of the village is a lovely privately owned cricket pitch, which adds to the village atmosphere on a sunny summer afternoon.

Bulwick ❧

Bulwick is a small village situated in a hollow of the Willow Brook valley about ten miles east of Corby. It is a 'Cotswold' style village with only three or four post-war buildings and is mostly built of stone with part of the village in a conservation area. Formerly it formed a notorious bottle neck on the main A43 trunk road to Stamford, but has now been bypassed.

Whilst there are only about 100 people on the electoral register, Bulwick has elements often peculiar to larger communities in that it is still a 'complete village' in the traditional sense, having a church and rectory complete with live-in rector, a public house, a post office cum shop, a village school and a Squire in residence at Bulwick Hall who still owns most of the land and property.

Any claim the past citizens of Bulwick have had to fame starts with a Knight from Bulwick who was said to be so infamous as to assist in the murder of Thomas Becket in the 13th century. Of more recent date, however, is the story of John Sarrington, one time miller, who operated the now defunct water mill. The miller's coat sleeve caught in the machinery with the result that first his hand and then his arm was caught up and crushed until he so feared for his life that he begged his apprentice to cut off the mangled remains. After some delay caused by the necessity to sharpen a suitable knife the operation was completed and the miller freed. It is recorded that the unfortunate miller was taken to Stamford by horse and cart to receive attention from a surgeon, but that he survived the ordeal.

Bulwick church is a notable building with a tall spire in the Perpendicular style and its first rector was appointed in 1227. Memorials on its walls chronicle history such as the death of Admiral Tryon who perished in HMS Victoria when it was accidentally rammed by HMS Camperdown in the Mediterranean in 1893. Owners of the village at that time, since they first came from Holland and built the Hall in 1676, the Tryons were well respected, some being of a military and some of clerical bent, but most unfortunate in that all five males were killed in the First World War as recorded in another memorial.

The ecclesiastical parish includes Blatherwycke where the small but ancient church was closed to services and put under the care of English Heritage a few years ago. Formerly the home of the O'Brien family, the Hall was pulled down about 60 years ago, but a splendid lake still remains. The O'Briens were Earls of Stafford and there are some fine tombs of the family inside the church. All its previous grandeur gone, the estate is now very much a commercial enterprise devoted mainly to grain, a characteristic of its bigger neighbour Bulwick, and indeed the surrounding area for many miles.

Byfield 🌿

Byfield is a large village situated on the main Daventry to Banbury road, the A361. Anyone travelling along this road and through Byfield will see a very smart and modern village with its supermarket, butcher/grocery, post office and two filling stations along the main road. The village also has its own pottery.

The church is one of the most attractive features of the village. Built in 1242, the bells are rung regularly by a very capable team of bellringers.

The Byfield you see today is far removed from the village remembered by those who were born here. Where modern houses now stand, rows of cottages and farm buildings once stood; there were nine dairy herds, one of which delivered milk in the village – now there is only one. Byfield once had its own railway station, and the ironstone workings, so that there was plenty of work for the local people, besides employment in the local shops, which included a grocer, butcher, general store and the small family shops – the children's favourite for sweets and toys. Going even further back there were many crafts in evidence, including a boot and shoe maker, watch and clock repairer, saddler, blacksmith, wheelwright and carriers, who were the only link for many of the villagers with the shops in the towns.

The cattle market at Fiveways brought many local farmers to the village and, having driven their cattle to market, they would then adjourn to one of the five public houses before making a somewhat unsteady return home!

Castle Ashby 🌿

Castle Ashby is situated on the south side of the flood plain of the river Nene between Northampton and Wellingborough. The Nene forms part of the northern boundary of the parish, while the A428 Northampton – Bedford road approximates to its southern boundary. The 'Castle' part of the name dates from 1306 when Langton, Bishop of Coventry, obtained a licence from the Crown to embattle his mansion at Ashby.

Today the village has some 112 inhabitants and one of the Great Houses of Northamptonshire. It is a classic estate village, with no other freeholders except the Marquess of Northampton and the church. Contrary to what might be expected, however, most of the buildings are relatively modern. It is clear from such documentary evidence as survives that the village has over the past 300 years been moved from east to west. Today the church, set well to the east of Castle Ashby House, is the only visible indication of this shift. The first stage of this removal appears to have been in 1695 when 'a long stone building near the south side of Ashby church' which had become 'a receptacle for idle persons . . . and a harbour for strumpets ... woodstealers and vagabonds' was pulled down. In return a new almshouse was built (now 19–24 Castle Ashby.

The second major clearance happened in the 1760s when the area immediately to the north of the house was cleared by Capability Brown in order to create the Dairy Walk. Given that there are no surviving dwellings in the village which clearly date from this period, it would not be unreasonable to suppose that the cottages which were built to replace those that were destroyed were of poor quality.

Most of the existing dwellings date from the 1860s onwards. The most distinguished is 43–46 Castle Ashby, which is date stoned 1874 and is by the Northampton architect, E. F. Law. A number of features from this row of cottages – most obviously the gable as an extension of the front wall – were blended with the vernacular tradition to create a distinctive estate style of architecture which can easily be recognised in the surrounding villages. Next door to this row is a school designed by G. E. Street, who was responsible for restoring Castle Ashby church in the 1860s. The reason for his nickname 'Stripey' Street is immediately apparent from this building, which is now used as a residential centre by the Northamptonshire Girl Guides. 43–46 Castle Ashby and indeed most of the rest of the houses in the village are roofed with tiles made on the estate between about 1880 and 1930. In design they are unique.

The parish itself extends to approximately 1,900 acres. Some 1,300 acres of this is farmed in hand, and most of the rest is let on agricultural tenancies to farmers growing chiefly cereals. The Home Farm includes the Capability Brown parkland, which provides some 200 acres of grassland for a dairy herd of about 200 and a flock of over 1,000 sheep.

Chacombe

Chacombe nestles in a well-wooded valley with hills on all sides except in the direction of Banbury, three miles away. On the road to Middleton Cheney, farmland on either side has been used to make the well-patronised Cherwell Edge Golf Course. On the north side is the county ditch, which, through the centuries, has created its own deep, winding valley; walk over one of its little wooden bridges and you are in Oxfordshire.

On the Banbury road is the Priory, with its medieval chapel. Augustinian monks lived there and some of their fish ponds are now the site of the neat, modern, village sewerage system, some distance away. The Priory house is a handsome mansion, in a setting of trees, partially surrounded by the original ponds. The nearby Old Vicarage is now a private house and, beyond, the beautiful early 14th century church, set a little apart from today's village, is dedicated to Saint Peter and Saint Paul. At the heart of Chacombe is a well-supported Methodist chapel, built in 1873.

Near the church is the George and Dragon, an ancient hostelry, and source of good food and drink today. Not far away are other well-kept, carefully restored houses with names reminiscent of their former use 'The Old Forge', 'The Old School', 'The Old Farmhouse'. 'Bell Cottage' probably occupies part of the site of the famous Bagley Bell Foundry (1600–1785) which supplied bells for local church towers and far beyond. 'Weavers', in Banbury road, recalls that, for over a century, weaving and plush making was a busy cottage industry.

Silver Street, half a century ago, had three working farms and a wheelwright's shop. Here, only the farmhouses are set back from the street. Most of the others adjoin the pavement and there are no front gardens. A farm orchard has been used as a site for three modern bungalows. There are no working farms in Silver Street now, but the old thatched houses make pleasant homes. Only two farmers live in the central part of the village.

Some of the old names have disappeared too. Silver Street North was once Saucepan Alley, part of Banbury road was called Catchall, and School Hill was known as Upper Tubs.

The village was in serious decline in the 1930s. One third of the cottages were condemned as being unfit for human habitation. Mostly picturesque and thatched, they were, in some cases, little better than hovels and were pulled down. Population slumped from 488 in 1841 to under 300 in 1937. Today the population is thriving, at 650. A new primary school was built in 1972, with extensive playing fields nearby. The village hall is in great demand, and the village shop and post office is a valued amenity.

Charlton & Newbottle 🎋

Charlton is a small village on the edge of the southern ridge of Northamptonshire. It is home to nearly 500 people and has a post office/village store, a pub, a chapel and a primary school, but no parish church. This is half a mile away across the fields, at Newbottle, one of Northamptonshire's many deserted villages. All that remains of this medieval settlement, with its beautiful views westward across to north Oxfordshire, are a couple of cottages, the Old Rectory and the Manor, with its striking octagonal dovecote, beside the lovely little church, dating from the 12th century, with a Norman font.

Newbottle made the national press in 1872 when a whirlwind struck. There is a dramatic, well researched account describing eyewitnesses seeing a 'rope' come down from the heavy storm clouds with a 'ball of smoke' at its base, felling huge trees and knocking down walls along its path, and pulling up the water from a pond, to deposit it like rain further along. It travelled for nearly two miles, but miraculously nobody was hurt. Newbottle Spinney is now a Nature Reserve, much visited for its primroses in the spring.

Along the main street of Charlton the oldest houses, built of dark golden stone, turn end on, facing toward the south, often with no windows in their north walls – a sensible arrangement in the days before central heating and double glazing. It is a true 'ribbon-development': one long row of dwellings with the only side-streets being fairly recent developments to the north.

Almost opposite the attractive, thatched Rose & Crown, the last remaining public house of the four that the villagers had to choose from once, stands what must be the grandest cottage in the land. Here lived Charlton's most notable resident – F. E. Smith, the first Earl of Birkenhead, lawyer and statesman, close friend of Churchill and once Lord Chancellor of England. He moved to the 'small hunting box' in 1907 to make a country home for his wife and young family. Over the years 'The Cottage' was extended and transformed into an imposing house, unusually, right on the village street, with gardens behind stretching down to a lake. Here, every July, the village fete and tennis tournament are held. 'F. E.' died in 1930 and his tomb, designed by Lutyens, can be seen in the cemetery to the west of the village.

Near the small triangle of grass at the junction with the road to King's Sutton stands the smithy, where you can still watch the blacksmith working at his forge. He fashioned the crown on the lamp-post on the green outside to commemorate the Queen's Jubilee in 1977.

At intervals along the main street odd blue-brick arched constructions can be seen. These were built through the generosity of Mr F Myers, a Victorian benefactor living at the Lodge, and provided a piped water supply, the pump house being at the top of Hogg Lane. Four of the original outlets survive – it seems a sophisticated arrangement for a small village, when others had to rely on a single pump, but it had its problems, as early in this century it was reported to the Parish Council that 'children were wasting the water'!

On the southern outskirts of Charlton is Rainsborough Camp, believed to date from the Iron Age, with earth ramparts held by stone walls 2,000 years old, enclosing about six acres. It was later used by the Romans, whose coins have been found in the area.

Charwelton ❧

The motorist may well pass through Charwelton without realising that a peaceful village street, leading to rolling countryside, lies just off the main road.

You may drive or walk along the gated road to the site of the original village, known today as Church Charwelton. Here can be found the ancient church, dedicated to the Holy Trinity, Church House Farm and one cottage. These, together with the old fish ponds and earthworks are reminders of a busy and prosperous community which flourished here in the Middle Ages.

With the advent of the Great Central Railway and station in 1897 a new prosperity was brought to the village, especially during both World Wars. In less than a century the station, platforms and bridges have been demolished. Now the railway line is a haven for many species of birds and wild flowers.

The river Cherwell once came into life in the cellar of Cherwell Farm (situated on the Helidon Road). Sadly this lovely old house was demolished and the Cherwell now rises, unnoticed, in a pool near to the new farmhouse.

In 1821, Cherwell Farm was the setting for a very strange murder. Mrs Mary Clarke and her lover Phillip Haynes were hung at Northampton Gaol for the wilful murder of Mary's elderly husband, John Clarke. After making several futile attempts on Clarke's life, Phillip Haynes finally succeeded in shooting the old man in the arm. A few days after the incident, a local surgeon amputated the arm, but Clarke died due to loss of blood.

The tiny school, on the main road, was donated to the village by the Knightley's of Fawsley in 1858. Its doors were closed for the last time on 2nd August 1935. Delightful daily accounts of school life may be read in journals kept at Delapre Abbey. The Knightleys also donated the village hall which had its opening on 2nd November 1922.

Just below the village hall, in Church Street is the former Wesleyan chapel, which was built in 1887. Purchased by the Church of England in 1932 and dedicated to The Good Shepherd, the chapel is used regularly for church services and Sunday school.

Opposite the chapel is the post office which has provided a necessary service to the village since the 1870s.

On the corner of Daventry Road and Church Street is the house known as Foxhall Farm. This was once a coaching inn but has long since been de-licensed. The Fox and Hounds public house however still caters for travellers and villagers alike, as it has since the 1600s.

Ten outlying farmhouses complete the parish. Most of them are still working farms, carrying on the tradition of centuries.

Clipston

It was St Swithin's Day, the 15th of July 1880, a beautiful summer morning. As they busied themselves about their daily tasks, the villagers of Clipston had no idea of the calamity that was about to befall them. Halfway through the morning, the weather began to change. The wind increased from a breeze to a gale, the sky darkened and distant thunder rolled ever nearer. Then down came the rain in torrents. Hour after hour, it rained and the mown hay which lay in the fields was swept into the dykes and drains, completely blocking them. The brook could not contain the sudden increase in the flow of water and before long, a swiftly rising tide was rushing along the village street.

A row of mud-walled dwellings were swept away by the swelling tide. The occupants had already fled their homes and no lives were lost. From the comparative safety of brick-built cottages, neighbours watched in terror from their bedroom windows, as doors were burst open and belongings were swept away by the surging water. Late in the day, there was an abatement and eventually the flood began to recede. The devastation revealed was heart-breaking and the drying-out and mopping-up was a long and laborious process. Small wonder that this story was handed down from parent to child over many years.

Times were hard here in the 1840s and 1850s, and many folk knew hunger and privation. Families were large and desperation drove many to emigrate and those who remained, to take the ultimate measures to feed themselves and their families. Sheep stealing was a way of providing food, but how could the carcass be concealed, once the animal was slaughtered? Certainly the owner would investigate the loss and if the guilty were discovered, the penalty would be severe. Men had been deported for lesser offences. So, banding together in a small group, they took the meat to a brick-built culvert and crawled some distance inside, where, fixing metal hooks in the roof, they were able to hang the meat and cut off pieces as required. Complete secrecy must have been maintained for no-one was ever discovered and the action continued as long as opportunity arose to steal an animal. In later years, lads skating on the frozen brook, crawled into the culvert and found the metal hooks still embedded in the brickwork.

In the past nicknames were a necessary, distinguishing title among communities where so many families bore the same surname. The story is told of two brothers who rejoiced in the nicknames of 'Dabs' and 'Wusser'. During an epidemic of measles, a neighbour enquired of their father, 'How are the boys, this morning?' 'Oh,' he replied, 'Dabs is bad and Wusser's wuss.' This became a much-used phrase, to everyone's amusement.

In thinking of famous 'sons' of the village, mention must be made of Thomas Jarman (1776–1861), a composer of sacred music. His hymn tune, *Lyngham*, sometimes known as *Nativity*, has literally gone round the world. After her coronation in 1953, Queen Elizabeth II toured the Commonwealth. Turning on the radio to listen to a service she attended in Tonga, what a thrill it was to hear, *O for a thousand tongues to sing*, sung to *Lyngham*, Thomas Jarman's tune, composed in this village.

Cogenhoe 🌿

Cogenhoe (pronounced Cookno) is situated six miles east of Northampton, on rising ground overlooking the Nene valley.

The architecture ranges from the Elizabethan rectory to present day buildings, and the earliest dwellings are situated around the village green. The population of the village was rather static until the 1930s. Since the 1950s there has been a great expansion, more than doubling the size of the village.

The present church building was started about 1225 and completed in 1280 by Nicholas de Cogenhoe, and additions were made by William de Cogenhoe at a later date. The heir to the estate died at the age of 10 and Agnes, his sister and the last of the de Cogenhoe line, built the tower as a memorial to him in about 1380. There are many interesting features in the church including an effigy of a Crusader, believed to be Nicholas de Cogenhoe.

During the 19th century many changes took place in the village, with the coming of new trades and occupations. These show up in the church registers, where earlier entries show that most employment was farmwork or other rural trades. During the early 1800s you find other job descriptions appearing, eg rail workers, navigators and iron ore miners.

Iron ore was mined in the vicinity during the middle of the 19th century, but the slump in the 1880s proved too much and the company closed in 1888. During the latter half of the 19th century shoe making was making its mark. Hand-sewn shoes and boots were mostly made in small workshops in the houses. A small factory making high quality boots and shoes was built by the Mann family and this continued to employ local labour until it closed in the late 1940s. There are now two small factories making electronic components, which employ local people. Yorks Coaches are based in the village.

One old lady was a well-known village character. She was married to a man who farmed in a small way, and was fairly comfortably well off, but was so parsimonious she would look through other people's dustbins looking for scraps for her husband's dinner. She was the 'laying out' person in the village and is supposed to have acquired her false teeth from one of the corpses she was attending to. They were much too big for her and she was unable to close her mouth and had a perpetual grin. 'Teeth like gravestones', the villagers used to say!

Cold Ashby 🌿

The village is situated on the north-west outskirts of Northamptonshire, and certainly lives up to its name because in winter snow can still be seen for two or three weeks after it has gone from surrounding districts. There

'The Cedars' in Cold Ashby

is an area renowned for its beauty about one mile from the village, known as Honey Hill. This attracts sightseers most days of the year, and on a clear day one can see five counties. Close by is the site where a beacon was lit to celebrate the Queen's Silver Jubilee. Warning beacons were first set up in 1588 when England faced the Spanish Armada.

The river Nene rises from a soft water spring on the western side of the village. The church of St Deny is chiefly Early English, but contains several Norman decorations, it also has one of the oldest bells in the country, dated 1317. The clock was given in 1917 by Thomas Francis Hazelhurst, squire of Cold Ashby. The register dates from 1560. In 1710 a Mr W. Wicks left £18 to the vicar, which was for hearing the children's catechism during Lent, and the interest of £6 a year for the education of the poor boys of the parish.

Although a comparatively small village (population approximately 250) Cold Ashby enjoys to the full a very active social life. In recent years an 18 hole golf course was opened. This has really put the village on the map. In the winter, if there is sufficient snow, the golf course is transformed into a ski slope and this attracts hundreds of enthusiasts.

Over the past years there have been many changes, but fortunately they have been to the good in some respects. There are no new housing estates, so Cold Ashby remains almost as it did years ago, although in 1881 the population was 385. The thing that has changed most of all is the volume of traffic. With the main Daventry to Market Harborough road going through the centre of the village the traffic is quite heavy. A far cry from the days when one would see cows passing down the main street twice a day for milking, and on Sundays villagers could be seen making their way to the local baker with a joint of meat in a tin, and Yorkshire pudding mix in a jug – the baker did the rest! Sometimes the end result almost resembled the oven it was cooked in and it was not uncommon to finish up with someone else's dinner.

Cold Ashby now has one public house, The Black Horse, and the post office and general stores, compared with days gone by when there were two bakers, a shoe maker, butcher and slaughterhouse, dressmaker, two public houses, Congregational church, school and a blacksmith. The blacksmith's shop still remains although it is no longer in use. The school is now converted to a private house, but the exterior has not been altered.

Collingtree

Before the First World War the village had no proper roads or pavements and in the winter the streets were a sea of mud. There was an old man employed to rake the mud in the street and he would pile it up in Barn Lane by the old rectory. In summer grass would grow in clumps as the High Street was really just a cart track. On the lane to Milton, the hedges on either side met overhead. The first real road was tar with chippings in the early 1920s. It was not until 1949, after the Second World War, that the first tarmacadam surface was laid. Also at the time, the village had sewerage and piped water. There had been electric lights available since 1928.

In the first years of the century, the 'big house' was owned by the Phipps family, who also owned the brewery. They employed most of the village people either in the house, its gardens, the farm or the brewery. The Phipps family left Collingtree in 1911 and the house was altered.

There were two pubs in the village until after the Second World War, when the Royal Oak closed. Bread was baked in what is now the shop and the village women used to take their Sunday dinners to be roasted in the ovens at a penny a time. This practice was only given up during the Second World War. Also in the early days, there was a smithy in the High Street, but in 1913 it moved to Slade's Farm, now across the M1 (but still part of the village then).

Most of the houses were originally thatched, but the only thatch left in the village is the pub, The Wooden Walls of Old England.

Every Christmas, the Phipps family arranged a party for the village and every child received a present. This tradition was continued by Mrs Sears when she moved into the big house and was carried on by her son John until the late 1960s. There was also a pig club in the village as nearly every family kept a pig. There was an annual pig club dinner which was strictly men only!

Holidays as we know them were unheard of. Even on Christmas Day and Good Friday, one was expected to go to church at least twice.

We tend to look back on those days with nostalgia and think how charming it all was, but one cannot help feeling how hard the lives of the women must have been when you think of the dreadful mud, the lack of running water, no washing and drying facilities, the cold and lack of central heating. We are very lucky today!

Collyweston

The name Collyweston is synonymous with the stone slates that adorn the roofs of the houses in this and many other surrounding villages. From the 14th century up until the last slate mine closed in 1967 slates were produced in the traditional way. Although called 'slate' it is actually a form of limestone containing layers of soluble lime 'sap' which allows the stone to be split into thin sheets.

It is only found in this unusual form in the vicinity of Collyweston, but this band of limestone comes all the way from Dorset right up to the northern part of Lincolnshire. In Southern England it emerges as the famous 'Portland' stone and is used for facing many London buildings. It is also seen as the lovely stone of towns and villages in the Cotswolds and Northamptonshire.

The language of the Collyweston slate workers goes back 600 years, they talk about the art of 'foxing' and 'cliving' and they prepare Wibets and Large Mumffets for your roof. The slate is located about 30 feet below ground level and reached through shafts excavated from the surface. Once brought to the surface the process relies on the action of frost, which freezes the 'sap' and causes the stone to split into the wafer-like slates. Consequently most of this work took place in the winter months, and many miners worked the farms during the summer, returning to the slate mines when the weather turned frosty.

Now that Collyweston slates are no longer produced, repairs to old buildings or new roofs requiring traditional materials rely on re-claimed slates from demolished buildings.

The church of St Andrew was rebuilt by Ralph Cromwell, who was born at the end of the 14th century, one of several brothers who fought at the Battle of Agincourt. He was also governor of Nottingham Castle. The church has a fine tower with pinnacles and the arch of the south doorway is surrounded with a moulding of carved flowers. The choir stalls are decorated with carvings of pelicans, which are the Christian symbol of sacrifice.

The manor house, also known as 'The Palace', was occupied in the 15th century by Ralph Cromwell and later by the more famous Lady

Margaret Beaufort, mother of Henry VII and thence the Tudor dynasty. After passing through several hands, all that remains of the site of the gardens that overlooked the Welland valley are the terraces, the remains of the fishponds and the dovecote, inscribed 'ER' 1570 (or 1578).

Like many Northamptonshire villages the advent of the Second World War brought an airfield to the outskirts. Collyweston Airfield became the base for Flight 1426 whose principal task was to evaluate and rebuild enemy aircraft.

The wide village street is lined by limestone houses, mostly 17th century, roofed with local slates. The school is still open for the education of infants and with barely 30 pupils. There is a public house, The Cavalier, although it was formerly called the Slaters Arms.

Cosgrove 🦢

Although Cosgrove is only a few minutes drive away from the new city of Milton Keynes over the county boundary, it has retained its village charm. Its geographical position, bounded by the Ouse and Tove rivers, attracted settlers as far back as Roman times. In fact evidence of Roman occupation was unearthed on the outskirts of the village a few years ago.

Cosgrove would have remained relatively isolated until 1805 when the Grand Union canal was built, bisecting the village. It then found itself not only on the main London to Birmingham route, but also at the junction of the canal arm that led to Buckingham. These days the canal brings visitors in their holiday boats to the village.

More visitors come by road to the leisure park at Cosgrove Lodge, which was formerly the site of a huge sand and gravel pit. It employed many men from the village and surrounding area, but was finally worked out after supplying materials for the stretch of the M1 that runs through north Buckinghamshire and south Northamptonshire.

Tablets in Cosgrove church give details of the local squirearchy over the years – the Mansells, the Thorolds and the Atkinsons. Captain P. Y. Atkinson who died a few years ago is particularly remembered as a great benefactor, while his father Joseph lives on in the memories of older villagers as 'Puffer' Atkinson – the first man in Cosgrove to have a motor car.

The Atkinsons lived at Cosgrove priory, a fine house standing slightly apart from the village and close to the river. Nearby there used to be a very picturesque water mill which was working busily until the 1920s but has sadly now been demolished.

Cosgrove Priory features in the village's ghost story which is a sad tale concerning the daughter of a family who lived in the house. She fell in love with a shepherd but her family forbade her to see him and, so the story goes, then had the hapless lad deported on a false charge of sheep stealing. Broken-hearted the girl threw herself into the nearby mill race and sometimes at full moon her ghost can be seen in that area.

As well as a ghost, Cosgrove can boast of something more tangible from the past. In a field behind the old National School lies St Vincent's Well, one of the genuine Holy Wells safeguarded by an Act of Parliament. The water is high in iron content and said to have great healing properties, being especially effective in curing eye troubles.

The oldest building in Cosgrove is the church of St Peter and St Paul, with its attractive tower rising high above the houses at the 'top end' of the village. The best view of it is obtained by entering Cosgrove along the Stratford road, past Cosgrove Hall and its pretty thatched lodge. Here in the neighbouring spinney every spring can be seen hundreds of daffodils, which makes this one of the most picturesque spots in the village.

At one time there were three village pubs in Cosgrove, but two have been converted into houses, leaving the Barley Mow to flourish in its canalside setting. The towpath along the canal provides a very attractive walk and gives the best view of the fine stonebridge that links the two halves of the village.

Although Cosgrove has changed and grown over the years, the lack of a through road has helped preserve its air of tranquillity.

Cotterstock

Cotterstock Hall was built in 1658. The poet Dryden was a frequent visitor and wrote his *Fables* here. One room is still called 'Dryden's Room'. The Hall was bought by Colonel Henry Wickham in 1912. Life in the village centred around the Hall. In addition to the staff employed at the house, there were the village blacksmith, carpenter, stonemason, builder, miller, baker, gamekeeper, road man, tenant farmers and farm workers. The estate was sold in 1927.

The Vicar of Cotterstock was also vicar of Glapthorne. The parishes were divided in 1921 and Cotterstock was then linked with Tansor, later Fotheringhay and finally in the re-organisation of 1986, with Warmington.

The only public house was the Gate Inn, but this was closed in 1961 and became a private residence. The mill, built in the 19th century, was destroyed by fire in 1968. The main bridge over the river had been rebuilt in 1956 to carry heavy vehicles to and from the mill.

Electricity was brought to the village in the early 1930s, but the village street remains unlit. Piped water came in the late 1930s, and before that all water was obtained from pumps and a well.

The village school was closed in the early 1930s, although it was re-opened temporarily during the Second World War to accommodate evacuees from the cities. The only occasion that brought the war closer to the village was when a bomb fell in the field near Church Farm.

Since then life has not changed a great deal and Cotterstock remains a peaceful, small, rural village.

Cottesbrooke ❧

Midway between Market Harborough and Northampton, Cottesbrooke is a village of 100 souls. With the kennels of the Pytchley Hunt close by, it is in the centre of hunting country.

In the 19th century, Cottesbrooke Hall had the honour of being occupied by the Empress of Austria, who regularly rode to hounds and brought a certain amount of publicity to it when local 'Bay' Middleton piloted her for the season. The Hall is a beautifully kept 18th century building of good proportions, with gardens that give much pleasure to the public on the occasions when they are open for charity.

Several houses of local stone have thatched roofs and larger properties, together with modernised cottages and a row of almshouses, add very much to the village atmosphere. The almshouses were erected by one of the early squires and are for local pensioners, two widowers and six poor widows who have been village residents. They have been beautifully restored with money from the charity itself plus additional gifts, and are very pleasant retirement homes.

In medieval times there was a flourishing company of monks who occupied a cell, situated to the north-west of the village. Kayland's Cell (hence Calender Farm) was part of the order founded by St Norbert in Laon, France, in 1150. The order lasted in England until the Dissolution of the Monasteries and they were known as the 'White Canons'. The field next to Hinson's Meadow (where there is a spring known as the 'Monk's Well') has sometimes been known as St Norbert's field.

The church, situated in the village, dates from 1220. The interior has a three-tier pulpit and has been carefully restored. Some of the pews were originally from the Brixworth workhouse chapel. There is a squire's pew in the organ loft complete with a fire grate. Some destruction to the memorials occurred when Cromwell's army was in the vicinity, indeed cannon balls now in Northampton Museum were found in local fields.

In spite of being only ten miles from Northampton, Cottesbrooke is truly rural. It has no post office, shop or public house, but it does have an original Victorian post box that the villagers fought to retain.

Courteenhall ❧

Courteenhall is a tiny village situated just five miles from the town of Northampton, consisting of a church, 20 houses, a farmhouse, the Old Rectory and a tiny art gallery, a virtual time capsule in this day and age and a village that cannot be driven through; an estate village which is more or less privately owned. A drive through country lanes brings you to this delightful haven of peace, where the most serious 'crime' appears to be children scrumping apples. The biggest transition into the 20th century came in the 1950s when the M1 was cut across the countryside just half a mile from the village. With hundreds of trees planted to obscure the sight and sound of a motorway, it is no longer a blot on the landscape and the continuous roar of the traffic has become part of everyday life.

At this time too, major changes were made to the stone built cottages, when all the thatched roofs were removed and indoor sanitation was installed. The village pump remains and, although waterless now, the open top provides a nesting site for great tits, who risk eggs and nestlings if curious visitors operate the handle.

Parts of the church date back to the 12th century, with the names and dates of the rectors being recorded from 1272, but it is now quite modern inside. It is light and airy because of a clear glass east window, and has chairs instead of pews. An unusual feature is the leper's window, which has recently been restored.

Another very fine building on the estate, just a short walk across parkland from the village, is The Old Grammar School, an endowed school which was used as a grammar school until just before the turn of the century and as a classroom again during the Second World War. It was built more than 300 years ago, with a dormitory over the main hall. This hall is now used for all village activities, while maintaining the desks and benches, and the oak panelling with many names and dates carved in it, thus retaining its atmosphere as a school.

As well as a grammar school, there was also a small primary school. Now sadly closed, the actual building is incorporated into The Grammar School House. From the endowment of The Old Grammar School comes an apprenticeship fund which is still in operation today. All children when leaving school are due to receive a sum of money to buy books or tools of their trade to help them with their career.

Cranford

The two villages of Cranford St Andrew and Cranford St John are divided only by the Alledge brook, a tributary of the river Nene, and to all intents and purposes are one community. In the 11th century the name of the village was Craneford, after the birds which came to the ford to catch fish, and the village emblem recalls this tradition.

Each village has its own church, both 12th century in origin. St Andrew's is now used for services only in the summer and its four bells no longer ring out over the village. There is also a public house in each village – the Woolpack in Cranford St Andrew is thatched and dates at least from the 18th century, while the Red Lion is even more ancient.

Cranford St Andrew has the village hall, and several interesting buildings. Cranford Hall is an 18th century Georgian mansion, the home of the Robinson family, who have a connection with Cranford going back

Cranford Post Office

300 years. Nearby is Dairy Farm, once the manor house, parts of which date from the 17th century, and a tall circular dovecote, with 400 nesting places.

There is also an early 17th century manor house in Cranford St John, and this part of the village has the 18th century building housing the post office/shop and the primary school, built in 1857. At No's 2 and 4 High Street, built in 1849, there was a dormitory, where famiies would send their eldest children to sleep so as to give more room at home!

Next to the post office are two 17th century thatched cottages, formerly an inn called The Stag.

Creaton

Creaton village, lying eight miles north-west of Northampton on the road to Welford, used to be in two parts, Great Creaton and Little Creaton. Now, however, there is little or nothing to be seen of the village that once was Little Creaton and lay a mile or so to the south in Spratton parish. 'Top Orchard' holds its secrets but one or two can still be told. Turn off the Welford Road by Highgate House and walk some hundred yards through the Norwegian elms till you near an old stone cottage. Look to your right into the field and call on the ghost of Amphyllis Twigden.

'Top Orchard' was a place she knew well. John Twigden was a yeoman of Little Creaton who married Anne Dickens of Great Creaton, whose family had connections with the Spencers of Althorp and the

51

Thorntons of Brockhall. Anne and John had five daughters, one called Amphyllis. Her early years must have been spent in the gardens and fields around here, her home, now a mere trace, was somewhere just below this turf. She and her four sisters must have walked the path to Spratton church where they had been baptised and as she grew into womanhood she was wooed and won by a man of the church, the Reverend Lawrence Washington of Purleigh. They became the parents of two Virginia emigrants, John and Lawrence.

Well-masoned stones in the field wall and clear lines of foundations in the field betray the old settlement – in living memory some buildings remained there – but only grass grows now where once the Twigden children played.

Point out this place to your friends from the New World; this is where the great-great-grandmother of America's first president, George Washington, was born.

Crick 🌿

Crick, perhaps better known to travellers on the M1 motorway as Junction 18, is situated on the A428, the main Coventry to Northampton road.

The large beautiful parish church, St Margaret of Antioch, stands in the centre of the village, built of local yellow sandstone with a splendid tower of red Warwickshire stone added sometime after the main building. St Margaret's in its present form dates from the 13th century. At one time Archbishop Laud, martyred in 1644, was rector. A copy of his portrait by Van Dyke hangs in the south aisle.

The present county primary school was opened in 1915 and replaced two small schools built in 1846 and 1847 on either side of the church-yard gate. A remark in the log book for 4th February 1895 states that as the ink was frozen, other activities than writing were to be undertaken!

The two former schools are still in use today, one is the Ex-Service Social Club and the other, known as 'The Old School', is used for meetings, houses the village library, and on Sundays is the meeting place for the children's church.

Many new homes have been built in recent years but there are still older ones left, mainly of stone but some are thatched. The principal houses in the village are Vyntners Manor and Crick Manor. Phoenix House in the High Street is unusual because it is built entirely of blue bricks, which were left over after the building of Kilsby tunnel.

Queen's House in Lauds Road, formerly known as The Cabin, was presented to George Smith of Coalville by Queen Victoria in recognition of his efforts to improve the conditions of children working in the brickworks and also his great care and efforts to educate the canal people.

Crick has three public houses, The Red Lion, The Wheatsheaf and the Royal Oak. All have a long history. In 1900 there were an additional two, one of which only closed in the 1960s. Crick has very few shops, mainly a post office, grocery stores and a hairdresser's. There is a popular antiques shop, and other small businesses.

The Leicestershire branch of the Grand Union Canal passes along the edge of the village. Boat Horse Lane was where the canal horses walked whilst the barges went through the tunnel.

The Crick Treacle Mines are now out of production and a great village myth has grown around them. At festival times their old implements are displayed in the village. Sometimes one of the miners, who is dressed rather like one of the seven dwarfs, can be seen in the village!

Croughton ❧

Croughton lies in the southern corner of Northamptonshire, almost on the borders of Oxfordshire and Buckinghamshire. It is a friendly, active village, with some 300 to 400 houses. There is a good local pub, The Blackbird, and a post office and general store.

The medieval church, in its peaceful setting, is famous for its 13th century wall paintings, uncovered during reconstruction work earlier this century. Facing the gate is a tree with a gnarled old trunk, 35 feet round. If you stand and look you can see all sorts of things nature has carved, including an elephant!

Children are catered for with an excellent primary school, fresh and bright and built in the grounds of the old Church school, which now houses a thriving playgroup.

On the borders of the village is the US air base. Fortunately it is a communications base, not an operational one, so we are hardly aware of its existence except at Christmas when they throw a wonderful party for all the old folk.

Unusually for a small village there is a small industrial estate providing work for some villagers, while the farming community still plays a large part in the economic structure of the village. The local quarry is kept busy providing stone for the M40 extension.

Culworth ❧

Culworth is an ancient site. Stone Age people walked here on old track-ways, and a Roman coin has been found in Banbury Lane. A mound and ditch beside the church, known today as Berry Hill, is said to be the remains of a castle built in King Stephen's reign.

St Mary's church dates from the 12th century, but was much restored in 1841. There are six bells in the tower. In the last century these were often

Memorial in Culworth

rung, and an occasion most trying for the inhabitants must have been the hour-long ring starting at 5am on each Monday in Advent.

A product of Culworth was white paving stone which, with blackstone from Byfield, was used to make chequered floors imitating marble, as can be seen in the hall of the manor.

For nearly 20 years in the late 18th century, the notorious Culworth Gang terrorised the countryside for miles around, attacking stage-coaches, robbing travellers and plundering houses. There were about 15 of them, one of the chief being John Smith, described as 'of advanced years, but of great strength and daring.' His two sons also took part, as did the parish clerk of Sulgrave (a shoemaker), who was said to carry pistols when about his duties in the church.

They hid much of their booty in Sulgrave church, and for years none dared give evidence against them. Eventually carelessness gave them away. Two members spending the night at an inn at Towcester had two bags with them, said to contain fighting cocks. While they slept the landlord peeped into the bags and found smocks, and blackened masks, which had been the guise of robbers in the district. He told the Constable, and when the villains broke into a house near Blakesley they were caught red-handed. This led to most of the gang being tried at Towcester Assizes in 1787. One was transported and four executed, among them John Smith. He left a last message to his son from the scaffold, asking that 'you take care of these letters, and cause them to be read to my children every Sabbath Day, and I hope God will give them grace to take warning: it is the prayer of a dying father.'

Culworth still has a village green, where lies the remains of a stone seat. Until replaced by the war memorial this stood upon a plinth nearby, for the auctioneer on cattle market days.

When older villagers were young there were two public houses (now one), four shops (now one), a baker, cobbler, butcher and forge (fortunately these two last remain). The carrier did errands in Banbury twice weekly, the coalman called, and Mr Hobbs from Railton's shoe shop was in the village fortnightly. The doctor lived in the village, but it was wise not to be taken ill whilst he was out hunting!

At Christmas a group of mummers toured the villages and farms, and the members of the church choir played handbells – to the big houses on Christmas Eve, and to the rest of the village on Boxing Day. Nowadays the young people still ring the handbells at Christmas for charity.

Deanshanger

Deanshanger, once a forest hamlet in Passenham parish, with two hamlets to the north, Holywell and Little London, is now a large village and still growing.

Up to 1791 Whittlebury Forest was still dense, but in the early 19th century clearing began and cottages were built around the many springs of excellent water in the area, that came out of the limestone faults.

The origins of this forest village probably date back to Roman times, as workmen found remains of a Roman villa when building Kingsbrook School. The school got its name from the brook running through the village.

Dove House Farm (called Duffus, meaning food house) is built in the shape of a cross and was once Deanshanger monastery. It is said to have been visited by Archbishop Thomas a Becket in the 12th century, who also stayed at Dagnel Farm. While the Archbishop was here he was asked to bless the water at Bears Watering, thought to be poisoned.

Although the parish church was in Passenham, when Deanshanger began to grow in 1850 another church was built here as a chapel of ease. Now Holy Trinity church, it was licensed for weddings in the 1940s.

The first chapel in Deanshanger was on the Willow Green, and in 1833 it became an infant school. Older villagers remember that at Christmas time the children would suddenly see Father Christmas run across the playground, but he had always disappeared leaving a sack of toys and gifts before the children could get out!

Although the village was small with no water or elecricity, candles or oil lamps were used and water was carried from stand pumps. There were five public houses, two butchers, three coal merchants (Wharf House – dating 1849), a post office, cobbler, five farms, a policeman, tailor, and three bakers. It was a common sight on Sunday mornings to see people taking their joints of meat and Yorkshire puddings to be cooked in the large ovens.

Dove House was once Deanshanger monastery

Village characters included Mr Luke Roberts, known as Dr Guffy, for he would do anything from taking out teeth to replacing dislocated collar bones (real doctors had to come to the village on horseback).

The Deanshanger Iron Works was established in 1820 by Edwin and Henry Roberts, making farm implements, baker's ovens, windmills and so on. After a fire destroyed much of it in 1912 the factory remained derelict until 1935, when Mr A. Wreschner came to this country and started a chemical factory making lead and iron oxides. It is now owned by Harcros Chemicals and is still sending the same products all over the world today.

Deene & Deenethorpe

As you leave Corby and travel four miles along the road towards Stamford you come across the sister villages of Deene and Deenethorpe. These two are among the last remaining estate villages, both belonging to Deene Park and inhabited by estate workers and old retainers. Deene Park estate has been owned since the 16th century by the Brudenell family, who are descendants of the Earls of Cardigan.

Deene is a tiny, unspoilt limestone village, hiding among the trees on the edge of the Willow Brook to the west of the A43. Deenethorpe is on the opposite side of the main road, nestling on the hillside. The dwellings in both villages are occupied by a host of estate workers: farm workers employed on the 10,000 acres of mixed farmland, gamekeepers to tend the birds for the shoots – both commercial and private, gardeners for the park grounds, foresters for the woodlands and a bevy of domestic staff. There are many fathers and sons and mothers and daughters employed in this tight little community.

During the Second World War an American air base was located behind Deenethorpe. One night a bomber returning from a raid crashed in Deenethorpe, damaging properties and shattering the stained glass windows in the Hall. Luckily most of the coloured glass was salvaged and the window has been restored to its former splendour, although the surrounding glass is now clear.

The church of St Peter in Deene was originally built in the 12th century, but was extensively restored in 1868 by Lady Adeline Cardigan in memory of her husband, James – 7th Earl of Cardigan, who was famous for his part in the Battle of Balaclava and the Charge of the Light Brigade.

The 7th Earl was probably the most colourful owner of the estate and the house contains a collection of Crimean memorabilia, including his uniforms and medals. It also houses the stuffed head of the charger *Ronald* that he rode into battle. Lady Adeline, who lived at Deene until 1915, was remembered as being rather eccentric. She wished to be remembered as a beautiful woman, so when her husband died – although she was still comparatively young and outlived him by 46 years – she had her own death mask made at the same time. She kept her coffin in the house and would lie in it and ask people how she looked. Her extravagance finally led to the arrival of the bailiffs and the sale of many of her clothes, carriages and horses. She was often seen bicycling around the village wearing Lord Cardigan's regimental trousers.

Denford

Set apart from other villages by its attractive riverside setting, Denford enjoys a quiet Nene valley location. Early settlement is evident from crop marks, with a major site being on the edge of the flood plain on the boundary with Ringstead. Other settlement existed at higher levels on what is now some of the best agricultural land in the region.

Like most villages in the region it was recorded at the time of Domesday. This tells us that two mills yielded a higher value than those of surrounding villages, suggesting a village of relative importance. Little is known of the following 500 years until church records began and a number of stone houses and barns were built, some of which remain. The main High Street provides examples of several 17th century buildings, indicative of the great rebuilding that occurred on the Midlands stone belt at that time. The local abundance of stone could have been a factor behind the construction of a church as early as 1237, possibly on a site of earlier worship.

A Wesleyan and Methodist chapel was built in 1872 to cater for a fast growing population. At times its congregation overflowed into the street outside. A victim of falling population, it ceased to be a place of worship several years ago.

Denford's population in the early 18th century was around 250 with about 70 houses, and changed little for the following 100 years. Throughout the 19th century the population expanded sharply and reached 500 around 1880. Brick kilns in the parish provided some employment and the scars left on the landscape can still be seen. Most residents however were agricultural workers. The decline in population began in the late 19th century and continued steadily. Today it is around 220 and in these terms the community has contracted to its lowest total for centuries.

A school, presumably charitable, is mentioned in 1670 although its location at that time and later remains to be confirmed. A new school for the younger children was begun in 1870 and remained open until the 1950s. In its early years over 40 children attended lessons. Older children would walk the mile across the fields to Ringstead in the summer and walk on the road in the winter. If lucky they might catch a lift on the brewer's dray to make the journey easier.

Denton

The village of Denton lies some five miles from Northampton, off the A428. The village is fortunate because a bypass was built in 1929, so most of the time it is relatively tranquil and traffic-free.

The village church of St Margaret stands in a perfect setting – in immaculately kept grounds in the centre of the village. This parish church of Denton is one of four churches under the care of the one vicar, with a good congregation and a large Sunday school. There is a key available from the post office, which is situated in Church Way, behind the church. The walls inside the church have been decorated with a series of large murals, painted by a well-known local artist, Henry Bird.

The church overlooks Main Street and to the left, over the roof tops, will be seen the dovecote, long since disused, but the subject of a preservation order. In fact the whole of the village centre is designated a conservation area. There is an old horse trough on the village green, fed by a spring and always full of water. It is said that you were not a Dentonian until you had fallen into the horse trough! One of the original village pumps still stands on the village green.

Further down the green, on the right, there is an archway between two old thatched cottages. This pathway leads uphill to our most recent buildings, including the health centre, village hall and primary school.

At this end of the village lies the cemetery and there is a Baptist chapel at the top of a flight of stone steps. All roads out of Denton are uphill as the village is in a valley with a stream through the centre. The only evidence of this now is the bridge by the church, as the stream was channelled underground in a big flood relief programme many years ago.

There is a public house, the Red Lion, a well-stocked Co-operative store and a family butcher's shop along Main Street, with the post office in Church Way. There are two 'new' estates within the village which blend in well with the older properties, The Leys and Bridgemeadow, bringing the population up to approximately 800.

Duddington ✑

Duddington was originally situated within the old Rockingham Forest and a settlement was recorded in the Domesday survey of 1086.

It is one of the prettiest villages in the area and benefited greatly when it was bypassed twice, so that the A47 was re-routed to the north over a new road bridge and the A43 was re-routed to the east. This was initiated in 1971 when Duddington was designated a conservation area.

The approaches to the village are particularly attractive. From the west the road from Leicester crosses the river Welland over an ancient bridge, medieval in origin, and passes by the 17th century water-mill with its mansard roofs.

There are many lovely buildings in the village and probably the best is the manor, which has belonged to the Jackson family since it was built in the early 17th century. It can be glimpsed from the road through its wrought iron gateways, nestling in its enchanted garden which sweeps down to the banks of the river.

The parish church of St Mary now shares its rector with 3 neigh-

Duddington village

bouring villages, but regular services are still held here. It is most notable for its 12th and 13th century architecture and the abnormal siting of its tower – on the south side. This probably occurred because of falling ground on the west side where the slope to the river begins. Inside there remain some boxed pews, many retaining their 17th century panelling, and a large number of monuments to commemorate the Jackson family, who still reside at the manor.

The adjacent Church Farm still has a two-cell 18th century dovecote with 800 nesting boxes and, although it is now the only working farm in the village, from 1775 until 1834 it was the parish workhouse.

Duddington was originally an agricultural community centred on the manor, but although many of the farm buildings remain their usage has changed and most of them are restored as residential properties. Many small cottages have been combined to form single dwellings and consequently the population has fallen from 321 in 1918 to around 200. There is no longer a village shop and the school was closed in 1962, but there is a flourishing public house, the Royal Oak, to refresh visitors.

Earls Barton

Earls Barton is a busy village situated about six miles from Northampton. It is well known for its footwear industry and its products are much sought after world-wide.

The most famous landmark of the village is the Saxon tower on the church of All Saints. This attracts many visitors from all parts of the world, the most famous visitor to date being Her Majesty the Queen Mother, who paid her visit during the Millenium Year in 1970, and planted an oak tree in the churchyard. The village was also honoured by another visit from Her Majesty when she came to open the new shoe factory owned by A. Barker & Sons.

The village boasts several listed buildings, which include the Manor House in the High Street, the red telephone kiosk on the Square and the gate posts at the entrance to the Manor House Flats. Earls Barton also has its own museum, which is well worth a visit.

Since the 1960s the village has doubled in size, the new housing estates and the new people blending exceedingly well with the old. The village is well served by a good assortment of shops, a library, a modern family medical practice with an equally modern chemist shop, and a good bus service link to adjoining towns.

Spiritual needs are catered for by the parish church, the Roman Catholic church and the Methodist and Baptist chapels. There is also a good primary and infants school, and play schools for the toddlers.

The village is surrounded by lovely views across the Nene valley and some interesting walks can be enjoyed without having to go too far away.

East Farndon 🪶

East Farndon is situated on the borders of Northamptonshire and Leicestershire, about two miles south of the town of Market Harborough. It is surrounded by rolling countryside. Most of the village borders each side of the main street, which is the B4036 road to Daventry. The houses are a mixture of old and new, many fronting the road without gardens. A small stone manor house stands on the Back Street which has the date 1664 carved on it.

There was a village at East Farndon at the time of the Domesday Book in 1086. In the 1800s the population was about 250 people and the trades included bricklayer, shopkeeper, baker, tailor, carpenter, publican, bootmaker, corndealer, maltster, miller and several farmers and graziers – the local countryside being very suitable for fattening cattle.

Today's population is about 245 and apart from five farms, most of the people work outside the village. Both of the public houses are now private dwellings. There are two small businesses but these employ few people who live in the village. Descendants of the miller, George Haynes, still farm in the village but the mill, standing in a field off Marston Road, was burned down.

In a field nearby stands a large stone reputed to be a glacial deposit from the Ice Age. It is known as 'The Judith Stone', referring to the fact that at the time of the Domesday survey local land was held by Countess Judith of Huntingdon.

The church of St John the Baptist, which stands at the top end of the village, has ancient foundations, though most of it has been restored. It has five bells in the belfry; the tenor bell is dated 1587 and the second bell 1675. The United Charities administer bequests, the earliest of which dates from 1640.

The National school, situated opposite the church had 60 pupils in the late 19th century, but this was closed in 1965 and the few children now living in East Farndon are taken by bus to either Clipston or Guilsborough.

Although there are now no shops or a post office, the village is a very pleasant place in which to live and is within easy reach of Market Harborough and the larger towns of Kettering, Northampton and Leicester.

East Haddon 🪶

In the Domesday Book 'Eddone' is recorded as having three manors each owning 'two ploughs of oxen', with a mill and a church with a clerk, in the gift of the Abbey at Leicester. Church registers later show a pattern of an agricultural peasantry with a population of 300 to 400.

The village appears to have been self-supporting during the 1800s with three large farms employing ten or more men, selling butter, milk and eggs, and a baker, where villagers could also take their Sunday dinner to cook – the signal was the tolling of the 'Pudding Bell' (or Sanctus Bell) in the church tower. It was collected at mid-day, cooked to a turn, and all for 2d! There was also a butcher, a saddler, a dressmaker, and most cottagers had their patch of wheat or barley as well as vegetables and fruit trees. There were at least twelve pumps and many wells.

At the time the Lord of the Manor was a Mr Sawbridge who built East Haddon Hall and many cottages for his innumerable staff. He and other public spirited gentlemen built the village Church School and a school house in the grounds for the master. There were 87 pupils.

When the railway was built the population rose to 650 and a few more houses were erected. The Co-op and the Methodist chapel were built and the Hall changed ownership. The new lord of the manor was a member of Parliament with liberal views. He turned one of the inns into a Trust House and encouraged church and chapel to join together in social activities.

Although the village is no longer a farming community – there being only two farm labourers and many machines to do the work – it is a very alive and 'villagey' place. Local events are always well supported and the prmary school – now Church assisted – goes from strength to strength.

East Haddon is a very pretty village with a warm stone towered church, thatched cottages with beautiful gardens and a thatched village pump. Although there is no village green there are still Mayday celebrations with a May Queen and dancing around the maypole. The present owner of the Hall has developed a squash court complex, including a creche for infants, which means there is plenty of activity in the village throughout the day.

Easton Maudit

Easton Maudit takes its name from the Mauduit family who bought the estate at Easton (East Farm) in 1131. It was not until 1578, however, that the village had its first resident landowner when Sir Christopher Yelverton bought the manor house and estate at Easton. Sir Christopher became Speaker of the House of Commons and his contacts instigated a flow of important visitors over the years.

Easton Maudit vicarage was also the subject of frequent visits. Dr Samuel Johnson, Oliver Goldsmith and David Garrick were often the guests of the then vicar, the Rev Dr Thomas Percy, who was a fellow member of Dr Johnson's London club – the Garrick. A plaque marks the pew used by them in Easton Maudit church.

An interesting story concerns the Rev Francis Tolson, who was vicar from 1732–45 and is buried in the church. Apparently he was not wrapped in wool at his interment according to the then laws of England; a practice designed to help the farmers of the day! Through this neglect he could not rest in his grave and it was said that he 'walked' at night by the pond in the vicarage garden. He is said to have been eventually laid to rest by twelve clergymen throwing 13 lighted candles into the pond after him so that the ghost should not walk again until the candles were burnt out!

There is another story concerning the mysterious Holy Grail or chalice which apparently disappears from the church for years then, suddenly, reappears again. Much has been written about this strange phenomenon.

In the village square are the stunted remains of an historic elm tree planted many centuries ago. Its great age is indicated by its girth, measuring some 23 feet. Both John Bunyan and John Wesley are believed to have preached the Gospel beneath its canopy. Only in recent years did it die and present its now sorry appearance.

There have been few changes to the village over the years apart from a declining population – down from over 200 to about 60. Several houses and barns are listed as of architectural merit, though inevitably the fine church, which can be seen for miles around, remains the focal point. Originally dating from 1050 it was totally rebuilt in 1350, with the spire being added in the 15th century.

Easton-on-the-Hill ✍

Easton-on-the-Hill is situated in the very north-eastern tip of the county of Northamptonshire, on the borders of Cambridgeshire, Lincolnshire and that part of Leicestershire that was Rutland.

A lane lined by small limestone houses, topped with Collyweston slate roofs, leads up the hill to the church, standing among trees in the churchyard. The parish church of All Saints is the dominant landmark of the village and dates back to the 12th century, but it has been enlarged and altered over the centuries. Some of the pews have been there since Stuart times and retain the oak pegs where men hung their hats while they were at prayer. Before the organ was installed the hymn singing was accompanied by a long bassoon – housed in the vestry. There is also a tablet to the memory of Lancellot Skinner – a rector's son who was lost in the famous wreck of *La Lutine* off the coast of Holland in 1799. The ship's bell was recovered and has become historic in the City of London, hanging at Lloyds.

The oldest building in the village is the 'Priests House', now belonging to the National Trust. Formerly the Old Rectory it was built around 1500, but probably ceased to be a clergy house as early as 1553. It was then used as stables, extensively repaired in 1867, and finally passed to the National Trust.

Easton is one of the larger villages in the area and as such boasts a well used post office and general store, a modern infants school and play school and three public houses. In the early 1920s, however, business thrived in the community with a butcher, two blacksmiths, two carpenters and a wheelwright, an undertaker, a tailor, cobbler and market garden as well as a barber's shop. It also took eight public houses to quench the thirst of the population! The old school building has been renovated for use as the village hall.

In the late 19th century the whole village was lit with gas lights, powered from a gas works in the village, and served with piped water from a reservoir to street taps, provided by Mr Neville Day – at his own expense as a memorial to Charles Day. The reservoir has now been filled in and Neville Day Close has been constructed on the site, remembering the generosity of this village resident.

'n the early part of the 20th century a great many men were employed at the Easton-on-the-Hill ironstone quarry. This was only operational for about 50 years and it was never a great success, probably due to the fact that the closest ironworks were in Scunthorpe and the inclining ground made working the site very restrictive. They did, however, enjoy a few years of prosperity during the First World War when the demand for iron was at its peak.

Ecton

The 13th century church of St Mary Magdalen is the centre of Ecton in more ways than one. The comfortable parish room is the venue for many organisations, and the generous use allowed of the retreat rooms, for charitable as well as personal celebrations, helps to integrate the many and varied people who pass through Ecton House.

There is an historical link with America through the Franklin family. The aunt and uncle of Benjamin Franklin are buried in the churchyard; the connection brings many interested visitors.

Hogarth is said to have painted a sign for the Worlds' End Inn, in payment of a debt.

The village still holds the medieval pattern and has expanded very little, infilling only having been allowed for some years. Two splendid barns have been converted into fine houses. Ecton Hall, almost a ruin, has now been restored and made into luxury flats, with several houses in the grounds, an addition of 26 homes.

Sheep still safely graze within sight of the village, though shots may be heard culling the pheasants so lately strolling in our gardens. Cricket is played across the A4500, and there is a Youth Club. There are not many young people in the village as there is no industry to employ them.

A feature is the large number of deep wells in the village, there are four within a stone's throw of the Old School House. There was a bakery, blacksmith and thatcher at one time, and there are still a number of thatched homes. In the playing field there is a fine walnut tree.

Evenley ❧

The village of Evenley stands on elevated ground about a mile south-east of Brackley. It lies near the point of junction of the three parishes of Turweston, Evenley and Mixbury and of the three counties Buckinghamshire, Northamptonshire and Oxfordshire.

For visitors to the village the first impression is that created by the village green, which is roughly square and is bounded by a roadway on all four sides. The green is flat and the turf is well-tended, providing an area for children's recreation and well-suited for cricket.

The manor house situated near to the north-west corner of the green is one of the oldest buildings in the village. Diagonally opposite at the south-west corner stands the Red Lion Hotel. At one time there was a roadway between these two buildings to give easy access out of the village for horse-drawn vehicles. This roadway was later taken over by the County Council and closed and grassed over. During the hot summer of 1976 the route of the old road could be clearly seen as a band of parched grass.

The village shop and sub-post office lies about midway along the north side of the green and serves the local community and the nearby village of Mixbury. These premises were formerly the malt-house barn, which in 1925 was altered for use as a working men's club by Major Allen of Evenley Hall, and it acted as the village hall until the school building became available for this purpose.

The Anglican church of St George is located to the north-west of the village. The original building may have been Norman or Saxon in origin. Almost all records of Evenley in early times perished in a fire that gutted the church. The present St George's church is a stone structure in the Early English style and was rebuilt in 1865 at the expense of the Hon Mrs Pierrepont of Evenley Hall in memory of her husband.

The Hall is set back some distance from the A43 and is reached by way of an avenue lined with lime trees. Viewed from a distance these trees look like a row of guards wearing busbies! During the Second World War the Hall was used by the Yorkshire Regiment. In 1941 ownership passed to the trustees of the National Children's Home and after the war the premises were adapted for the residential care of children.

Over the years there have been many changes in the pattern of farming in and around the village, where at one time sheep and dairy farming predominated. Many of the pastures have been ploughed for arable crops. With reductions in the manual labour required for farming, there have been movements out of the village and an influx of newcomers following a variety of professions and occupations.

Everdon ✑

Everdon is situated about two miles south of the A45. It has grown in a valley, surrounded by rolling countryside, having the beautiful woodlands of Mantles Heath and Everdon Stubbs nearby. Visitors from many miles away come each spring to see the bluebells in all their glory.

The village is old. It is mentioned in a charter dated AD 944, and at the time of the Domesday Book (1086) it belonged to the Bishop of Bayeaux. Later, much of Everdon was the property of the Benedictine Abbey of Bernay in Normandy.

This century has seen the closure of four of the five public houses and of the butcher's, the baker's, the Co-op, the post office and two other small shops – a trend common to many more villages. The Baptist chapel is disused, and the village school became a Field Study Centre in 1974.

Like London and Northampton, Everdon has had its Great Fire. This occurred on 13th April 1786 when a serious fire broke out at 2pm. In a short time it had engulfed some 20 houses as well as outhouses and workshops. It spread rapidly across the thatched roofs, but fortunately there was no loss of life. Both College Farm and the Stone House still have scorch marks on beams in their roofs.

The poet, Thomas Gray frequently stayed at Everdon Rectory with his uncle, the Reverend William Antrobus, who was rector here from 1729 to 1744. Many believe that it is Everdon churchyard rather than Stoke Poges churchyard which was the inspiration for his *Elegy*.

St Mary's is a huge church for a village the size of Everdon, more akin to one of the Suffolk 'Wool Churches'. It is thought that prosperous local people combined with the monks from Bernay to build this fine place of worship. It is constructed partly of local ironstone, which although lovely to look at, weathers badly. Much repair and restoration has been carried out since the early 1970s. Funds for this have been raised annually since then at the August Bank Holiday fetes.

The south aisle is said to have been reserved for the parishioners of Snorscombe. The manor house, now a disused farmhouse, one cottage and a converted mill are all that remain of the once flourishing community of Snorscombe. The village was depopulated and its houses pulled down by order of Richard Knightley of Fawsley in 1520.

The hamlet of Little Everdon, about a quarter of a mile from Great Everdon, stands on the new Nene Way. It contains the Hall, built on the site of an old manor house and the Old House dated 1690. Now the vicinity is well known as the location of Captain Hawkins' cricket ground, and the parkland is the setting for the Everdon Horse Trials held every August.

Eydon

The small and attractive village of Eydon lies close to the centre of England, in the southern corner of Northamptonshire. It is well positioned on a hill, surrounded by idyllic undulating countryside. The village contains many fine historic buildings, including Eydon Hall, built by Francis Annesley in 1788 and designed by James Lewis. There is a shop, a public house and a post office. The public house has traded as such at least since the mid 1600s. There is still a 'School House' in Eydon which first opened as a school in 1854, but unfortunately it was forced to close in 1968.

Eydon was recorded in the Domesday Book in 1086, but it is thought by some to have been inhabited long before this. Whatever its Saxon origin, Eydon grew at the side of the ancient Roman road from the villa at Chipping Warden to a settlement at Daventry.

It is believed that a church has been standing in Eydon since 1154. The present church has a Norman font and 14th century tower. Although the medieval records for Eydon are not complete, some of the villagers must have been quite wealthy because the church records show generous gifts at this time. The village suffered two fires, the first being on 13th August 1651, the second on 28th May 1905. Some of the stone in the village buildings even today shows the scorch marks from the fires.

The railways brought welcome alternative employment in the 19th century for the villagers, with the Central and East and West junction railways running close by the village. Apart from work and some prosperity, the railways also brought cheaper coal and newspapers on the day of publication! People were very keen to read of the latest news during the Boer War because three Eydon men were fighting in the armed forces. The railways gradually went into decline and on the 4th September 1966 it was all over. The last train passed by, leaving Eydon with a great silence.

In recent years there has been renewed interest in Eydon, partly due to the M40 motorway. The population in 1841 was 647, today it is approximately 410 and rising. Building within the conservation area is closely monitored and Eydon was first designated a conservation area in October 1970.

Farthinghoe

Farthinghoe is a village of approximately 300–400 people. It is five miles from Banbury and three miles from Brackley, within reach of Northampton and Oxford. The village is split by the A422, along which huge lorries travel at high speed, at times barely negotiating the very sharp corner at the end of the village.

Architecturally it is a mixture of old and new. The main building is the church of St Michael and All Angels. The tower is Norman, and was repaired by Sir John Egerton in 1654 – the date being carved under the one-handed clock, which is quite an unusual feature. The church bells have been dismantled owing to the unsafe bellroom. In 1443 John Abbott founded a school in the vestry, which was then a chantry chapel. Now the vestry is in need of repairs and to achieve this the village has to raise £30,000. Many varied events have and will take place to raise this money.

Next to the church is the village's oldest and most interesting house, Abbey Lodge. It dates from the 15th century, with later alterations. It has a fine carved and moulded fireplace and on the north side a newel stair leading to the upper chamber. Being so old it has a ghost, heard but not seen! In passing it is interesting to note that goats and bees thrive in the Lodge's paddock, thus providing goat's milk, cheese and honey.

There is a Methodist chapel, once a barn and then given by John George in 1894 to the Methodists. It is used for worship twice a month and occasionally for other events. The congregations of both church and chapel are small and once a month combined services are held.

There is still one pub. There were three! This is happily run and besides drinks serves food daily. The friendly village shop and post office provides most local needs. The village school has been in use since 1846, and the modern village hall was designed and built by local men.

Farthingstone

Farthingstone's population in 1801 was 230 increasing to nearly 400 by the beginning of the twentieth century. As the years have passed the population has decreased to 150 souls due to the fact that cottages have been knocked into one house as the present day families require larger spaces to accommodate washing machines, dishwashers, two cars, etc.

The Norman Church is dedicated to the Blessed Virgin and was restored in 1852. In 1874 a vestry was added and the chancel restored.

The village school was built in 1875 originally to accommodate 80 children. Unfortunately, due to falling numbers of children in the village and rising costs, the school was closed in the late 1950s. The children now attend Blakesley School, and the village school has become the Village Hall used for social events by the villagers.

The village pub called the King's Arms dates back as far as the 18th century at which time it was an inn. In 1801/2 there was a fire and all the accommodation area was destroyed. When it re-opened it was just as a public house but it still retains its character.

In the early 20th century, the Agnew family moved into the village and were generally looked upon as the 'squire' as they employed many villagers as gardeners, house-keepers, etc. Mr Philip Agnew J. P. became the High Sheriff of Northamptonshire and was principal proprietor and director of *Punch* magazine. He contributed a great deal to the village of Farthingstone.

Unfortunately, the lost both his son and daughter. His daughter, Enid Jocelyn (Joy) died in 1921 at the age of 22. His only son, Lieutenant Ewan Siegfield Agnew of the 5th Royal Irish Lancers was killed in the First World War. In memory of his children, he gave the village a garden of remembrance called 'Joymead', named after his daughter. Every year to this day the villager hold the Joymead Tea as near to the 13th July as possible in memory of Joy Agnew to which everyone is invited. In the cloisters there is a memorial to the war dead erected in memory of his son. The Joymead Gardens are very well kept and are open to the public.

In 1913 the Agnew's built a beautiful stone stable yard close to their home. The U shaped yard, set around a sun dial, housed both staff and horses. Today it remains virtually unchanged and is known as Littlecourt Yard and Equitation Centre. Immaculately maintained and in glorious surroundings, it is quite unique.

The village post office and stores still survives and carries a good selection of goods from food to stationery.

Farthingstone also has a golf club, Woodlands Vale, that is very popular and open to the public. It used to be a small farm. In the early 1970s the owner had the land cleared and turned into an 18 hole golf course.

Farthingstone is slowly becoming a very desirable village to live and consequently the cost of property is soaring. More and more people from the towns are moving into the village and village life as such is fast dying. A few new properties have been built recently but Farthingstone is still the beautiful village it has always been, surrounded by breathtaking countryside.

Flore

Situated on the south facing slopes of the Nene valley, at the time of the Domesday Book Flore was already a well established village, with a manor and two mills. It is thought that it originated nearer to the Nene than the present village, since the church is in the south-west corner, and the field adjoining it has mounds which indicate the existence of houses. In any case the older part of the village lies on the southern side of the main road, once a turnpike and now the busy A45. Council and private developments on the north side date from the 1930s.

Once a farming village, the community is now mainly composed of commuters. The proximity of the M1, A5 and A45 make Flore a popular village for those whose work involves travelling, and village facilities are good. There is a post office, a resident doctor with his own pharmacy, a

Village green at Flore

vicar, two grocer/greengrocers, a newsagent, a hairdresser, a filling station and garage and a regular bus service.

May Day is held on the second Saturday in May, in a festival dating from 1895. The children of the village primary school elect their Queen from amongst the girls in their last year, the rest of the 'leavers' act as Maids and Knights and the infants' class provides two crown bearers, two page boys and two presenters of the Queen's bouquet.

For the Flower Festival, in the third week in June, the church and 19th century United Reformed chapel are decorated with beautiful displays of flowers, usually depicting a theme. August sees the village Flower Show, organised by the Garden Society, and in November comes the annual Feast Supper run by the church to celebrate All Saints Day.

Fotheringhay

The first written mention of Fortheringhay was in 1060, and it is listed in the Domesday Book in 1086 as 'Fodringeia'.

After many different owners, the manor came into the possession of Edward III who gave it to his son Edmund Langley, the first Duke of York and founder of that powerful house. He it was who founded the College whose chaplains and choristers were to pray for the souls of the founders and their families. Edmund's son Edward Langley continued the work until he was killed at Agincourt in 1415. His body was brought home and buried in the choir, although it was not finished until about

1430. To this private, collegiate church was added the parish church in the same style, begun in 1434. This is the only part which remains today.

Fotheringhay is most famous for the birth of Richard III at the castle in 1452, and for the trial and beheading of Mary, Queen of Scots in 1587. At the time of Richard's birth Fotheringhay had become one of the principal seats of his parents, Richard Plantagenet and Cecily Neville, Duke and Duchess of York, and he spent his first six years here. Members of the Richard III Society join villagers at the annual carol service, and have given a memorial window to the church and refurbished the chapel in memory of the House of York.

Mary Stuart was brought here in September 1586 after 18 years in captivity in different safe places and prisons in other parts of England. Her trial took place in the Great Hall of the castle on 14th and 15th of October and she was beheaded on 8th February 1587.

The castle does not seem to have been used after Mary's death. It fell into ruins and was pulled down in 1635. The stones have been used to build many cottages and walls around the village.

Fotheringhay in the 1980s has a population of about 120 within the parish boundaries and about 80 in the actual village. The primary school closed in 1970 and we lost the post office a few years ago.

The Falcon public house is in the centre of the village and is often used for meetings, which involve the whole village. The darts and domino teams are active in the winter months, and the large garden is popular in summer with its lovely view of the parish church, floodlit after dark. Next to the Falcon, the Fotheringhay Forge continues an age-old tradition supplying local needs. In the village you can also buy a wood-burner, have books rebound and restored, sample bed and breakfast at Castle Farm, or fish in the river Nene! There are also four busy farms.

Gayton 🌿

Gayton is a village in south-west Northamptonshire standing on high ground, with fine views to the east and west.

In the past much ironstone was mined in the area, which leaves some of the roads high above the surrounding fields. National Steel developed iron ore excavation in a large way but soon closed owing to the increased railway charges for transporting the ore to the furnaces.

On the ground sloping towards the river Nene were, at one time, three brick-yards. The dangerous deep pits have now been filled – two as council rubbish tips.

Travelling south-west from the village on still rising ground one comes to the highest point – a flat, clay, waterlogged land with the watershed of the river Nene to the north and the river Ouse to the south. There by the wayside of the road to Eastcote is Millmott, where there was once a water-mill. The site is surrounded by high and ancient willow trees and a large deep drain ditch still remains around a hardcore centre.

In the village by the five roads called Five Ways is a small green called The Pound, originally a wall-surrounded place for impounding stray cattle.

To the north-east of the village is the parish church of St Mary the Virgin. In 1815 the church was restored from its ruinous state by the Rev Dr Butler, but the tower was not restored to its former great height. Standing on high ground it must once have been a noticeable landmark from the upper Nene valley. A further restoration was carried out in 1881–83 by Rev J. C. Williams Ellis, when the chancel was rebuilt and the organ chamber and vestry added.

One of the several tombs in the church is the 14th century one of Lady Scholastica, daughter of Sir Philip de Gayton, who is reputed to have murdered her husband. The child Mabilla, cradled between the corbels above the tomb is not her child but that of her sister, Julianna de Murdak, who was burned as a witch.

Churnwell Spring supplied the village with fine, clear piped water for around 60 years until the area was taken over by the Anglian Water Authority.

In the past, as in most villages, Gayton had its own blacksmith, builder, carpenter, baker, shopkeeper, tailor and dressmaker – but alas none today. Opposite the Pound though is a very attractive thatched cottage which was once the home of the local cooper, or barrel-maker.

Geddington

Geddington lies on the main A43, three miles from Kettering and three miles from Corby.

One of the treasures of the village is the Cross, built in 1294 as a memorial to Edward I's beloved Queen Eleanor. He built a cross at each resting place of her funeral procession from Nottinghamshire to London. Geddington Cross is one of the three surviving and is thought to be the best, both in architectural purity and preservation. The bridge is older than the Cross by 40 years and travellers today may cross the river Ise the same way that Queen Eleanor's cortege crossed 700 years ago.

The church of St Mary Magdalene which received the body of the Queen overnight was then many centuries old. At the rear of the church was a medieval royal hunting palace. Nothing of this now remains except for some fragments of stone in the church, but it is possible that the steeply buttressed cottages in Wood Street originate from the same period. The name Wood Street emphasizes the reason for a palace in Geddington, for this was the heart of Rockingham Forest and very popular with kings and courts of the Middle Ages.

Many old traditions are kept. In the churchyard lies the tomb of Samuel Lee, a ranger in Geddington Chase who died in 1789. In his will he left £100 to be distributed by the churchwardens every Christmas Day. This continues even today.

The Queen Eleanor Cross at Geddington, built in 1294 by Edward I

Every May Day, May Bread is distributed throughout the village as it is in many other places. Some 'traditions' are not so old, but just as pleasant. On May Day the village children take posies to pensioners, singing a May Day song as they go. Then, in the afternoon the May Queen is crowned on the steps of the Cross and the children dance around the maypole. The day finishes with a May tea. At Harvest time the children make up boxes of provisions to take around the village, again to pensioners.

Another tradition which has started in more recent years concerns Geddington Volunteer Fire Brigade. The brigade was formed in 1977 in response to the national firemen's strike. They do not actually put fires out, but they do own a fire engine and they raise money at fetes to increase the funds of Lee's Charity.

Glapthorne

The stone-built village of Glapthorne lies almost unnoticed in its shallow, saucer-shaped valley. Yet it is an ancient settlement, dating from pre-Roman times.

For years Glapthorne was joined with Cotterstock for ecclesiastical purposes, and only comparatively recently has it been joined with Southwick.

Glapthorne's history has been closely studied through its ancient field names. Names like 'Swinner', a field which must have nurtured Saxon pigs, or 'Puckwell Hill Fielde', which conjures up the Old English 'puca' or mischievous goblin. It is interesting that Glapthorne goblins were friendly and helpful, rather than frightening or malevolent. 'Wheate Wong Lees' sounds almost Chinese, but it is merely a reference to an unenclosed area within the enclosed fields. Glapthorne was not enclosed until the early 19th century, and the old field names date back far into the past – the days of Saxon peasants and the confused days following the withdrawal of the Roman legions.

Grafton Regis

Grafton Regis is an historic village situated on a hill, nine miles south of Northampton and nine miles north of the new city of Milton Keynes, on the main A508 road.

There are about 90 residents and 30 houses, a manor house, the old rectory, a village hall (once a local school), the White Hart public house, the church of St Mary the Virgin and three farmhouses. Like most villages, Grafton Regis has changed into a commuter village.

The lords of the manor go back to about 1105 and included the Woodvilles. In 1464 Edward IV married Elizabeth Woodville. Richard III stayed at the manor in 1483. Later Henry VIII stayed here with Ann Boleyn and Grafton became Grafton Regis. The manor house is now a private hospital.

Charles II selected Grafton for the title of the dukedom conferred on his illegitimate son Henry FitzRoy in 1675. Like the Woodvilles before them, the FitzRoys have played a large part in British history.

The church is worth a visit to see the altar tomb of freestone with an alabaster top to the memory of John Woodville. There is also a panel of a medieval screen. The walls are rich with monuments in memory of the FitzRoy family.

The 12th century church consists of an embattled tower containing five bells, nave, north aisle, chancel, Norman font and south porch. The nave roof, windows and porch still require attention, and a number of 'Country fayres' have been held to raise money for the village hall and church.

Grafton Underwood

Grafton Underwood lies in the north of the county, and is located about four miles east of the town of Kettering. It is referred to in the Domesday Book as Grastone. The 'Underwood' was added in the 18th century, probably referring to Grafton Park Wood, part of the old Rockingham Forest which is nearby.

A small stream, a tributary of the river Nene, crossed by several bridges, runs down the side of the main street. The majority of the stone cottages are on the east side of the stream, some of these set at right angles to the road, which gives a pleasing appearance. The cottages are mostly 17th and 18th century, and quite a few of the roofs are thatched, intermingled with Collyweston slate and pantiles. The manor house, dated 1653, is also on the east side.

On the west side of the stream there are some green open spaces and paddocks, with several fine chestnut trees, that afford pleasant views of the parish church of St James. The old school and schoolhouse also lies on the west side. Erected in 1853 by the then Duke of Buccleuch, it is now a private home. The village was almost entirely owned by the Duke of Buccleuch.

The church is a mixture of various architectural designs and periods. The oldest parts are the tower and the nave, which are late Norman. In the vestry there is a record of Thomas Carley, 1757–1825. He was born without hands, and later went on to be parish clerk and schoolmaster. A sample of his copperplate writing can be seen. He held the pen in his mouth.

The most recent addition is a stained glass window, dedicated to the memory of the 1,579 members of the American Eighth Air Force who gave their lives while serving at Grafton Underwood airfield during the Second World War, and especially the members of the 384th Bombardment Group (heavy) who served there the longest.

The airfield to the north of the village was built in 1941. It has the distinction of having been the airfield that the first and last bombing raid by the American Eighth Air Force in Europe, took off from. A granite memorial has been erected on the airfield by the 384th Group, and in addition a banner was presented to the village. It now hangs in the village hall.

Until quite recently, the village was almost entirely owned by the Duke of Buccleuch. Boughton House, built by the Dukes of Montagu, is nearby. Through marriage, Boughton passed to the Douglas Scotts, they added Montagu to the name. The family name of the Buccleuch's is now Montagu Douglas Scott. Fifty years ago there were four farms in the village, today there is only one, and barns have been turned into attractive houses. There are still two thatched barns on the west side of the stream in agricultural use. Sadly there is no village pub, although the Dukes Arms, dated 1645, still stands at the top of the village, now a private home.

Great Addington 🦔

Great Addington or 'Addington Magna' is a small village situated four miles south west of Thrapston, bordered on the east by Ringstead, the south by Little Addington and the west by Burton Latimer. The village is situated in a prominent position overlooking the river Nene.

At one time the Northampton to Peterborough railway ran in close proximity to the river. Unfortunately the station buildings were burnt down about 1938, but the line remained open until the last train ran in May 1964.

Great Addington has today a population of approximately 300, and the acreage included within the parish boundary is 1,230 acres. In 1801 the population was 200, and in 1841 it had risen to 266.

Great Addington boasts an ancient burial ground near the south east end of the village. This elevation has always been known as Shooters Hill, and was used by the ancient Britons and Romans. In the spring of 1847 a Mr Cole writes:

'that whilst digging for gravel the spades of men employed came into contact with many perfect skeletons. There was no indication that a tumulus had been erected to protect them, the sand and gravel proving admirable preservatives. In some cases the face of the body had been placed downwards, others laid on their side, whilst three were recorded indicating rudely constructed urns or vases of unbaked clay, known as drinking cups, indications of Druid Influences'.

The church in Great Addington is dedicated to All Saints. The earliest recorded history of the church mentions that the manor and certain arable lands were given to the Abbey of Croyland in 829 by Wolnoth. There is a possible mention from a charter of 833 of a church at Great Addington in the 12th century. There was a Norman Church on the present site, but of that building only the south porchway remains. The church was dedicated in 1234, alterations followed including the building of the tower in 1350.

Within the church is a tomb with an alabaster figure of Henry de Vere Esq who died in 1516, the last of his particular line. Previously in 1125, an Audrey de Vere dwelt in the Manor, which through him passed to his second son Robert de Vere. Eventually Henry de Vere inherited the Manor and lands in the time of Henry VII. He had lived through the Wars of the Roses, fought on Bosworth Field and possessed two printed books.

The manor house where de Vere lived was thought to be situated somewhere near the present Home Farm. However, the present manor house stands near the church and is of Jacobean origin. The manor passed through various hands until in 1863 when on his marriage to the widow of Viscount Downe, a Mr Sidney Lane purchased and enlarged the manor. His wife's monogram, Mary Isobel, is to be found in the Billiard Room. Lt Col Romer was the next occupant for eleven years, when Miss Breitmeyer bought it in 1936, remaining there until her death in 1986.

Great Addington has record of a village school. It is thought that for a number of years the school met in the porchway of the parish church. In the old rectory there is evidence of a school room on the first floor, probably used until the first school building was constructed on the present site. This was completed with a grant from the National Society in 1875 and in 1876 given to the Rector and Church Wardens for education of the children of Great Addington.

Employment in the village in 1840 was basically agriculture – six farmers are mentioned in the Gazetteer of Northamptonshire. One of these farmers, a Thomas Coleman, was also a miller, the cornmill being situated behind the present Home Farm. Another mill – probably a papermill – was situated towards Ringstead Station. Other occupations recorded were, apart from the Rector, a carpenter, a victualler of the Hare and Hound, a blacksmith, a wheelwright and shopkeeper.

Recollections of the village in the 1920s reveal agriculture was still the principal employment, a blacksmith's shop, and two pubs, the present Hare and Hounds and the Leopard. There were two shops, one adjoining the Bakehouse kept by Ginger Wilson, where you could get a Sunday Dinner cooked for 2d. The other, kept by a Mrs Warr, was a general store and generally in a muddle. A chimney sweep, Fred Smith, was in residence, and there was Wesleyan Chapel with services on Sunday and a reading room/concert hall in the week, but strictly teetotal.

Today only two farmers remain and employment is mostly in the surrounding towns. The village boasts a community bus, but no public transport or shops. The village post office is the centre of communications. Life is quiet but the community spirit is strong and there is seldom a dull moment. Long may it remain so!

Great Billing

In common with other villages in the immediate vicinity of Northampton, Great Billing has been enveloped by the expansion of the county town. However, there are still villagers who can remember it consisting of one main street running from the Wellingborough Road to Billing station, with footpaths across the meadows to Ecton, Little Billing and Weston Favell.

The village is listed in the Domesday Book, and up to the 14th century was situated to the west of the parish church. The population was then decimated by the Black Death, and they abandoned the old village and rebuilt it gradually in its present location. It is fortunate that parts of the village retain much of the old atmosphere, centring on the 12th century church of St Andrew and the old rectory. The village store is in an 18th century property and the old village pump and horse trough can still be seen. There are several other notable buildings in both Church Way and Elwes Way.

The story of Great Billing is intertwined with that of the Elwes family, who at one time owned the whole of the village with the exception of one house and five cottages. They lived in Billing Hall, built in 1776 and unfortunately demolished in 1956.

The only tangible links between the family and the village remaining today are the names of the village inn, The Elwes Arms, and two roads named after members of the family, Elwes Way and Lady Winefride's Walk.

The expansion of the village has changed both the pace of life and the composition of the population, but older villagers thinking of earlier times remember such characters as Charlie Tipler the village sweep and lay preacher. He was always smartly dressed with a clean shirt and shining face. His mode of transport was a pony and trap. He was a great conversationalist, with tales of chimney sweeping in the past at Billing Hall and Horton House. Unfortunately when talking he ignored the passing of time, so that no matter what time he was due villagers learned to expect him only when they could hear the sound of his horse's hoofs!

When outsiders think of Billing today they often first call to mind the Aquadrome, created from old gravel workings, with its marina, caravans and amusements. However, a link between the new and old remains within its grounds, Billing Mill, now a museum, where villagers used to take their corn to be ground.

Great Doddington 🦚

Great Doddington is a long narrow village which lies between Wellingborough town and the village of Earls Barton. It is thought that it dates back to the Iron Age, since traces of four hut circles, storage pits and an internal ditch have been found. Quantities of Saxon and Roman pottery have also been found near the village. There is a limestone ridge, hence the road leading into the village is named The Ridge and the village is built mainly of grey limestone, unlike surrounding villages.

In Church Lane, the centre of the village, stands lovely St Nicholas' church, which is partly Norman. One of its fascinating features is a Jacobean pulpit with a wrought iron hourglass dated 1618. Of the four misericords, one of the carvings shows the artists at work carving the rosettes which adorn the seats. Also in Church Lane is the Old Vicarage, a listed building, no longer a vicarage and now privately owned. At the top of the lane is Doddington Manor Farm, a lovely old manor house.

There are four farms in Great Doddington and throughout the whole year there is much to-ing and fro-ing through the village as tractors and other farm implements go about their seasonal jobs.

The views of the Nene valley and river are beautiful, although since the 1970s much work has been going at the gravel workings. Once restored, there should be landscaped pastures and quiet lakes.

Hardwater Mill is a very pretty picture and a popular attraction for visitors. It is said that the Archbishop of Canterbury, Thomas a Becket, fled here after a clash with King Henry II at Northampton Castle. He was sheltered by the miller before going into self-imposed exile in France. The mill is now converted into a private house.

Great Harrowden

Great Harrowden, in the Hundred of Orlingbury, derives its name from having been a 'Hearg Dun', a place of worship on a hill.

The present place of worship is All Saints' church, which has traces of a 12th century foundation, but may be older. Under a brass in the chancel is the tomb of William of Harrowden (d. 1434) and Margaret, his wife (d. 1441). Their son married Margery Vaux, and so founded the family of Vaux of Harrowden. The family accumulated wealth by marrying heiresses. They built Harrowden Hall, and Nicholas (d. 1523) was made Baron Vaux by Henry VII. His son, Thomas, was a poet who contributed the poem in Act V of Shakespeare's *Hamlet*.

The Hall continued to dominate Great Harrowden sometimes inhabited by its owners, sometimes let, until, in 1876, it regained a brief glory when it was let to Mr Samuel Sharp, who established a girls boarding school there. In 1975, it became the home of Wellingborough Golf Club.

The Hall was, throughout most of its history, the distinguishing feature of Great Harrowden, which has always been a small village whose economy has been dominated by farming. Although it has had a post office, a post house and an alehouse, its present extent does not differ much from former days.

The church derives its present congregation more from Redwell Grange, a housing estate established in the early 1970s and lying within the parish of Great Harrowden along the road to Wellingborough, than from the remaining scattered houses in its own village.

Great Houghton

The prettily shaped spire of Great Houghton's church of St Mary the Blessed Virgin is a landmark, piercing its way through the many mature trees which surround it. Its visibility is made clearer by the elevation of the village, which is built on the southern slopes of the Nene valley, about two miles from Northampton town centre. The village is now encompassed within the Borough of Northampton but holds its breath in the hope that it will not be swallowed completely by the town's expansion.

The name of the village was originally Houghton Magna: the word 'Houghton' means 'settlement on the spur of the hill'. It was an Anglo-Saxon settlement, and it may have been in existence even earlier as it stands on the likely route from the once busy Iron Age trading camp at Hunsbury Hill to the probable river crossing at Clifford, near Little Houghton, on the way to Irchester.

Great Houghton has changed considerably since the early 1950s, when water and sewerage pipes were laid, making life much easier. No longer the need to give the village pump its straw overcoat to combat the winter frosts, and the discomfort of tripping down the garden path to the 'privy' is, thankfully, a thing of the past! However, it is inevitable that with growth and modern-style living, a less intimate atmosphere now prevails. It is remembered with nostalgia by many residents how village people often came together to enjoy 'The Social', and the Christmas Whist Drive.

At one time very few strange faces were seen in either of the two village pubs – a very different case today! In both the White Hart and the Olde Cherry Tree there could be heard the tumble of the skittles as the wooden 'cheese' found their targets.

There are some splendid large houses. The Old Rectory is still a very gracious building; the Hall is now a well established independent preparatory school; Great Houghton House is occupied by a firm of architects; and the pretty Manor House, overlooking The Cross, is attractively thatched – the only other thatched building now in the village is the White Hart public house.

The church is not large but its interior is light, welcoming and well cared for. It was built in 1754, replacing one dating back to the 13th century, and the sale of its bells to raise money for alterations or repairs (possibly to Little Houghton) gave rise to the following rhyme:

'Great Houghton folk, foolish people
Sold their bells to build a steeple.'

Great Oakley 🦢

Great Oakley is a small village situated approximately two miles from Corby and five miles from Kettering. Much of Great Oakley has been in the ownership of the Brooke family for over five centuries, and the present lord of the manor is Hugh de Capell Brooke. He lives with his family in Great Oakley Hall, which was extensively renovated in the 1960s.

In the grounds of the Hall is St Michael's church, which was built of stone in the 13th century. The nave roof is built of Collyweston stone slates. Both the nave and the small tower, which houses three bells, were added to the church in the 16th and 17th centuries. The church register dates from 1718. Inside the church there are several monuments to the Brooke family, and the oak choir stalls are said to have come from the Cistercian abbey at Pipewell.

In the centre of the village is the village hall. This was erected in 1921 by Sir Arthur R. de Capell Brooke for the villagers to use for social activities. Next to the hall is the old vicarage, in the grounds of which there is a large grass mound. Rumour has it that a vicar once had this made so that he could feel nearer to Heaven!

A stream flows through the village called Harpers Brook, and this stream was once a boundary of Rockingham Forest. There is a well in the village called Monks' Well. This was mentioned in the Domesday Book, and at one time the villagers used it as their water supply. It can still be seen, and is situated in the grounds of Bridge Farm in Brooke Road.

Although in recent years extensive new housing estates have been built at the top end of the village, much of Great Oakley remains unchanged. A preservation order exists on all trees and stone houses in the village, and this will help to ensure that the character of Great Oakley remains for future generations.

Great Oxendon

Great Oxendon is quite a small village, situated on the Northamptonshire/Leicestershire borders, with the A508 road passing through the centre.

The village has a long, interesting history. It is mentioned in the Domesday Book and its name derives from 'The Hill of Oxen' – quite an apt description as the village is built on a hill, measuring 600 ft above sea level at the highest point, from where one can see and count seven hunting counties.

Early church records disclose that many of the villagers of the past were weavers and farmworkers.

St Helen's church stands in splendid isolation on a hill to the north of the village but it has not always been so. Careful inspection of the fields north and west of the church reveals signs of foundations and wells where the old village was. It is said that the inhabitants moved south to the site of the present village when the original settlement was struck by the Black Death.

In more recent times the church roof collapsed, the rain came in and at the 1968 Harvest Thanksgiving service the rector preached the sermon from underneath an umbrella! The church became unusable and from 1968 to 1976 was closed. Much of the interior woodwork rotted. It was re-roofed and reopened for worship, thanks entirely to the efforts of the village itself.

Then came a period of near despair for Oxendon. The village school was closed after around 100 years of use. Village life without school as a focal point seemed dead. The post office/shop closed with the retirement of the postmistress. The Baptist chapel was forced to close and the one and only village pub was vacated and closed for quite a time. Dark clouds indeed before the sun shone!

Then the situation began to alter. The Hall grounds were developed and built upon, the Hall was converted into flats and the stable and out-houses into mews cottages. The village school became the village hall, and the old rectory was converted into a home for the elderly. The newcomers in the new houses have now become new friends to the old villagers.

Greatworth 🌿

Greatworth is situated on a hill, some 500ft up, and lies just to the south of an important old drove road, Welsh Lane, used for taking stock from Wales to London.

The houses on the west side of The Street were originally part of the hamlet of Westhorp, administered by Marston St Lawrence. In 1935 Westhorp became part of Greatworth. Before that the old minute books of both parishes record many disputes between them. Village folk in Westhorp had to be buried in Marston churchyard and it is recorded that in 1895 a bier was purchased to convey the corpses the one and a half miles down the steep hill to Marston, despite the fact that Greatworth church was only a few hundred yards away.

The layout of the village is such that the houses, old farmsteads and terraced rows of cottages form tight building lines winding along the natural contours and creating attractive streetscapes. The older part of the village was made a conservation area in 1985 and contains a number of listed buildings.

The row of houses known as Dering Cottages remind us of Lady Dering, who seems to have been an early supporter of education for women, as she endowed a charity for girls as well as boys which still gives small grants to students from the village.

The manor house has a commanding position overlooking the agricul-tural landscape. The present manor stands on the site of the two previous manors, the second of which was destroyed by fire in 1793 along with many of the village records. The pair of elaborately carved stone pine-apple finials still stand marking the entrance of the previous building. George Washington, America's first president, was descended from the Pargeter family of Greatworth manor.

'A little wayside church' is how Arthur Mee described the village church of St Peter. The battlemented tower is 15th century but the chancel is 13th century and the nave has been rebuilt in the style of the first English builders. In the churchyard a magnificent sycamore tree and a healthy old hornbeam stand among some very old gravestones. Early in the present century a row of cottages was demolished and the churchyard extended.

Between Cockley Hill and Greatworth lies Cockley Brake. This is the overgrown remains of early Victorian enterprise, the junction of the Banbury to Bletchley and the Banbury to Northampton railway lines. The second route was not all that successful commercially, but in its latter days the lads of the village would stand by the track to hear the Northampton football score called out by the driver, and to catch the newspapers thrown to them for delivery in the village.

Geographically the area is a watershed with streams running into three rivers, the Ouse, the Cherwell and the Tove. The fact that the village stands on one of the highest points in Northamptonshire accounts for the presence of RAF Greatworth to the north of the village. The tall masts, ugly in close-up but a landmark for miles are now redundant.

Greens Norton 🐦

Situated two miles from Towcester and with a population of about 1,700, Greens Norton is a pleasant and attractive village containing old houses and cottages built of the local yellow stone, as well as more modern developments.

The village is dominated by the tall slender spire of St Bartholomew's church, which is a landmark for miles around. A church was standing on the site in the 9th century but little of this is still visible as so much has been added over the centuries . . . and removed, too. There is a peal of six bells in the tower and this is rung regularly. By the belfry door, hangs the coat of arms of Queen Elizabeth 1; thought to be a rarity as Cromwell's armies often destroyed such things.

Opposite the church is the Chantry House, where priests used to live who were occupied in the affairs of the church, taking services at altars in the side aisles.

The big old rectory, hidden behind the church (and now a private house), boasts two ghosts, a tall lady and . . . a pair of legs! It has been suggested that a floor level has been altered at some time to account for this odd phenomenon. They are said to have been seen by Canon Wrangham Hardy and his sister whilst they lived there.

The centre of the village, marked by its green, has not changed too much over the past 50 years as the old substandard cottages, which have been demolished, were in yards off the main street, and most new housing has been built on the outskirts. By the green are two general stores, one of which contains the post office, a butcher and the village pub, the Butchers Arms.

The oldest house in the village has the date 1666 carved on the

The village of Greens Norton

chimney but as a priest hole has been found within the house, it would seem to be much older, probably early 16th century. Katherine Parr, sixth wife of Henry VIII, is claimed to have lived there and she is also said to have visited the rectory.

The original village school, which was a dame school, is still standing at the head of School Lane. Its successor, a red brick Victorian building in the High Street, is now in use as the village hall, itself having been replaced by a modern school.

At the turn of the century, Greens Norton lacemakers were well known and today the craft has been revived and there is a flourishing group in the village, making traditional and modern bobbin lace.

The latest joint venture is the creation of a 'Pocket Park' on the site of the old brickyard, about a quarter of a mile down a track from the village. The area has been cleared and fenced and about 150 young trees planted, including many oaks, though in early summer the site is a riot of dog roses.

Grendon

Mentioned in the Domesday Book, the village seems to have changed hands fairly frequently until in the early 14th century a John de Harrington was paying a rent of 'sixpence (per annum) on Christmas

Day, in lieu of other services'. De Harrington left the village to his two daughters, so that it became two separate manors – Over and Nether Grendon – which were not reunited until the Earl of Northampton took them over in the 16th century. At about the same time, Henry VIII gave the church and some land to Trinity College, Cambridge, on the College's foundation, and it has belonged to Trinity ever since.

Grendon Hall, as we know it, was built by General Hatton Compton, Deputy Lieutenant of the Tower, in 1685, on the site of an older and larger house. It was here that the 1901 Grand National winner *Grundon* was trained by Mr Bletsoe. That year the racecourse had a considerable covering of snow and *Grundon* won because his hooves had been buttered so that the snow slid off them, whereas the rest of the field got their hooves balled up and could not gallop! One pound of butter was used on each hoof and he led from start to finish – an unknown 'feat'.

During the Second World War, Grendon Hall was used by the Free French to train personnel who were parachuted into France to join the Maquis resistance movement. It became the Northampton County Youth Centre in 1946, and was opened by Princess Elizabeth (as she was then) on 29th July – only the second centre of its kind in the country.

Grendon is regrettably deficient in antiquities, except its wealth of old stone cottages with thatched roofs. Now mostly modernised inside, they are very comfortable to live in, which they cannot have been originally when they housed large families without any 'mod-cons', even a water supply. They were mostly the 'two up and two down' kind, with a patch of garden.

Gretton ✑

The parish of Gretton lies in the north of the county on the borders of Rutland and Leicestershire. It is a large village of approximately 1,700 inhabitants, overlooking the Welland valley. It is a pleasant happy village with its winding streets, nooks and corners and many stone-built houses and cottages of great charm and interest.

The church of St James, parts of which date from the 13th century, overlooks the village green where the stocks and whipping post still stand. The remains of the 17th century manor house in the High Street now houses three families. Most of the old houses have been carefully renovated without losing their character.

To the east of the parish stands Kirby Hall, designed by John Thorpe in 1570 for Sir Humphrey Stafford of Blatherwyke. After his death in 1575, it was completed by Sir Christopher Hatton of Holdenby near Northampton. This is an outstanding example of Elizabethan architecture. Over the years it gradually fell into ruins but fortunately, it was taken over by the Office of Works and now stands greatly restored, a building inspired by a great Queen who never came.

In times past Gretton was a very close-knit, self-contained community, the only means of travel being horse-drawn or Shank's pony (your own two legs), until the advent of the railway. The highlights of the year were looked forward to with eagerness and excitement. The crowning of the May Queen and maypole dancing on the Village green, followed by games, races and tea in the vicarage Glebe Field. The arrival of the fair for the Village Feast, where the whole family turned out to enjoy the fun, was a week to remember. Horse racing took place in the meadows by the Welland, and Christmas was brightened by the band touring the village playing carols, visiting the five public houses on the way. The band still plays, having gone from strength to strength.

Gradually a change came over the village. Work and prosperity increased owing to the arrival of an ironmaster from the north, Mr S. J. Lloyd, who lived here for a few years and who together with his partner started the nearby steelworks.

A factory producing electrical goods replaced the original clothing factory which for years employed the women and girls. Gretton House is now a home for disabled people.

Now, instead of relying on the ministrations of the late Mrs Reservoir Wood, of gipsy origin, for attention at births, deaths and general illness, and a doctor jogging along in his pony and trap, a modern surgery and nursing services provide care for the inhabitants. Many house owners live around the village and on the council and private estates.

Guilsborough

Guilsborough has always been a lively place in which to live, with many dramatic happenings throughout the centuries. Beautifully situated at 500 ft above sea level, close to two large, most decorative reservoirs, with sailing and fishing, it is a very old village. In one house there are the remains in the cellar of a Saxon dwelling, roughly dated at AD 867, and there was a large Roman encampment in the area, part of which is still visible.

In 1612 scandal ran riot over a case of witchcraft, when two unfortunate Guilsborough women were hanged for bewitching into grievous bodily harm a certain Mrs Belcher and her brother-in-law. Before their demise one of them, joined by two others, rode forth upon a sow's back to visit another powerful old witch residing at Ravensthorpe. This interesting scene is depicted on the arresting banner which hangs in the village hall!

In 1645, during the Civil War, General Thomas Fairfax camped here before the battle of Naseby, and one can imagine him and his soldiers marching down Nortoft Hill in colourful battle array on that morning of 14th June.

The Domesday Book mentions a church in Guilsborough, though there are now no traces left of this Saxon building. The church of St Etheldreda

Guilsborough village

(once dedicated to St Wilfred) was mostly built in the 13th century, with later additions.

The grammar school is the most handsome building in the village, a magnificent example of Jacobean architecture in apricot coloured Northamptonshire stone. It was opened in 1668 to 'provide free education for 50 youths within a radius of four miles'. It is said that some of the masters used to reside in the house just across the road from the school, which remained operative as such until 1909. It has now been converted into five attractive dwellings, which preserve the beautiful exterior.

This is hunting country and the many lovely, old houses in Guilsborough have, over the years, provided sturdy supporters for the local Pytchley Hunt. It is a regular, thrilling sight to see riders and hounds surging down the High Street en route to a meet. The Queen Mother used to stable her horses at the Ward Arms.

Guilsborough today buzzes with life and activity, with a pleasantly mixed population of all ages.

Hackleton, Horton & Piddington

The three close-knit villages of Horton, Hackleton and Piddington lie on the south-east border of the county, in the shadows of Salcey Forest.

The origins of the villages lie deep in history. A recently excavated Roman villa at Piddington shows there was a settlement there in Roman times. When the Domesday survey was carried out in the 11th century, William the Conqueror's niece, Countess Judith, is said to have owned the land around the three villages.

Horton church is adorned by the alabaster tomb of Sir William Parr and his wife Mary. Their niece, Katherine Parr, was the sixth wife of Henry VIII. Horton is also known to have been the birthplace of Charles Montagu, 1st Earl of Halifax, who established the Bank of England in 1694.

Hackleton's claim to history lies with William Carey and the Baptist chapel dedicated to his memory. He was the first Baptist missionary and lived and worked in both Hackleton and Piddington as a cobbler. He called the little cobbler's shop at Hackleton 'Carey's College', and it was from here that he walked six miles to be baptised in the river Nene. Night after night he would read about the voyages of Captain Cook and this kindled the fire of his missionary work, which eventually took him to India.

Hackleton was once a hamlet of the parish of Piddington and hence has no parish church. In 1709, however, the Northampton to Stoke Goldington turnpike road was opened, bypassing Piddington, which subsequently diminished in importance while Hackleton thrived and is now the hub of the community.

There is the usual variety of activity to suit all age groups in the three villages, plus a thriving primary school, two public houses, three shops, a garage and renowned restaurant.

The surrounding countryside offers a wealth of flora and fauna with interesting walks into the nearby forest and to neighbouring villages. Wherever you walk there are ever-changing views of Piddington church visible from miles around, a welcoming and friendly beacon as you tread your way home.

Halse

Halse (pronounced 'Hawse') is a small hamlet two miles south of the village of Greatworth. It was incorporated into Greatworth parish in 1935.

In the Domesday Book of 1086, Halse, an independent parish, was more important than nearby Brackley. The now demolished parish church of St Andrew is thought to have been at or near the site of the present Manor Farm. Local information records that in 1912 to 1913, many skeletons were discovered during alterations to the buildings north-west of Manor Farm. Fragments of medieval window tracery are built into the garden wall and an octagonal basin, possibly a late medieval stone font, survives in the garden. The earthworks to the south-west of the village indicate a medieval deserted village.

More recently and until the early 1950s Halse consisted of a church, six farms and a number of farm cottages. Today development has extended the village either side of the main road. Halse has a mission church built in 1906 by Lord Ellesmere, who owned most of the land round Halse. He also owned the large manor house in Brackley High Street which is now a preparatory school for boys.

The main employment in Halse is farming. In 1970 a local farmer made available the use of a field near to the road, with the young of the village in mind, and from this generous gesture, a football club was formed. A sports pavilion was built in the field with the help of a local builder, who donated both materials and time. The club is flourishing today, though the players now are mainly from outside the village.

Halse does not normally suffer from extremes of weather, but being 500 ft above sea level, and rather exposed to the west, the village can be windy at certain times of the year!

Hannington

Hannington, with its 62 houses, a population of just over 200, no shop and no pub, is typical of so many small villages, though lucky to be off a busy main road.

The church, almost unique, is the village's claim to fame historically. It was built in the 13th century. There is a local tradition that Gilbertine monks had established a cell on the site before then and even that Thomas a Becket spent a night there in 1164. There is said to be only one other church in England which has a similar bisected nave. In Hannington there are two pillars down the centre of the aisle supporting an arcade of three arches which in turn support the roof.

By the middle of the 19th century the building was in disrepair with holes in the roof and nettles in the mud floor. After 1866 the church was repaired and a new rectory built. Now the rectory is a private house and, since 1954, one rector has served the two neighbouring parishes of Walgrave and Old as well as Hannington.

All this time the village has been in a state of continual change; old houses replaced by new, old occupations by different ones. Population figures, though, have not varied much. From 1801 to 1861 it rose from 144 to 201. By 1957 it was down to 137 and has grown, though by no means spectacularly, since then.

Few of the old families are represented here now. Some of the older houses remain, including the former inn, now privately owned. The original stone walls still give an impression of how the village must have looked in the past, as do some of the names – The Old Bakehouse; The Old Forge.

The village school closed in 1931, since when most of the younger children have travelled to Walgrave and, when they are older, to Moulton, Kettering or Wellingborough. The old school is now the cherished and much-admired village hall.

Hardingstone

There's a 'skeleton in the cupboard' of Hardingstone's county primary school! Skulls were found when the foundations were being laid, and a complete skeleton unearthed from just below the surface. Fine Iron Age brooches and 1st century pottery kilns were also discovered in the area, certain proof that Hardingstone is a village with a past.

If ghosts there were, perhaps they could be found down Barrow Stile, for this is where Henry VI battled during one of the Wars of the Roses. He lost but was cared for by nuns in the Cluniac abbey of De la Pre (unconnected with the present Delapre Abbey). Or perhaps in Hardingstone Lane, where on the night of 5th November 1930, the infamous Alfred Rouse set fire to his car, and with insurance in view let his passenger burn. Rouse was hanged in Bedford on 10th March 1931 and his unknown victim is buried in the churchyard; several thousand people have since visited his grave.

Finally, may be a ghost walks near the Queen Eleanor Cross; the magnificent edifice erected by Edward I to the memory of his wife. He and the funeral cortege stayed at De la Pre Abbey for the night on his journey to London.

There was no shortage of water in Hardingstone in the 'old days', when even in the severest drought the now extinct Back Lane pump could be relied upon to produce water, but the 200 wells were filled in when a typhoid scare was traced to the village in 1874. Underground streams still filter through the ground, one having been utilised as a garden waterfall, while another flows forth down Houghton Hill.

The lords of the manor were the Bouverie family, who took their duties very seriously, ruling, guarding and guiding villagers since 1723. Miss Mary Bouverie was President of Hardingstone WI from 1918, when it was formed, almost until her death in 1943. Older members describe how she expected and was given due homage, a curtsey, whenever she appeared on the scene.

It is not so long since Hardingstone comprised only Coldstream Lane, Back Lane, the High Street and houses in the vicinity of the green. Now local people jealously guard their village status.

Hardwick 🐝

Just a few miles from Wellingborough, reached by narrow, winding lanes running from both the A43 and the old A45 is the tiny village of Hardwick, tucked away in a fold of typical Northamptonshire countryside. The cottages are grouped around a green dominated by the lovely little church, built of local stone. Lanes lead in from Orlingbury and Little Harrowden but with no main road access Hardwick remains a quiet backwater, little changed by the passage of time.

St Leonard's, built in about 1200, seats 98 and has some fine furnishings – especially the pulpit of Italian marble which was exhibited in England in 1860 and was bought as a gift for Hardwick church by an unknown benefactor. There are two bells (one dated 1484) and until quite recently they were rung every year to commemorate Guy Fawkes Day – an unusual custom.

The manor house, once used to house the Knights Templar, and the old school, now the village hall also stand alongside the green but Hardwick children have had to travel to Little Harrowden for schooling since the early days of this century.

Farming is still the main way of life. As there is no inn, shop or other kind of meeting place most activities centre around the church and village hall and are well supported by the villagers. At present these number 59. The Domesday Book recorded '25 souls' dwelling here and by the 19th century numbers had increased to 120 but have since dwindled again – probably because we are so isolated. Hardwick Woods, covering over 100 acres, are, however, famed for their lovely views and still attract visitors who come to enjoy the primroses and bluebells which grow abundantly under the trees in the springtime.

Hargrave

Hargrave is a small village lying just inside East Northamptonshire on the boundaries of Bedfordshire and Cambridgeshire. The population today is about 250, although in the 19th century it once topped 356 in 58 dwellings.

During the Roman occupation of Britain there was a settlement here, the name Hargrave means 'the army camp', and several stone coffins dating from that period have been unearthed in the area and are on display outside the church.

The 16th century Nag's Head public house, Hargrave

In the 19th century Hargrave had a thriving clay pit and brickworks, used for building the local houses. The clay pit is now a pond and the brickworks are ruins which are supposed to be haunted! At that time most of the village inhabitants were employed as farm labourers but others were shepherds, shoemakers and lacemakers. There used to be many shops in the village, though none remain today, and the names of the older houses reflect their past uses – Forge House, The Old Bakehouse, Cobblers and The Old Post Office. The track of the old disused railway line between Kettering and Cambridge is still partly visible in farmland near the village outskirts, the nearest local station was at Raunds. On the Bedfordshire side of the village near to a farm, named after it, is the site of Hargrave Mill, now lying in ruins, but at one time producing flour for the village bakery.

At the entrance to Hargrave on the main A45 road stands a house beside a water-tower called Three Shire House, so named because that is where the three counties actually meet. In 1837 the owner was an eccentric old farmer whose wife died suddenly. For various reasons it was impossible to have her buried at Hargrave church. The farmer then refused to have her buried at all, but had the body bricked up in the house, and when his daughter died in 1843 he placed her body beside that of the mother. It was only 24 years later, when the old farmer himself died, that his surviving son buried the bodies in a neighbouring churchyard.

At the rear of a private house just past the village hall, is the post office, run since the 1960s by a lady, born on the premises, who had relatives as long ago as 1890 running the service for the village.

At one time there was a Methodist chapel in Brook Street, but this closed in the 1960s leaving only the small but picturesque church of All Hallows, or All Saints as it is generally called. The present church dates from the late 12th century although evidence of an earlier wooden church has been found at the site. It was extensively restored in 1869 and is now a Grade A listed building.

There were once two pubs in Hargrave. The Waggon and Horses closed years ago, but the Nag's Head is still thriving. It dates back over 400 years and is popular with both residents and visitors alike.

Harlestone 🐚

Bonnie Prince Charlie almost came to Harlestone – but not quite. It was in 1745, and Prince Charles Edward Stuart, the Young Pretender, had marched into England leading the kilted clans of his Scottish army, intending to force his way to London. The further south Charles marched, the greater became his concern at the lack of support for the House of Stuart. From his agents, Charles Edward learned that the

Northamptonians were mustering at Harlestone, five miles to the north-west of the county town, so as to place themselves astride the road from Rugby and the North. It was the last straw. The Prince halted his army, turned them about and set out on the long return march to Scotland, a journey which culminated in the desolation of battle at Culloden and the ending of Stuart hopes.

Harlestone is one of the county's loveliest villages. Lying in the folds of the Northamptonshire uplands, it is a favourite spot for the county's walkers and country lovers. The area was once a rich source of the warm, brown sandstone of which many of the village's old thatched cottages are built. Whilst the last Harlestone quarry was productive until fairly recently, the locally-known 'hills and hollows' bear witness to a tradition of quarrying which must have begun in the days before Duke William of Normandy's followers founded the great castle of Northampton.

Most recently, the virtually exhausted local quarries provided the 'donkeystone' with which houseproud Lancashire housewives would clean the doorsteps and outside window ledges. The stone, in small square portions, took its name from the donkey carts driven by the rag-and-bone men, who collected unwanted clothing and other household items in exchange for the cleaning stone.

Since the early 19th century, when the Andrews family sold their Harlestone estate to the Spencers of Althorp, the forebears of the present Princess of Wales have had a significant influence on the social and economic fabric of the village. Virtually all local people depended upon agriculture for a livelihood, and most workers were employed directly by Althorp and lived in houses owned by the estate. Now, of course, the pattern of life has changed. At the end of the working day, no longer do battalions of estate workers walk back down the country track from Althorp, past the ancient 14th century circular dovecote. Those days are long past and most villagers are now likely to work in Northampton, Daventry, Rugby or even London.

On the Spencer parkland between Upper and Lower Harlestone, a new international golf course is under construction. The site encompasses many hundreds of acres around the historic parish church of St Andrew. Studded with venerable chestnut trees, the course includes Harlestone lake with its fine arcaded dam and also the site of the former Harlestone House, demolished just before the Second World War.

Harpole ✏

Bricks and mortar give the frame to a village but it is the people who breathe life into it, and one such character of Harpole was William J. Burt, born in 1899 and who died in 1985. Here, in his own words, is his story.

'My great grandfather came to Harpole in the mid 1830s with a portable steam engine, and he fell in with a certain William Smith in the village. They went out as a team, threshing. In that field opposite the church they used to stack little ricks, people had only got half an acre or so, and they went there to thresh.

'My grandfather had no schooling. He was about seven when they settled in Harpole, and he had to go to work scaring crows, from light in the morning till dark at night seven days a week, and for all those hours he received the lordly sum of one shilling. These times were the hungry 40s and my grandfather was packed up two slices of black bread, and when he had eaten that he lived the whole of the day on what he could get off the farm.

'The main industry in the village was outwork shoe-making and farming. With regard to the shoe operatives, there were three agents when I was a child, there was Robinses, Pinkards and Edwin Starmer. He was the biggest agent, he was agent for Manfields. He fetched the work on a four-wheeler and a strong cob.

'I started school in 1904, 4 years old, and I left school at 13. The last question we used to ask the school master was "Please sir, have I made me times?" and he used to look and he used to say "You're alright" and he used to shake us by the hand, and that was it, we never went back no more, never went back in the afternoon.

'I learned my work as a shepherd at Church Farm. We used to assemble at Harpole church, 6 o'clock in the morning, and as soon as that bell struck the first note, the biggest man amongst us said "There she gus, well have to gu", and we used to work from 6 o'clock in the morning till the Hunsbury Hill buzzer blew at half past five. The wage for a man, except for a waggoner, a cowman, a shepherd and a specialist, was 15 shillings a week.'

And so Bill Burt, a real village character, worked and lived, a true man of Harpole.

Harrington

Harrington is a quiet, unspoiled village, about seven miles west of Kettering, on a hill above the Ise valley with wonderful views over miles of open countryside. Recorded in the Domesday Book as Arintone, today the population of Harrington and the hamlet of Thorpe Underwood is about 150.

Old stone farmhouses, attractively restored cottages and mellowed brick council houses form one main high street, bounded by old stone walls. There are a number of outlying lodges and farms. Snowdrops, aconites and daffodils, flowering trees and chestnut blossom add charm to the village.

Behind the chestnut trees in the middle of the village is the Falls Field, once the site of a monastic manor owned by the Knights Hospitallers of

St John of Jerusalem and later laid out as an ornamental garden with fish ponds, sunken gardens and terraces. The site has been carefully preserved and the fish ponds are some of the finest in the county.

The Tollemache Arms, which has established a wide reputation for its old country pub atmosphere and excellent restaurant meals, takes its name from the Rev Hugh Tollemache, who was rector of Harrington for 58 years and died in 1890 at the age of 87. He objected to villagers attending the pub on Sundays so he bought the public house, took it over and installed his coachman as landlord, closing the inn from Saturday night until Monday morning.

In 1865 Harrington estate was sold to the Naylor family and in 1913 was purchased by the Desborough Co-operative Society. A red chestnut tree standing at the top of the village was planted to commemorate this event. In 1927 the estate was broken up and the properties sold to private buyers.

A short distance from the village down the lane leading to Thorpe Underwood is the 13th century church of St Peter and St Paul, originally dedicated to St Botolph. This is a listed building. In a glass case at the west end of the church is an ancient wind instrument known as a vamping horn, one of only eight still surviving in the country, two of them in Northamptonshire. It is thought to originate from the 17th century and may have been used as a primitive loudspeaker or speaking trumpet to 'vamp' an accompaniment for hymns and psalms.

By the side of the road to Lamport is an impressive modern memorial to American airmen who lost their lives in the Second World War. The crews known as the 'Carpetbaggers' flew hazardous night bombing missions from this secret base, also dropping munitions and supplies and parachuting agents to underground resistance forces in Nazi-occupied Europe.

Haselbech 🐑

Haselbech, with its medieval church of St Michael and All Angels, stands on a hill, some 600 ft above sea level and one of the highest points in the county.

Always a small village, the population is now around 80. In 1921 a population of 132 was recorded. The fall results from the social changes of the intervening years – from estate village to a community of owner-occupiers. In 1921 Haselbech Hall was the centre of a village in which grooms, gardeners, farm workers and indoor servants played their part in a way of life, then traditional, now history. So although superficially Haselbech looks remarkably similar to its appearance 70 years ago, the similarity is only skin deep. Farms and cottages alike are now owned and lived in by people who for the most part, work outside the village.

In the Middle Ages the original village stood in the fields opposite the church, but the lord of the manor, Sir Thomas Tresham, in 1598 enclosed over 700 acres of the land for use as a pasture for his own sheep – land which had previously belonged to the villagers. This policy of enclosing land eventually resulted in the eviction of over 60 people from their homes in Haselbech. However, serious debts forced the Tresham family to sell the manor and the lordship passed to the Wykes family, who also built the original Haselbech Hall. In November 1917 a disastrous fire destroyed the Hall and it was subsequently rebuilt.

The parish church of St Michael dates from the 13th century. It houses a peal of eight bells of which two are ancient, cast in Leicester in 1621, and the remaining six are of 1930. The old custom of the village whereby thrice three tolls were given on the death of a male and twice two for a female, is no longer maintained.

Visitors to Haselbech will discover several listed buildings – the former rectory (1768) which lies to the south of the church; the farmhouse Ortons Holdings, of 1800 or thereabouts, adjacent to the working forge; and the Manor Farm, of which the handsome 18th century red brick facade fronts the Naseby Road. The former school (1872) lies just below the Manor Farm. It was built on the instructions and at the expense of Selina, Viscountess Milton who is responsible for most of the housing in the parish. Viscountess Milton built the stables and walled garden at the Hall, and put up walls and iron railings throughout the village. Many of the houses of the 17th century were pulled down and replaced with red brick or stone.

Hellidon 🌿

The village of Hellidon, reputedly one of the highest in Northamptonshire, lies adjacent to the Warwickshire border in the southern part of the county. The rivers Leam, Cherwell and Nene rise in or around the village.

The church, which is dedicated to St John the Baptist, lies at the centre of the village. A date over the entrance door proclaims that it was built in 1591, although the tower is older and is said to have been built in about 1350, whilst the north aisle and chancel were added at later dates in the 19th century. The four bells were hung in 1615 and 1635. They came from the foundry of Hugh Watts and were rehung in 1860. During the Second World War when church bells remained silent, bees made over one hundredweight of honey in the clock works. Today they are silent once more as they are in need of rehanging.

The windmill, situated at the eastern end of the village, has long since lost its sails and been converted to a private home. It was probably around the turn of the century that the last sacks of flour were milled there. The miller himself lived in what is now the only thatched house in the village and itself was the subject of extensive alteration and renovation in 1948.

At the eastern boundary of the parish there is still some evidence of the once productive ironstone quarries which closed in 1961. The ironstone system was connected with the Grand Central Railway by a small branch line which ran for three quarters of a mile parallel to the road until it reached Charwelton station.

Although the building of the Grand Central Railway in 1895 did not much affect Hellidon – it passed under the parish rather than across its land – there are four men buried in the churchyard who died in the construction of the tunnel, which at one and three quarter miles in length was the longest on the line, and took just over two years to construct. The necessity of a tunnel was because the owner of nearby Catesby House would not allow a railway line across his parkland – it therefore had to be put beneath it.

The post office which has been in the village since the mid 19th century serves only that one function – there are no shops nowadays. At the beginning of the 20th century Hellidon was a bustling community with two pubs, two churches and a variety of shops from tailors to bakers, as well as a Co-op and several cobblers. A carrier too called regularly in the village. Today there is only one church, one pub and no public transport.

Helmdon 🦡

Called 'Helma's Valley' by the Saxons and recorded in the Domesday Book as Elme Dene, Helmdon is in the south of Northamptonshire near to Brackley.

The oldest thing in the churchyard of the parish church of Saint Mary Magdalene is the yew tree, reputed to be about 2,000 years old. The present church dates mainly from the 13th and 14th centuries, with later restorations and the rebuilding of the tower in 1823. The oldest item in the church is the Early English piscina near the north door.

One item of great interest is the Campiun window, in the north wall, in which William Campiun is represented at work as a stonemason. This medieval glass window was still in its original lead when it was cleaned and reset in 1976 and it is thought that it is still in its original site. William Campiun may have been a Helmdon mason and possibly the dominant mason in the building of the church at that time. (The name Campin remained in the village until 1969). By the beginning of the 14th century Helmdon was already renowned for the quality of its limestone and the work of its stonemasons.

There are still some of the older Helmdon people who can remember when it was a self-supporting village. Most of them kept hens for eggs and food and also a pig and a Mr Campin would come to kill the pig and then butcher it for them the next day. There were two bakehouses where bread and cakes were baked during the week and on Sundays the family joints of meat and Yorkshire puddings were cooked. There were four public houses, the Chequers and the Bell which still exist, and the Magpie and the Cross, which are now private houses. A butcher's shop opened at the weekend and there were four other shops. There were two black-smiths, two builders and carpenters, two pillow-lace makers (Mrs Cadd and Mrs Winmill), two dressmakers (Miss Isham and Miss Hawkes) and a tailor (Mr Charles Brown), who made, among other things, riding and hunting jackets for people who lived as far away as Banbury. Tom Pitt, the carrier, with his horse and cart, brought goods on approval from Banbury twice a week, delivered parcels and often supplied transport between the villages.

When the older inhabitants reminisce, they talk of the dances held in the hall at the back of The Bell, paying 1/- if the music was on gramophone records and 1/6d if Billy Mold's band played. One of the highlights of village life was the Annual Holiday held by the Helmdon Sick Society on Whit Monday. Men with staves walked from the square to the church, headed by a band which accompanied the hymns at the church service, and Joe Mayo who had a wooden peg-leg. Dinner for the Society members followed, cooked in the bakery, the vegetables being cooked in coppers at Langlands. A visiting fair was held near the village cross with roundabouts and side-shows and this went on until Saturday evening.

Of course the village has its ghosts. One story is told by three members of the WI who remember cycling home one moonlight night after a dance and seeing a man suddenly appear in front of them and cross the road, disappearing through the hedge into a field. When they described him to their parents they were told that it was the ghost of Jimmy West who had killed a young boy in the field.

Because of the T shape of the village, with fields backing on to many of its houses, there are many public footpaths which are in constant use for getting about the village. There are still five working farms with farm-houses and one of them has provided a cricket field and a nature reserve for the village school.

Hinton in the Hedges

Hinton in the Hedges lay on the main route between Banbury and Brackley until the end of the 18th century, when the Banbury to Buckingham turnpike was built. Nowadays Hinton is some distance from a main road and people visit it more by desire than by necessity. The village has a population of about 160, somewhat less than in Victorian times but more than in the 1960s.

In the way of many villages, Hinton has grown up around the church, and the small triangular green close by is still its centre. The old rectory on the north side of the green is a building of substance and Manor Farm just off the south-east corner is the largest of the four old farmhouses within the nucleus of the village. Only one of these farmhouses still has its land attached. In the 1960s many of the old cottages and Lord Crewe's almshouses were in a poor state of repair but since then much renovation has taken place, new houses have been built and a number of old barns have been converted into houses. Other buildings besides the barns have changed their use, and some have fallen into disuse: the old school and the village shop are now houses, the smithy is a garage and the malthouse a ruin.

The green is the focal point of the village but it has no special function because of its small size. An old village pump stands on it and so does an oak seat where children often congregate. Local Morris men come here by tradition to perform the Morris dance which originated in Hinton. From the green it is only a short step to quench the thirst with Real Ale at the Crewe Arms! The village pub is an attractive old building and it fulfils an important role in the community as a social centre, for the village has no village hall, shop, school or regular public transport.

Hinton church lies in a quiet churchyard at the end of a drive running up from the north side of the green. Traces of Saxon masonry suggest that the building replaced an earlier simpler church. The present church, built of limestone, has a nave, chancel, north aisle and a Romanesque tower which leans to the west in a rather picturesque way.

Farming families and their workers no longer dominate the community. Modern agricultural practice is changing the landscape and its effect on the rural villages, combined with everyone's greater mobility, has been dramatic. As late as the 1930s most of the village people would have worked in the village or at local trades. Today, families whose adult members work outside the village, often at a considerable distance, make up more than three-quarters of the population.

Holcot ☙

Holcot stands in undulating countryside six miles north of Northampton, three miles to the east of Brixworth and in an area of natural beauty. The Parish lands were originally drained by a small tributary of the Pitsford Brook; this was dammed in the 1950s to form the Pitsford Reservoir. This reservoir now covers a large area of the north-east of the Parish and ornithologists and naturalists come from many miles around to view the wild life of this nature reserve.

The Church, dedicated to St Mary and All Saints, is in the middle of this small village and over recent years has been the object of fundraising to preserve and restore its 14th century wall paintings. Appropriately enough, one event took the shape of a 'mediaeval week-end' when Holcot returned to ages past and had jousting in the fields and village folk sold their wares around the lanes.

In the churchyard, some 5 metres south of the church, there is a limestone cross probably 15th century. A map dated 1839, amongst the parish records, shows that the cross originally stood in the middle of the crossroads at the junction of the Brixworth and Moulton roads. The early years of the 19th century saw the establishment of the Wesleyan chapel in Holcot, and the Chapel itself was built in 1814.

Farming played a major part in Holcot life. Most of the parish has been under cultivation at some time during the medieval period. Open field mixed farming was practised in Holcot until the common fields of the parish were enclosed by Act of Parliament of 1777. At the end of the 18th century it is documented in the Church records that there was a village shepherd who looked after all the village sheep; he was also responsible for dipping these sheep and used the wash pit in Holcot for this purpose. In recent years this wash pit has been cleaned and restored and is now a village pond and is attractive to both people and coots alike!

The wash pit naturally drains onto nearby farmland, where a farmer has recently restored two medieval fishponds. These fish ponds are also sourced by underground streams, and are now stocked with trout, and encourage a wide range of wildlife. However in medieval times, these fishponds would have been stocked with carp and other fish by the villagers to help provide food for the winter. Fresh water for the village came from the Town Well, which is situated in Main Street, just a few metres down the road from the Church. In the Church records, it is noted that in 1776 Edward West was paid the sum of 2/- for the work of cleaning the Well.

Holcot seems to have always had a caring community and the indications are that this trend will continue in this delightful village.

Holdenby 🐌

Holdenby, pronounced and sometimes spelt Holmby, is a small village situated in some of Northamptonshire's most picturesque countryside, with wonderful views to east and west.

The village lies just off the Church Brampton – East Haddon road and consists of small cottages, farms and a well preserved stone built school-room (not now used for education). These buildings surround a village green where once children would play and celebrate May Day in true traditional style.

Alongside the village green are the grounds of Holdenby House, once the site of the palace of Holdenby which was built by Elizabeth I's chancellor, Sir Christopher Hatton. The original place has been replaced by a 'modern' house of great beauty and dignity in Tudor style, incorporating parts of the old building. Now only the two lonely gateways of the outer courtyard of Hatton's mansion remain – they stand in isolation in a field next to the present house.

Charles I was brought here as a prisoner of Parliament from Newark and he stayed here for four months in 1647. His recreation was to play bowls at Boughton, and when crossing the long bridge at Brampton he used to meet some of his supporters, who gave him secret messages. This was reported by the then miller who lived at nearby Brampton Mill and sadly (legend has it) the mill never prospered from that day and fell into disuse. On the night of 2nd June 1647 Cornet Joyce came to take the King in the custody of the Army to London. When Charles asked for his warrant he pointed to the men behind him and the King observed wryly that it was a warrant that needed no spelling.

The church at Holdenby stands remote and isolated beside a pond and is reached by a field path under a dark and heavy plantation of trees, where one can expect to see wild life in abundance. It can boast of having had one prior, one prebendary, three canons and five knights as rectors. The ancient and battered screen with carved Roman soldiers on top no doubt came from the original palace.

The years since the Second World War have seen the closing of the post office cum village store, and the large red-bricked rectory is now a restaurant. There are riding stables in the vicinity and the village has not been spoiled by any housing developments. The present Holdenby House has been the venue for many Pytchley Hunt Balls and is the centre of the hunting fraternity.

Irchester 🐿

Irchester, with its roots firmly in the Iron Age, is situated just off the A45 between Wellingborough and Rushden. The site near Chester Lodge which has yielded evidence of settlement from that ancient time, has also revealed finds from the Romano-British period. Indeed the name Irchester comes from the Anglo-Saxon Iren Ceastre – iron fortress or town.

Quarrying took place in Wembley Pit until 1941 and although many used to be employed from the village itself, the extraction of iron ore was the cause of much aggravation. The huge shovel that used to dig out the ore, also belched out thick black smoke, and blasting had to take place to remove the hard core of rock.

Conifers were planted in the 1930s and 1940s over the hill and dale formation left by the workings, and grass, shrubs and wild flowers gradually covered the scars left by quarrying. In 1971 Irchester Country Park was established.

While clinging stubbornly to its village status, Irchester has seen a great deal of expansion since the 1960s and the population now stands at around 5,000. Three housing estates have been built, Bradshaw Way, Woodlands Road and the Arkwright estate, which is the largest. Part of this estate was built on the site of the 'Halle' or manor house mentioned in historical documents of 1385.

Irchester village with St Katherine's church

Chester Lodge, which dates from Elizabethan times, is of great historical interest and has not one but two priest holes. Knuston Hall too, on the borders of Rushden, is an attractive building, being a mixture of Jacobean, Georgian and Victorian styles. Occupied at the turn of the century by Robert Arkwright, grandson of the Arkwright who invented the Spinning Jenny, the hall was opened in 1952 as an Adult Education Centre.

Architecturally, most villages are dominated by their church and Irchester is no exception. St Katherine's stands on a site occupied by buildings of worship since the 13th century. A very attractive building of limestone and ironstone, one of its many points of interest is the bread oven in the north wall of the chancel. Bread used to be baked there for communion use and was also one of the church's ancient charities. Another interesting feature is the weathervane, which incorporates a Catherine-Wheel, the instrument of torture on which the saint was thought to have met her death.

During the 1850s when men were working on the railway viaduct at Wellingborough and the tunnel at Sharnbrook, an enterprising family in the village fed them. With meat from the local butcher and pastry ingredients from the grocer's, the Parsons family made their first pork pies. The pies proved so popular that a factory was soon built in the High

Street and the business thrived. Mr Parson's grandsons were trained in the business and this, inadvertently, led to a family split. The Saxby brothers set up a rival firm in Wellingborough, causing the families not to speak for years. Saxby's pies are still being made, but the makers of the original ones eventually sold out to Bowyers. Fortunately the hatchet was buried years ago and the two families are now on the best of terms. So next time you bite into a delicious pork pie, just think of Irchester and those hungry men working on the railway!

Isham

The village, situated midway between the busy market towns of Kettering and Wellingborough, has always been readily accessible to travellers. Indeed, it used to have *two* stations on the Leicester-Hitchin Midland Railway, (known later as the London, Midland & Scottish) which actually came within the parish boundary! Finedon station was closed to passengers in 1940 and the Burton Latimer/Isham station closed in 1950. Now the main A509 road runs through the middle of Isham and soon the A1/M1 link road is to be built within one mile of the centre of the village.

The Ise was once a far greater river than it is now and over succeeding generations made itself useful in driving the local mill. In the 1770s it was a paper mill and its various uses before and after made it the centre of activity in the village. Sadly, now all that remains are a few rows of weatherbeaten stones.

Passers-by cannot fail to notice the beauty of the 12th century village church, in its prominent position by the side of the main road. St Peter's church is lovingly cared for by its congregation and possesses a fine early Jacobean carved oak pulpit. Six bells peal out, calling folk to church, and often attracting visiting teams of bellringers. The beauty of the church's exterior is almost magically brought to life with the soft glow of floodlighting, installed and financed by Wellingborough Council.

There are 297 homes in the village, including a sprinkling of picturesque limestone, thatched cottages, including one where the thatcher has cleverly topped the porch with a straw pheasant. Isham is well supplied with shops, three in all, including a newsagent and sub-post office, and also has two well supported public houses, The Lilacs and The Red Lion. Three farmers tend their crops and cattle – and one provides the area with succulent plump turkeys.

Isham Independent Wesleyan church, in the old part of the village, is faithfully cared for by its members. Whilst several villages can boast of having retained their ancient dovecote, Isham is proud that *two* excellent examples still exist – one with 570 nesting places!

Islip

The picturesque village of Islip stands on high ground on the west bank of the river Nene. Approaching from Thrapston you will cross the 12th century 'nine arch' bridge, originally a packhorse bridge, but widened and strengthened over the centuries, until today it carries the full load of modern juggernauts on the A604.

Set back behind a high stone-faced wall lies Islip House, which is often floodlit by night. This was the home of Thomas Squire, who played a large part in making the river navigable from Peterborough to Thrapston. The grand opening was in November 1737. At that time wharves had been built on both sides of the river and the old warehouses still exist today. Beneath Islip House were the bonded wine vaults.

In the High Street most buildings are of Northamptonshire limestone, many being thatched and presenting a charm of their own. School Lane is a short cul de sac with several interesting houses including the old rectory, and terminated by very old farm buildings, indicating the original function of the village. The school is still in use, with 72 pupils. Standing opposite is St Nicholas church, whose spire stands proudly above the village's 800 inhabitants. Parts of the church date back to the 12th century.

Beside the village hall stands what was a row of very old cottages, which were virtually derelict until refurbished and made into a delightful dwelling. Beyond this lies the working men's club, which back in the days of horsepower was a horse collar factory, and has since played an important role in village life. On the right is one of two public houses in the village, the Rose and Crown, and alongside this lies the 'Nene Way' a recently waymarked footpath which runs diagonally across the fields to Islip Mill.

In Mill Road lies the only village shop. Next door is a thatched cottage called 'The Old Shop' which was in use within living memory, but now is a private dwelling. Near this is a narrow three-storeyed red brick building with a bay window. This was once the home of the manager of the other horse collar factory, which stood behind and to the side, but was demolished for housing. It is said that at that time there was no bay window and the factory owner's wife dearly wanted one, but he saw no reason to waste money on such trivialities. However he was called away on business to London and upon his return he was greeted with this window!

The old mill was there in the early 1700s, as records show that Thomas Squire leased it whilst working on the navigation project. It continued to grind corn right up to 22nd August 1960. It is now a private residence and is in remarkably good preservation. A narrow footbridge crosses the river at this point, over the parish border into Thrapston.

Kelmarsh 🌿

Kelmarsh is a small village situated in the Northamptonshire uplands. The village itself is to the north and east of the crossroads formed by the A508 and the by-roads leading to Clipston and Harrington. Lovely stone cottages line the east side of the main road, and more of red brick are on the north side of the road to Harrington.

It is difficult to believe the tragedy which overtook the stone cottages on the 4th May 1943. On that day, as lunch was being prepared, a spark somehow ignited the thatched roof of the middle house. A strong wind was blowing, and all the 13 houses were destroyed, rendering 44 people homeless. No one was injured, but few possessions were rescued. The cottages were rebuilt in their present form in 1948.

One of the first line of cottages on the Harrington road has a porch. This was the first school in Kelmarsh, built in 1850. Evidently there was trouble in the village in 1849 and Lord Bateman, owner of the village and occupant of Kelmarsh Hall, gave all his tenants notice because they had lapsed into bad habits. They were called to the Hall where they were told to attend church regularly and live in peace with each other, conducting themselves honestly and soberly. A school would be built so that children would learn to read, write and sum, and a charge of 1d per child per week would be made. Notices would be withdrawn if the tenants signed an agreement promising to behave themselves in the future!

Kelmarsh church, dedicated to St Denys, is a short distance from the village on the road to Clipston. As with most village churches it goes back far into history, but was altered considerably in 1874 by the Naylor family, who were the owners of the village at that time. It is now in the grand Victorian manner, unusual in a village church.

Opposite the church is the park belonging to Kelmarsh Hall, where it is usually possible to see a herd of British White cattle grazing. It is one of our rare breeds, distinguished by white or mottled bodies and black noses, eyelids, ears, teats and feet.

Kelmarsh Hall is a beautifully proportioned building of mellow red brick. It was built in 1728–32 by Francis Smith of Warwick to the design of James Gibbs for Mr William Hanbury, a noted antiquarian.

Kilsby 🌿

Kilsby is an unremarkable, but ancient village, half a mile from the Warwickshire border, between Daventry and Rugby.

Ridge and furrow marks visible in local fields bear witness to a farming community in medieval times, which it still obviously was in 1642, when a group of Royalists led by Sir John Smith tried to search cottages at Kilsby for hidden weapons. News had leaked out that the villagers were

Parliamentarian supporters. When they met with resistance they shot and killed Thomas Winkles and Henry Barfoote and severely wounded John White with a pitchfork.

At the end of the 18th century the Oxford canal linking the Thames with the Midland coal fields passed within a mile of Kilsby to the west. In 1838 Kilsby tunnel was opened, connecting the existing sections of the London to Birmingham railway. During the five years the navvies took to build the tunnel Kilsby must really have been woken from its rural calm. A thousand navvies lived in a shanty town on the edge of the village, using 200 horses and 13 steam engines to construct the tunnel. Drinking heavily in the Devon Ox pub when they got paid, these rough men were a force to be reckoned with. It is recorded that on one occasion soldiers from Weedon barracks were brought in to quell a riot.

A local legend tells how some were killed as a result of drunken bets. After a specially heavy session at the Devon Ox, it is said, men would bet each other that they could complete a circuit of the huge brick ventilation shaft, jumping from one turret to the next. Several lost their bets and their lives, falling about 160 ft to their death. Their ghosts are said to still haunt the shaft, which towers above the village beside Watling Street, now the A5.

The coming of the railway and the Industrial Revolution were the beginning of the end of Kilsby's agricultural way of life. Now the village only supports four farms, most of its workers travelling to Rugby or Coventry to work. It is still a thriving and happy community of around 1,200 people with two pubs, a post office, three shops, a restaurant, a school and a reasonable bus service.

Kings Cliffe

The village is 14 miles from Peterborough and at the present time the population is around 1,500 inhabitants. Much restoration of buildings has gone on and new people have come here to live. The village has a Co-operative shop and a greengrocer's, together with a butcher's shop and bakery. There is an Ex-Servicemen's Club and the Cross Keys Inn, and also two fine schools.

Kings Cliffe has a large village hall and a church room which is used for many activities. This room was originally part of the old water-mill and the sluice water can sometimes be heard, which tends to drown the proceedings! The church room holds the archives of the village, with pictures and photos of every part of village life. This was the work of a previous rector and is of great interest to villagers and visitors.

The library of William Law is housed in the Library House on School Hill. William Law was born in the village, the son of a grocer. He was a non-juror – a clergyman of great standing – but who never became rector of a parish. He helped the poor and was instrumental in founding the

Law and Hutchinson Almshouses, for six or seven widows or single ladies. These are near the old school where boys and girls went to school, around 2d a week paying for their education. The girls wore bonnets made of a cotton material, and aprons. The old school is still preserved with the master's desk in one corner. In Bridge Street are the Cornforth Homes, endowed by a wealthy lady of the village.

Kings Cliffe was noted in the old days for wooden ware – and is known as the wooden spoon village. The men had lathes in their backyards and lovely pieces of work were made. Even now there is one gentleman carrying on wood turning. Pottery is also made here.

The Miles family were timber merchants and great trees were brought to the big wood yard near the station. The Miles property was later a Youth Hostel and crowds of cyclists would be seen around the village in the 1930s.

The Second World War brought American airmen to the big aerodrome on the Wansford Road near the village. Some of the local girls married and went back to America after the war. The great number of children who came to the village as evacuees must remember the days at 'Cliffe now they are grown up.

Kings Sutton ༄

Kings Sutton is a large village with nearly 2,500 inhabitants. It is, however, quiet and peaceful, being at least two miles from the nearest classified road. This is just as well, its narrow streets and blind corners were not designed for motorised vehicles.

The heart of the village is The Square with the church of St Peter and St Paul on the west side and the 17th century manor on the south-west corner, next to the Bell Inn. The 16th century court house is now occupied as a private dwelling. Also in The Square are Lovells, a large residence which presumably owes its name to the 14th century lords of the manor, some of the very few remaining thatched cottages, the White Horse Inn and a general stores.

To the north of The Square, Whittall Street (formerly High Street) and Red Lion Street run downhill to Richmond Street and Wales Street respectively. There is a great mixture of architectural styles but many houses are built of the ironstone which was quarried locally until the 1920s. Many were rebuilt after the disastrous fire of 1785 which destroyed 40 houses and caused damage amounting to £3287 16s 5d. Several houses still bear the badges of the companies with whom the inhabitants insured.

The Butchers' Arms and The Three Tuns are both in Whittall Street. The Three Tuns has the original inn sign and the date 1695 in the front wall but is probably not the original building. The Red Lion, which gave its name to Red Lion Street, is now a general stores. This area is called

Spinney Bank and contains the post office, the one surviving bakery and the Baptist chapel. Follow the 'Railway Station only' sign and again you will find a wonderful mixture of architecture, including the oldest cottage in the village, 'Q' cottage.

In 1664 the spring at Astrop was 'discovered' by two doctors, Richard Lower and Thomas Willis, and thereafter they recommended their patients to take the waters at St Rumbold's Well rather than travel to Tonbridge. The next hundred years was a time of fame and prosperity. According to a pamphlet published in 1668, the waters were beneficial to 'all kinds of general disorders of the stomach, liver, spleen, kidneys, heart, brain, nerves and muscles'. A new well, the Bog Spring, was opened in 1749 but by 1777 Bray says 'the place is now out of fashion, the lodging houses are miserable', and Leamington Spa had become 'the' place to take the waters. The path through Astrop Park passes the site of St Rumbold's Well and the Bog Spring can be viewed in the field by the railway station.

Lacemaking was an occupation of many women in the village in the 19th century and girls would attend the lacemaking school behind the stores in The Square rather than the general school in Astrop Road. The latter is now a private dwelling but still called The Olde School House.

Kislingbury ✒

Kislingbury is a pretty village four miles west of Northampton on the southern bank of the river Nene, and was mentioned in the Domesday Book of 1086.

Although the village has acquired some modern houses over the last few years, there are many old stone houses with thatched roofs, including one of the pubs, The Sun. Two particularly fine buildings are the Old Rectory and The Elms at the top of the High Street.

Oliver Cromwell is reputed to have stabled his horses in the church-yard here in 1645, the night before the battle of Naseby. As one comes into the village from the A45, a narrow stone bridge crosses the river giving a fine view of the Cromwell Cottage, originally three cottages in which two old ladies ran a tea room. It is now a popular licensed restaurant.

The church of St Luke was built about 1330. It stands away from the road behind a wall made of mud, a rare type of construction, of which there is one other example in the village. The building is quite lovely, beautifully kept and decorated with a display of delightful floral arrangements. Inside the porch used to hang some very old leather fire buckets, but sadly some years ago these were stolen and nothing more has been heard of them.

Kislingbury is at present surrounded by open countryside, but for how much longer is in doubt, as we are on the edge of the planned South Western Development.

Lilbourne ✦

The village of Lilbourne in the north-west of the county could easily be missed by travellers speeding along the A5, as it lies back from that part of the road well-known for the masts of Rugby Radio Station. It is a little rural oasis, closely bordered by Warwickshire and Leicestershire.

The centre is sturdily attractive with various older houses round the village green, planted with young trees by the Parish Council. The roads leading from the green are mainly built up with modern houses but there are no housing developments as such. The population is around 350, compared with 243 in 1801 – the village has not grown like many others in the county.

There is very little documentary evidence to piece together Lilbourne's history. It is not far from the Roman site called Tripontium. Many tantalizing archaeological sites abound, including a windmill and a watermill. The remains of two mottes and a bailey close to the river Avon make an impressive and unexpected sight from the motorway. Close to these castle mounds lies All Saints church, whose earliest construction goes back to the 13th and 14th centuries, although in recent years two Saxon doorways have been discovered. The squat tower is balanced by the huge chestnut tree growing by the gate. Now the church, the Victorian rectory and Glebe Farm are all that remain of the former village, which became relocated on the hill top.

In medieval times the proximity to the Watling Street and its merchants and sheep trade made Lilbourne a wealthy village and it is thought that some of the land was owned by Simon de Montfort. There was a market larger than the one at Rugby in the field now known as the Butts, and cobbles still remain in the yard of Glebe Farm. Its prosperity can still be seen in the many fine old houses and farms, including the black and white timbered manor house. There were several inns but these have been converted into houses.

The Methodist chapel dates back to 1824 but it was closed in recent years and has subsequently opened as an Evangelical church. There was once a railway station on the Northampton to Market Harborough line and a village school, but these have both closed. The shop and post office also closed – all that has stayed open is the pub, the Bell Inn. Lilbourne was for a while bereft of any public transport until the County Council fostered the introduction of a voluntary community minibus in 1977.

Little Billing ✦

Little Billing is a village situated three miles east of Northampton town centre. It is mentioned in the Domesday Book of 1086. Also mentioned is a mill attached to the village, with a value given as two shillings, and also a thatched cottage in Orchard Hill. A plaque to this effect is situated on the outside wall.

The large house to the north of the church, known locally as the Priory, is in fact on the site of the original manor house and some 14th century features still remain. There is a rumour that there is a secret passage that leads to the church.

The church, locally thought of as Saxon, is in fact 14th century, with extensive restoration having taken place in the 1850s. The interesting cylindrical font is probably no earlier than the 11th century. It is interesting to note that in the 1920s construction work in Church Lane, next to the church, uncovered a Saxon burial ground, the remains being taken to Northampton town museum.

In the late 1800s the population comprised eleven families and one of these was the Knight family, who have lived in Little Billing for over 400 years. Their cottage stands at the corner of Orchard Hill and Knights Court. Knights Court was named after the family when they were rehoused and the original cottage sold for development. The original Knights were farmhands and thatchers.

One remarkable feature about Little Billing is that it never had a school, pub, shop or village hall. In the early 1900s the rector of All Saints used to let a room out for the locals, who met for games and to make their own entertainment. The population of Little Billing has grown tremendously since the 1960s but it still has no school, pub or village hall. A small shop was opened in 1958.

Little Harrowden ❧

The parish of Little Harrowden, in the Hundred of Orlingbury, is long and narrow, running north-east for about three miles along a ridge until it meets the valley of the Ise.

The heart of the village is the long Main Street. Its buildings are grey and mellow in the middle and modern at either end, with a row of houses at the eastern end separated from the main part of the village by fields. Modern development is to the west, comprising two small compact council estates, and recently a small cluster of privately-owned houses.

Though essentially rural, Little Harrowden has an industrial aspect. Reynolds' Foundry, dating from the mid-19th century, stands back from the centre of Main Street. The Glendon Iron Ore Co, now closed, operated six blast furnaces in Furnace Lane near the boundary with Finedon. The present Gammidge's shoe factory, in Orlingbury Road, was built after the Second World War, but previously the closing-room ladies worked in an upstairs room at the Lamb public house, down the road.

Within living memory there were three bakehouses and two butchers, all now closed. There remain two shops, one a newsagent, and a sub-post office which now receives mail by van, but a hundred years ago the letters arrived by 'foot post' from Wellingborough. Indeed, not so long ago, people would walk across the fields to and from work in Wellingborough. Nowadays the villagers 'commute' longer distances by car.

The present church of St Mary dates from the late 14th century and was restored in 1851, although, regrettably, the ancient Norman tower became unsafe and had to be demolished in 1967.

The school has existed since 1661, when, as William Aylworth's Endowed School, it started as a grammar school for the children of Great and Little Harrowden and Orlingbury. Its present buildings, dating from 1851 with subsequent alterations, now house a county primary school.

The village used to be served by three public houses. Now there are only two, The Lamb and The 10 O'Clock (believed to be the only pub with that name in England). Social life has been enriched by two innovations: the working men's club, opened in 1925, occupies a former shoe factory and now houses and fosters a bowls club; and the village hall, opened in 1973.

Little Houghton

Little Houghton, lying to the east of Northampton, while originally founded as a satellite of Great Houghton in early Saxon times, owes much of its prominence and prosperity to the River Nene which flows along the north boundary of the Parish. The ancient ford by the Cliff was in use 4000 years ago, and was still in use during the first half of this century. By AD 800 Clifford Mill was already operating and brought early prosperity to the village.

The strategic importance of the ford was recognised by the Romans and there is evidence of several Roman settlements within the Parish. By 1100 William de Houghton, Chamberlain to Henry I, had built the motte and bailey, or fortified artificial mound known as Clifford Hill, to protect the mill and the river crossing. He also founded and built the first church in Little Houghton and was the first of a long line of resident Lords of the Manor. There are no visible remains of William's church. This was rebuilt by his two grand-daughters. However, the main body of the church which can be seen today was rebuilt again in 1872–1874 when the north aisle was added.

Little Houghton has had two great fires. The first was in 1333, when almost all the houses were destroyed. The second, in 1780, appears to have occurred in the Lodge Road area and destroyed or badly damaged almost a quarter of the village.

The village stocks can still be seen near the post office. They were last in use about 100 years ago, when one William Baucutt was placed in them for being drunk and ill-treating his wife.

The village has many fine old buildings and farm houses of architectural interest, mostly built between 1600 and 1750. These together with a number of beautiful stone cottages are in such an excellent state of preservation that a conservation order has now been placed on most of the village.

Much of the appearance and character of the village is due to the fact that the Lordship of the Manor has been held by only three families since the Conquest. Each family has left its mark. The de Houghtons built the church, while during the 18th century the Wards rebuilt in stone the old medieval village of timbered houses and, in essence, it is their village which survives today. Finally the Smyths built Little Houghton House and The Mere and laid out the whole of the landscape and field system of the Parish which now surrounds the village.

Lois Weedon
& Weston by Weedon ᢟ

The small hamlets of Lois Weedon and Weston by Weedon nestle in the south-west corner of Northamptonshire. The two hamlets combine to make a single community, with Weston claiming the pub and Lois Weedon the church, and the school conveniently placed halfway between the two.

In the 11th century Gilo de Pinkney built a castle in Wedone and the village became known as 'Weedon Pinkney'. All that remains of it today, is a tree-covered mound beside the village green, which is greatly reduced from its original size.

The 11th century priory has also vanished and all that is left are the monks' fishponds in the field known as 'Church Close'. When the monks discovered a mineral spring to the south of the church they made it into a well and dedicated it to saint Lucien. It became known as St Loys' well – this was the beginning of the village being known as Weedon St Loys. The water from the well was believed to have healing properties and it attracted many pilgrims.

The peaceful church, dedicated to St Mary and St Peter, witnessed a violent scene on Sunday 2nd July, 1643, when twelve Parliamentary troopers rode from Northampton to arrest the Anglican priest, William Losse. An account of the story is printed on a plaque to his memory within the church.

There is a very weathered tombstone in the churchyard showing a woman handing a cup to her husband, which is supposed to contain poison. It is linked with the story about a woman who poisoned her husband and was burnt at the stake in a field near Weston. She was supposed to have been the last person to die at the stake in England.

Weston takes pride in possessing one of the oldest Baptist chapels in Northamptonshire, which was built in 1791. Up till then baptisms took place in an open air baptistry at Cathanger Farm, near Woodend.

Until his death in 1988, Sir Sacheverell Sitwell, the youngest brother of

Sir Osbert and Dame Edith Sitwell, lived at Weston Hall. Sir Sacheverell is buried beside his wife and his mother Lady Ida Sitwell in the church-yard extension. Dame Edith is also buried there, her grave marked by a tapering stone pillar on which is fixed a bronze plaque, by Henry Moore, depicting two delicate hands, the hands of Youth and Age.

Why the village is called 'Lois Weedon', when all the modern maps and signpost record it as 'Weedon Lois' remains a mystery. To many of the locals in fact it is still called by its ancient name of 'Loys Weedon'.

Long Buckby 🐾

Long Buckby is certainly long, it stretches for one and a half miles, and has done so since the time of Elizabeth I when the prefix was first recorded.

Historically it was an open village, independent, adaptable and radical. Now it contains several modern housing estates, which do not destroy the original character. It has a population of approximately 4,000 and is mostly a dormitory village, with many amenities including a modern library.

Behind some Victorian terraced houses stand the 'shops' where the hand-sewn shoemakers formerly worked. The village was well known in the 19th and early 20th centuries for these shoemakers, who gained a considerable reputation. There were several shoe factories but sadly only one remains. The largest factory had a world-wide reputation for riding boots and supplied the Royal Horse Guards, the last major order being for the coronation of Elizabeth II.

The castle, which now comprises an oval ringwork surrounded by a ditch, is undocumented but may have been built by the de Quincy family, later the Earls of Winchester, who held the manor from the mid 12th to the mid 13th century.

The parish church is dedicated to St Lawrence, the tower dating back to the 12th century. The main part of the church was added later with subsequent alterations to the north and south aisles.

Nonconformity has been a very strong feature of this village. The

The market place in Long Buckby

113

United Reformed church was formally constituted in 1707 as the Independent chapel and the present building was erected in 1771. The Baptist church on the Market Place was founded in 1759 with the present church being built in 1846.

A charter dated 1280 provided for two fairs in May and August. The August Fair was quite a holiday time when friends and relatives visited. Families made the Buckby Feast plum pudding, a rich bread pudding baked for about ten hours, which is still made today. Both fairs are retained but the one previously held in August has been transferred to September.

A very noticeable feature of the village is the variety of the forms of transport that pass through the parish, including the Roman Watling Street (now the A5) which forms the western boundary of the parish. In 1790 the Grand Junction Canal (now the Grand Union) was built at Buckby Wharf, linking London and Birmingham and in 1830 the main railway line from Euston to Rugby passed within yards of the canal. The railway line near Northampton which provides Long Buckby with its station, one of only six in the county, was not built until 1880. Then in 1959 the M1 motorway was built near the canal and the railway. These features have in their time had some effect on life in Long Buckby.

The tiny hamlet of Long Buckby Wharf is encompassed in the village of Long Buckby alongside the Grand Union Canal and the A5. At one time this hamlet was a thriving community with post office, church and village hall. The post office was closed and the church became redundant and almost derelict, until in 1980 it was purchased and has been turned into a house.

Lowick

Lowick is once more a haven of peace and quiet since the village was bypassed at the end of 1981. Set amongst undulating fields and woodland, with the very fine medieval church dominating the landscape, it is easy to feel at one with the generations of villagers who have gone before.

It is a genuinely old village; of the 80 or so houses, 20 have been built this century and only eleven of these are brick-built, the rest are of stone blending in with their surroundings. Many of the original 'two-up, one down' cottages have been joined together and modernised to make larger more comfortable homes but the thick walls, low thatched or pantiled roofs and attractive gardens present a very welcoming and homely picture to both resident and visitor alike.

About half the cottages still belong to the Drayton estate, with all the surrounding land. Situated in parkland between Lowick and Slipton is the lovely Drayton House, home of the squires of Lowick since the mid 14th century. The present owner is Mr L. G. Stopford Sackville.

The life of the village is mainly centred round the parish church, St

Peter's, which has a magnificent pinnacled lantern tower and many other noteworthy features and draws a great number of visitors.

The village school was closed in the 1950s and the building is now used as a parish hall, known as the Germain Rooms, after Lady Betty Germain of Drayton House, a generous benefactor to the village in the 18th century.

The public house formerly called the 'White Horse', now the 'Snooty Fox', has changed completely over the last few years from a small village pub to a large popular eating-out venue.

There is a recreation ground in the middle of the village where the children can play, and this is being altered to include a pond and copse to encourage wild-life and to make it more attractive.

Agriculture and domestic work are the only sources of employment so most people have to travel out of the village to work – a great change from the days when the cottages housed mainly farm and estate workers.

Luddington-in-the-Brook 🦊

The village, never large, developed as labourers' dwellings in meadows on both sides of the brook, until the landlord Duke of Buccleuch and Queensberry had new cottages built beside the Hemington-Gidding road, above flood levels, in 1863.

The village layout then established has not changed, save one new house built in 1969, somewhat apart and end-on to the road in a plot of a few acres. Other houses have been extended and one bungalow replaced by a new one. The old bungalow still had an outside nightsoil closet until demolished in 1981, and stood like a tollhouse at the T-junction of the Hemington-Gidding and Thurning roads.

This junction boasts a signpost yet this little village is rarely named on maps and road atlases. With equal rarity, a red VR letterbox is let into the wall of a small red brick former bakehouse at the end of a terrace of cottages moved up from the river meadows. Some 20 metres from the junction signpost is a red telephone box which, with the antique but functional postbox, provides the total public utilities of this quiet rural place. All houses have mains water, electricity and telephones, but the village is without gas, street lighting, main drainage, roadside kerbs or public transport.

The 14th century church tops a low grassy knoll close to the brook, but sufficiently high to escape the frequent floods before the extensive land drainage of recent years.

At its eastern, Gidding, end, an enlarged cottage, once an off-licensed house, is some 200 yards within the Northants county boundary with Cambridgeshire, yet the village has no nameboard of identity. It's a place drivers often come upon by surprise, wondering just where they are and starting to look around as they're pulling away from it again!

Those who must have the blessings of urban life do not choose to live at Luddington. Folk here appreciate Nature in all its forms and moods. Officially classified as 'Open Country', no new building is allowed other than adaptations or extensions, at any rate up to the next County Structure Plan Review from the year 2001.

Maidford ✿

This is a small village with a very long history. Surrounded by lovely country and still a few woods, it is within easy reach of centres such as Daventry and Towcester.

Inevitably the life-style of the place has changed considerably. A few residents are old enough to remember it as a busy agricultural place and practically self-sufficient with a post office, general shop, blacksmith, carpenter cum undertaker, shoemaker, tailor and dressmaker etc, but today it is a commuter village, busy with traffic only at the beginning and end of the day.

In much earlier times it was a busy place with a silk stocking industry employing many people. Pillow lace was also made and sold to help the family income. In the 1850s Leopold Stanton, a lace-designer, lived at The Villas, now Brook House, Maidford. His lace designs were exhibited in many parts of the world. The gate, made by the village carpenter, to the driveway of his home, was made up from his own design based on a Maltese lace pattern, and it became known as 'The Old Lace Gate'. Sadly it no longer exists, but in the driveway at the rear of the house remains can be seen of the same pattern laid out in bricks in the ground.

The church dedicated to St Peter and St Paul has a fine saddle-back tower and a very long history, the first rector being appointed in 1219. The manor house, now known as 'Manor Farm', adjacent to the church is thought to have been a monastery connected with the priory of St Augustines at Canons Ashby.

Most of the buildings are built of ironstone, a soft restful colour, and some have become listed buildings with interesting architectural features. Several springs in the area are impregnated with iron and mineral salt, and water from the chalybeate spring in the village was used for curing eye infections.

The peace and serenity of Maidford must have suited Elizabeth Wilson, for it is recorded that she died here in May 1767 at the extraordinary age of 122 years!

A part of village life disappears when the school closes, as was the case some years back. The building itself was brought into being by the generosity of the family living at Maidford House and subscriptions from others in a position to help. Before this there was a dame school, one penny per week being paid by each pupil who attended. The school has now become the village hall, bought from the education authority in 1973 by the efforts of a band of devoted workers.

Maidwell

Maidwell is a small community of about 300 people in all, which is about the same number as at the time the Domesday Book was compiled.

Evidence of Roman and earlier Iron Age settlements exists in fields just outside the present village boundaries. The ownership of the manor was divided for many centuries, with two manor houses and even two churches; somewhat of a rarity for so small a village. Around 1540, the church of St Peter was either destroyed (one account refers to a fire) or fell into disrepair. The only clue to its location is the field known as St Peter's Close, behind the Old Rectory, in which a grassy mound gives some indication of where a building might have been. Similarly, the second manor seems to have decayed without trace though it is likely to have been near, or part of, Manor Farm to the west of the A508.

The other manor became Maidwell Hall and continued as the residence of successive lords of the manor until the death of Mr R. B. Loder in the early 1930s, when the whole estate was broken up and sold by auction. Maidwell Hall then became the well-known and respected boys school which it remains today.

On the right hand side coming in from the north is the one remaining pub, The Stag's Head. Behind the pub is Manor Farm, the home of Miss Sylvia Stanier who, until recently, was for many years the stand-in for Her Majesty The Queen at rehearsals of Trooping The Colour. Miss Stanier and her staff maintain and train horses, including many from a well-known circus. Beyond the pub is the Loder Hall, provided for the village's use by the last lord of the manor around the turn of the century. On the crossroads are two of the remaining working farms – Hall Farm and Home Farm – now worked as one.

Draughton Road contains perhaps most of the village's interesting buildings. These include the old post office, the old bakehouse, School Farmhouse and its Old Barn and the School House. All alas no longer functional in their original roles but converted into very desirable homes. The parish church of St Mary the Virgin, the excellent primary school, the Old Rectory and Rectory Farmhouse are also in Draughton Road before it turns right at the end of the village on its way to Draughton.

In 1823 Joseph Moore was transported for 'stealing and breaking Maidwell Hall windows'. In 1842 Annie Gardner was whipped at the post against The Chequers for 'standing on her head while being drunk' and was 'sent out of the village for ever'!

Marston St Lawrence

Marston St Lawrence lies in the rolling countryside of south Northamptonshire, approximately half way between Brackley and Banbury. The village houses a population of just under 200 people in 80 dwellings. Amenities include a well-used village hall, an inn and a visiting post office service provided weekly in the village hall. Development within the area has been negligible and the village maintains its rural image more than many places.

Findings in and around the village suggest that a community existed here as far back as the 5th century and there are sites of interest relating to Roman times. Mention is made of 'Merestone' in the Domesday survey of 1085–6. The church of St Lawrence dates from the 11th century and has a Jacobean carved screen, separating the Lady Chapel from the north aisle. A yew tree, certified to be over a thousand years old, can be seen standing stout and strong outside the north door of the church.

Situated nearby is Marston House, once the home of the Blencowe family whose roots dated back to 1446. Much evidence of this family can be seen on the memorials placed in the church, along with the hatchments displayed high on the wall at the west end of the church.

Within the grounds of Marston House is a lake surrounded by lawns and a shrubbery, with a bridge dated 1759 over its south end. This provides an enjoyable walk around the edge of this attractive Northamptonshire village.

Mears Ashby ✺

The Domesday annals give the first official evidence of the existence of the village, and the name quoted was Asbi. Richard III gave the Manor to Robert de Meres, from whence evolved, through four changes (including Esseby Mares) today's name.

Today's manor house is relatively modern but does have a story to tell, relating to the fish pond in its grounds, overlooked from the secluded Church Walk west of the graveyard. Northampton's *Mercury* reported on 1st August 1785 that 'A poor woman, Sarah Bradshaw, accused of witchcraft, in order to prove her innocence, submitted to the ignominy of being dipped (in the manor pond) when she immediately sank to the bottom, there to remain. This was reckoned incontestable evidence she was *not* a witch'. Locals still talk of the ghost, believed to be that of this unfortunate, walking across the graves every anniversary of August's first midnight toll.

The church dates back to the 1100s. The vast 'Doom Painting', restored in 1984, has been widely described. The south aisle holds the 'Wheel Cross', possibly of Viking origin, circa AD1000, and may well have been the designation of a pre-conquest burial place and preacher's stand – a first pulpit maybe? Standing proudly by the south doorway is the magnificent 12th century font, beautifully lined with lead.

On the rise of School Hill there once stood a superb elm. The yarn goes that a tinker, taking ease from his mid-day 'jar', his stave pushed into the soil, departed after a post-prandial snooze, without his stick, which duly took root to ensure future shade for artisans spending enjoyment at the alehouse. So the 'Tinker Tree' came to be an original pub sign. Some 50 years ago the hollow bole (for long a 'cave' for youngsters after lessons) was removed. A grass roundel is the tiny vestige of the past, and the drinking 'den' has given way to a bungalow, proud to bear still that famous name. There remains only the hostelry once called the 'Boot', until a less common name was found by employing the Stockdale family crest – The Griffins Head.

The school grew on the present site from 1870, to today's spacious groups of classrooms overlooking the brook and its valley. The name 'Kinloch' peers out from countless angles. Sarah Kinloch, sister of a past incumbent's wife, willed in 1711, not only a silver flagon still central to the parish's communion plate, but also £200 for investment to ensure the education of Ashby's children.That seed of generosity has grown into grazing land in Arthingworth generating returns undreamed of so long ago.

Well known to the county is the Hall, erected in 1637 by Thomas Clendon. The Stockdales have owned, and occupied the house since inheritance in the late 1700s.

Middleton Cheney

Middleton Cheney lies about three miles from Banbury, and approximately six miles west of Brackley on the A422. It is the largest village in the area and in 1981 the population was 3,297.

Middleton Cheney has a long history and derives the second half of its name from the Chenduit family who were the Norman lords of Middleton at the time of the Domesday Book in 1086.

One of the first battles of the Civil War was fought at Middleton Cheney in May 1643, the site is now the Moors Drive housing estate. After the defeat of the Parliamentary forces, 46 of the Parliamentary soldiers were buried in the churchyard.

The 14th century church, built in the Decorated style, has a tower with six bells and a spire which rises to 150 ft. The church porch is of an unusual construction and only two other similar ones are known of, at Chacombe and Corby, the roof being made of stone sloping at an acute angle.

The church contains some of the best Edward Burne-Jones and William Morris stained glass in the country. Two windows in the chancel were created by Edward Burne-Jones as a memorial to his friend the Reverend William A. Buckley, who was a rector of Middleton Cheney from 1853 to 1892. The church was restored in 1865 under the direction of Sir Gilbert Scott. The church register dates from 1558.

Many of the older houses have historic associations such as tanning, glove-making, clockmaking, baking and hosiery weaving.

Middleton Cheney today is a big village with a pleasant mixture of older stone cottages and farmhouses, modern private estates and council houses. It is a busy place and has its own library, post office, bank, pubs, garages, chemist, a wide variety of shops and even a garden centre.

Milton Malsor

Milton Malsor is an attractive village with several interesting buildings, most of them dating from the 17th and 18th centuries.

The church of the Holy Cross is situated along Collingtree Road and was restored in the late 19th century. It has a crocketed spire and there is a beautiful 'Catherine Wheel' window. Further down Collingtree Road is the Old Bakery, which was in use until the 1960s. Opposite is a thatched house called Rectory Cottage, thought to have been the home of the rectors of Collingtree in the 16th and 17th centuries.

The former forge has an anvil incorporated into the wall to mark it. On the far side of the road as it bends to the right is the 'little' green. This is the original village green, but has got smaller as roads and pavements were laid. A young tree has been planted inside the stump of a much larger tree, which had been a feature of the village for centuries until it became unsafe.

There are two manor houses in the village. Milton Malsor Manor has 17th to 18th century alterations to a much larger house, and is situated along Malzor Lane. The other manor house is built largely of stone and is 16th century with 18th century alterations. It was at one time the home of Sir Sapcotes Harrington and his son, James Harrington, author in 1656 of *Oceana*. A 16th century dovecote stands in the garden.

Facing the green is a terrace of six attractive cottages which have been converted from the malt house belonging to the Hope Brewery. The brewery itself, now disused, is next to one of the two public houses in the village, the Greyhound.

A portion of the old village pound survives and is marked with a plaque. The parish pump used to stand here but has now gone, though there are still numerous pumps and wells in private gardens.

Moreton Pinkney

Moreton Pinkney, named from the Norman family from Picquigney, lies in the south-west corner of the county, ten miles from the nearest town. However, places of interest such as Oxford, Stratford on Avon and Warwick can be easily reached.

Moreton Pinkney has many pretty gardens and there is a thriving Garden Club. The annual fete, which involves many villagers, attracts people every summer from far around. The village hall is an excellent home for village activities. There is also a playing field, goal posts and swings for outdoor activities.

Moreton is a conservation village with many beautiful cottages, some dating back to the 17th century or earlier, and there is an interesting early English church. The National Trust property, Canons Ashby House, is only a mile away – the restoration work being completed in 1984 and now open to visitors.

The village has a post office, and the milkman, butcher, baker, grocer and fishmonger call each week, while the mobile library visits fortnightly.

Moulton ∂🐚

Lying just north of the county town and surrounded by new estates, both residential and industrial, Moulton could easily have become a suburb of Northampton. However, this ancient village – mentioned in the Domesday Book as Moltone, but with a history that goes back to Roman times and even earlier – retains its individuality. The heart of the village, now a conservation area, remains essentially rural.

The parish church, dedicated to St Peter and St Paul, dates mostly from the late 13th century but Saxon remains, including the shaft of a cross, have been found nearby which shows that the site has been used for Christian worship since very early times.

A Methodist Society was formed in 1801. The present Methodist chapel was built in 1835 and has twice been enlarged over the years. Perhaps however, the most widely known place of worship in Moulton is the Baptist church dating from the mid 17th century. Visitors come to see where the great William Carey was pastor, whose vision led to the formation of the Baptist Missionary Society in 1792.

Agriculture continues to play an important role in the life of the village. It is home to the Northamptonshire College of Agriculture, which developed from a Farm School opened in 1913.

On examining the information given in the early censuses (1841 and 1851) it appears that there were many tradesmen living in the area – the usual bakers and butchers, but also stonemasons, cordwainers (allied to the shoe trade), engineers and what are described as 'sojourners' (sometimes travelling tradesmen). There were, of course, the agricultural workers employed on the many farms and most of the women and girls were lacemakers. This was a thriving cottage industry.

It is thought that the old church room, built as a warehouse for the Co-op, became a pinafore factory attached to the Brook Company of Northampton – an early example of the spread of industry to villages around the town. In the latter part of the last century when the shoe factories were opened in Northampton many Moulton men (and women) walked to and from work in the shoe factories in the town.

One family well known in the village is the Jeyes family, members of which were Philadelphus Jeyes, chemist, and his brother John who invented the famous disinfectant Jeyes Fluid, as well as many other products.

Naseby ❦

Naseby lies three miles east of Welford, not far from the county border. At 600ft Naseby can be snowbound in winter, and daffodils take two weeks longer to appear here than in Market Harborough, the nearest town seven miles away. The village stands on the watershed of the Midlands, and among several water sources gives rise to both the 'Warwickshire' Avon which flows west and the northern tributary of the river Nene flowing to the east coast.

The pattern of village streets is very similar to that on the oldest recorded map of 1630 – Church Street and High Street running parallel and nearly north to south, Newlands across the top, Nutcote at the bottom, and School Lane and Gynwell in between – Gynwell named after a cleric of the Middle Ages.

The famous battle of 1645 was fought between King Charles I and the Parliamentarians with Sir Thomas Fairfax as Commander-in-Chief and Oliver Cromwell, at that stage, as Lieutenant-General of the Horse. The Parliamentarians carried the day following Cromwell's decisive charge. The battle was not recorded in the parish register but there are two monuments in the parish. One, erected in the 19th century on the site of an old windmill to the right of the road to Market Harborough, warns of the dangers to peoples who rise against their King. The other was put up in 1936 on the way to Sibbertoft and marks the spot from which Cromwell led his cavalry.

There are now fewer people who work on the land, and most work out of the village – in fact several go to London every day. Since the 1960s a steady number of new houses have been built to fill in the paddocks, larger gardens and farmyards of old.

Inside the church of All Saints is the Cromwell Table, reputed to have been in the pub opposite (now Shuckborough House) on the eve of the battle, when advance troops of the King surprised Roundheads at rest and recreation. As usual, Cromwell is supposed to have stabled horses in the church. There is a Norman font, a very old brass of a man and his wife (though he has lost his head), and an enormous copper ball said to be loot from Boulogne in France in 1544. It used to grace the 'stump' on the tower before the spire was built.

There are two pubs in Naseby, both in Church Street – the Royal Oak and the Fitzgerald Arms (named after one of the two landowning families at the time of the enclosure in 1822). Near here is a small industrial development with several small factories and more jobs for local people than there used to be. On the corner of School Lane and High Street is an excellent village shop and post office.

Nassington

There has been a village settlement here since ancient times. An important archaeological discovery was made in 1942, during the reopening of an old gravel pit. A mechanical scraper, removing the top-soil, uncovered parts of an old Anglo-Saxon cemetery. About 50 graves were found, with quite valuable grave goods such as spear heads, shield bosses, bronze drinking cups and jewellery. Some were taken by Oundle School, but some examples are in Peterborough Museum.

The cemetery was rather near the river, and liable to flooding, so the settlement must gradually have moved higher up the hill, where the first Anglo-Saxon church was built, and around which the present village still clusters.

The prebendal manor house, 1230, is the oldest inhabited house in Northamptonshire, and stands over much of the old Anglo-Saxon site. Excavations of parts of the gardens prove this, and the excavations are still going on. From these works it has been deduced that King Canute owned a royal manor here. It would have been a large wooden building with a single aisled timbered great hall. Some of the post holes of the foundations have been uncovered, determining its size. Near this settlement site an old stone quarry has been excavated, from which the first church was built.

Within living memory there were seven pubs in Nassington, but four have now been converted into private dwelling houses. The Black Horse dates from 1674, though of course it has been altered and added to over the years.

Nassington was obviously a very close-knit community at the beginning of the 20th century, before agriculture became so mechanised. Most of the people used to work on the surrounding farms, but now most people have to commute, some as far away as London. There used to be a blacksmith's forge, a tailor's and a clock-maker's shops, a laundry and an undertaker's. These have all gone now, but there are still two general stores, one with a post office, a good butcher's, and recently a glassware and china shop and a bread and cake shop.

There is still a good community spirit in the village and many and varied organisations are flourishing. Nassington still manages to maintain its rural atmosphere.

Nether Heyford ﷼

Heyford, or according to the Domesday Book, 'Heiforde', is a village of under 2,000 souls situated to the west of Northampton in the valley of the river Nene and bordered by the Grand Union Canal. Since 1964 the village has expanded rapidly due to better roads and the proximity of the M1 motorway. The village is well served with a variety of shops including a hairdresser and patisserie, as well as the more usual small supermarket, butcher and newspaper shop.

The school, which was endowed by William Bliss, a native of Heyford, in 1674 for £400, opened on its present site in 1880. The village hall, financed and built by village volunteers, and opened in May 1960 by Viscount Althorp (now Earl Spencer), is the centre of village activities of all kinds.

The feature which strikes the eye as soon as one enters Heyford is the beautiful, tree-lined, five acre village green – certainly the most handsome for miles around. At one time cows and geese grazed there and washing was hung out to dry. Cricket has been played upon it and latterly, a very successful football team enjoyed Saturday matches. But with the new playing field, the green has reverted to its role of Heyford's 'lung'.

Perhaps the most famous (or infamous) character of the past was Francis Morgan, Judge of the King's Bench, who was said to have pronounced sentence of death on Lady Jane Grey and who then in 1558, full of remorse, took his own life with the lament 'Take away the Lady Jane from me'. His monument appears on the south wall of the church, showing him kneeling at an altar tomb with his wife and with their sons and daughters behind them.

Newnham ﷼

This friendly village is situated in the west of Northamptonshire, just a few miles from the Warwickshire border. It nestles in a little valley on the edge of the Northamptonshire Uplands – just a stone's throw away lies Arbury Hill, the highest point in the county and the source of the river Nene.

The community of approximately 300 persons was virtually self-sufficient when the parish was largely agricultural. Some villagers happily recall when, in their youth, Newnham boasted two blacksmiths, two bakers, a butcher, a sweet shop, a timber merchant, a wheelwright and a funeral undertaker. Today, with a present poulation of around 500, village industry is virtually non-existent.

Several nut orchards can be found in the village, which were under-planted with snowdrops and daffodils. The largest one of these still sends its snowdrops to Covent Garden each Spring.

The village is an attractive grouping of stone and brick houses with only minor development occurring until recently. Infilling has occurred but with a thoughtful approach. The timely development of the Bradbury estate in the 1960s probably saved the school from closure.

Since 1915 the school has been in its present wooden building. Previously it had been located in what is now the village hall, which had itself, years before, been the poorhouse. Adjacent to the village hall stands the church of St Michael and All Angels. The original building, of which little remains, is deemed to be 12th century.

Wandering from the church down School Hill brings us to the village green. The green is much cherished in Newnham and on it is located the Romer Arms. The one and only public house was so named by Romer Williams, who bought and reconstructed the old Bakers Arms after it was damaged by fire. A lawyer of Welsh ancestry, Romer Williams settled at Newnham Hall in 1898. Villagers became accustomed to his generous feasts when he was visited by his beloved Pytchley Hunt.

Newton Bromswold ❧

Newton Bromswold is one of the smallest villages in Northamptonshire, and is situated on the Bedfordshire border three miles south of the town of Rushden. The name of the village is derived from the fact that in Anglo-Saxon times the village was a new town in the Brunswald Forest.

Needham Langhorne owned the Manor in 1644. One of Needham Langhorne's children, Mary, married a Robert Townsend and before emigrating to America the couple had their daughter, Mary, baptized at the church on the 15th July, 1669. Mary Townsend junior later married Captain John Washington of Virginia, who is known to have acted as guardian to Augustine Washington, the father of George, the first American president. The only remaining trace of the Langhorne family today in the village, is a silver alms dish given by Needham Langhorne's second wife Barbara on her marriage in 1656.

The church, completed in 1272, is a small church of the Early English period and dedicated to St Peter. One of the church's more notable features is its medieval stained glass. A window in the north aisle shows the head of Hugh of Lincoln on a rare blue flower patterned background, and the only other glass like this in the Midlands is in All Soul's College Chapel in Oxford. The churchyard still retains the base for the old village cross, and in 1988 was awarded the Northamptonshire Award for Nature Conservation in Churchyards.

Electricity was installed in the village in 1951 and with it came the disposal of a large quantity of oil lamps into the nearest pond! They may be collectable now, and some villagers may regret throwing them out, but back in 1951 Newton was glad to have 'the electric'.

Records show that Newton has had a public house called The Swan since at least the 1840s. The present building was erected by Packwoods of Rushden in 1931, after the previous pub was burnt down in 1930.

Agriculture provides the only source of employment in Newton today as it has throughout the centuries. Unlike the past however, the women no longer supplement their income by such crafts as lacemaking. While some men still work on the three farms most people travel to neighbouring towns to work. The population of the village has fluctuated over the years, for example in 1871 there were 157 residents while today there are only 56. Despite being small however the people from the surrounding area are always willing to help and support the villagers whenever the need arises.

Norton 🐿

The pretty, mostly stone-built village of Norton lies two miles east of Daventry on a site it has inhabited since prehistoric times. It is mentioned in the Domesday Book.

Norton Hall was inhabited by the Knightley family of Fawsley in the reign of Elizabeth I. The marble tomb of Lady Elizabeth Seymour, second wife of Sir Richard Knightley, is situated in the beautiful 13/14th century church. She was the daugher of the Duke of Somerset, Lord Protector of England, in the Reign of Edward VI.

Before 1840, the village used to surround the church but local legend has it that Beriah Botfield, the then owner of Norton Hall, had the village demolished and moved because he had a lady friend who used to visit him whom he did not want observed by the gossiping villagers! One row of terraced cottages is known as Tattle Bank Row as the local women used to chat and swap tittle-tattle over the wall during the day.

Sadly in 1947 Norton Hall was blown up by the British Army as there was no-one prepared to restore this splendid old building. All that remain are the coach-houses, blacksmith's shop, stables and the ice house.

Today Norton is growing again, with fine quality sandstone houses being built.

Old 🐿

Nestling in the heart of the countryside between the main roads to Market Harborough and Kettering, just north of Pitsford reservoir, lies the little village of Old. First mentioned in the Domesday Book as Walda or Walde, it underwent several name changes before arriving at its present form in the 16th century. However, it is still referred to occasionally – particularly amongst the older residents – by its alternative name of Wold.

In 1791 there were about 90 families (of whom nearly 40 were freeholders), whereas today there are just over 100 homes, ranging from 17th century buildings such as the Manor House (1607), Brewery House and parts of the Old Rectory, to the latest modern homes, carefully blended in with the old.

St Andrew's church, though extensively restored in 1874–5, dates back in part to the late 13th century. Of the five bells in the tower, the oldest is medieval and is inscribed in Latin to the Angel Gabriel. Today the church is festooned each July with elaborate flower arrangements during the two-day Flower Festival, and in the late summer is home to the annual Arts, Crafts and Produce Show.

In former times Old also boasted a thriving chapel community, together with its own schoolroom in which teas were served on the popular 'Band Sunday', when villagers were entertained by musicians from Rothwell. Today, sadly, the imposing chapel building has been put to use as a workshop and its little schoolroom has vanished. Gone too is the old Church of England school, which was closed down in the 1960s and converted into cottages. Smithy, bakehouse, brewery and butcher's shop – all have gone the same way in the relentless march of progress, though most of the buildings still remain.

One village institution which has remained intact for over 300 years is the 'Townson & Ward Charities', so named after its two earliest benefactors. Originally set up to provide for the poor, the widowed and 'fatherless children', and giving aid in the form of bread or lengths of unbleached calico, today it still gives regular financial assistance to the village's pensioners, schoolchildren and students. It also arranges free Christmas shopping trips, serves a Christmas meal to the OAPs, and runs a thriving community centre, six bungalows for the elderly, a large playing field and a children's playground.

Old still retains one pub, the White Horse, and close by it stands the 'Jubilee Tree'. This lime tree, planted in 1887 to mark Queen Victoria's Golden Jubilee, is now the regular mustering point for all village trips and outings.

In recent years Old achieved a rather sinister claim to fame after the discovery of a bag of human bones in a local stream, the identity of which remains an unsolved mystery to this day. The village has also been well known for many years as the home of the quaintly-named family haulage firm, 'Knights of Old'.

Old Stratford ✍

Old Stratford is on the border of Buckinghamshire, the river Ouse being the natural boundary.

In 1769 Sallow Copse, part of Whittlewood, came down to the village

Bridge over the river Ouse, Old Stratford

and was quite dense, encouraging highwaymen, but by 1860 it had been cleared and turned over to farming.

The Grand Junction Canal, opened in 1801, was cut from Cosgrove through Old Stratford to Buckingham and finished in eight months. From the early 19th century Edward Hayes, from Stony Stratford, concentrated on the production of steam tugboats. Until its closure in 1925, these tugboats were launched on the canal at Old Stratford. The AS 161 tugboat started its journey down the canal to London and ended up working on the river Nile, while others went to Russia and India!

Around 1800–40 the population seems to have doubled with new houses being built. There were a number of inns in the village, The Falcon 1734, The Black Horse 1820, The Swan 1800 (the only remaining one) and the Saracen's Head, which did a roaring trade with canal and road traffic. In 1849 the Saracen's Head became a school, Trinity House, later the Green Parrot Cafe, and now is the River Garage.

Around 1885 the Stony Stratford and District Light Railway Company was formed and a tram ran from Wolverton through Old Stratford to Deanshanger for a time. Mr Louis Bonaparte, a resident of Old Stratford, was the second managing director.

The original bridge over the river was thought to have been a wooden one, but a stone bridge was mentioned in 1594. At some time a tollgate stood on the bridge.

A windmill once stood between Old Stratford and Passenham, possibly how Windmill Field got its name. There is another field in Old Stratford called Chapel Close, where it is said there once stood a chapel, hermitage, leper hospital and workhouse.

Orlingbury 🔖

The village of Orlingbury lies within the triangle of main roads linking the nearby towns of Kettering, Northampton and Wellingborough and so it still has much of its rural character without major developments and heavy traffic. Orlingbury Hundred, the ancient grouping which comprises fifteen parishes in the rural area between these towns, derived its name from this Parish in recognition of the earlier importance of this community which contained two Manors with all their associated feudal history. The present village population of about 360 is similar to that of a hundred and fifty years ago, notwithstanding the small clusters of new houses around the village, although few of today's villagers still earn their living within the confines of the parish.

The Village Green remains the heart of Orlingbury, and the focal point for much of the everyday village activity. Clustered around it is a medley of buildings old and new, including several traditional ones constructed in the local stone, often with ironstone used for the decorative masonry. These include the former Forge and School with adjoining Schoolmaster's House which was built in 1845. The three major listed buildings of the village – Orlingbury Hall, The Old Rectory and the Parish Church – are all around the edge of The Green.

Dominating the scene is the church whose square tower is a landmark visible from far afield. Older residents of Orlingbury still recall with a chuckle that – whilst they were told, as children going out to play, not to get out of sight of the church – they knew that this still gave them plenty of scope to wander. The parish church of St Mary was completely rebuilt in 1842 to a new design by the architect R. H. Hussey. It stands on the same site as the former church which had fallen into decay and was deemed to be a grave danger to all who entered it. The style of the present church is that of the early Victorian Gothic revival such that the church is often thought by visitors to be far older than it actually is. A detailed description of the church and its major memorials, many of which were transferred from the former building, is provided therein for visitors.

Orlingbury Hall occupies the site of the former Manor House which was lived in successively by the Lanes, Toftes and Chybnalles. In 1678 this contained twenty rooms and paid taxes on twenty hearths but was replaced early in the 18th century by the present Hall, built by Richard Young whose family held the Manor for the next two centuries. The Dower House can be seen across the road to the west of the Hall, opposite a gate in the wall which served as a short link between the Lord of the Manor and his widowed mother.

Other buildings which have survived from this time include the Dovecote opposite to the entrance of The Old Rectory, and various farmhouses and cottages which have now all been modernised internally. There remain numerous wells, from which the village derived its water in days of old, and several residents remember times before the arrival of modern amenities such as electricity and mains drainage. Today's villagers face the future with the assurance that many of the best aspects of village life have been retained for enjoyment by all, both those who grew up within sight of the Orlingbury church tower and those who came from farther afield to settle and make Orlingbury their home.

Overstone ⚘

Overstone is a linear village, with only one small estate of bungalows and houses. The reason for this can be traced back to the 18th century, when the 'new' village was built. The old village was in front of the manor house, but such was the power of the gentry that the old village was arbitrarily demolished and new houses built well outside the park. The church was also demolished and a new one built away from the manor house, giving the opportunity for the public road to be closed and the grounds round the house to be landscaped. Slight indentations can still be found on the site of the lost village.

Having the park wall on one side of the main village street led to ribbon development. Until 1920 Overstone was an estate village, houses only being built for estate or farm workers. With the sale of the estate, residents had to find work away from the village or become self-employed.

As you enter the village the outstanding feature is the Pytchley Gates, at one time the main entrance to Overstone House. These gates were originally erected at Pytchley manor, which for a time was the headquarters of the Pytchley Hunt. After Pytchley manor was pulled down the gateway was brought, stone by stone, and re-erected on the present site.

Overstone did have a ghost, which appears to have been laid when the old blacksmith's forge, part of the 18th century development, was demolished. Residents living in a nearby cottage remember hearing heavy breathing and doors opening and moving mysteriously.

At one time during the 14th century the rent of the manor was a single red rose due on 1st May. In those days it was very difficult to get a rose to flower at this time of the year and the gardeners went to great lengths to do so. There is a story that one year a young guest, seeing the beautiful rose, decided to pick it to present to his love. There was great consternation next morning when the gardener found that the rose was missing. We are not told how the omission was rectified, but as the family were not turned out presumably he was able to retrieve it!

A later owner was Lady Wantage, whose husband was a courageous soldier in the Crimean War, winning one of the first VCs. This is depicted in stained glass in the Loyd family memorial window in Overstone church. He is also remembered as being one of the founders of the British Red Cross.

Today Overstone House is the Head Office of the New Testament Church of God, Overstone Theological College and Overstone Hall conference centre. The buildings that were the workshops and stabling at the time of the estate have been converted to residences.

Passenham 🌿

Passenham is a hamlet consisting of about a dozen houses, and the church of St Guthlac. There is also a mill, a manor house and a tithe barn dating from 1500.

A church was first mentioned in AD 921, but the present one is 13th to 14th century. The chancel was beautified by Sir Robert Bannister in the 1620s. In recent years a unique set of murals have been uncovered in the chancel, part of Sir Robert Bannister's great scheme of prophets and evangelists, dated 1628.

Many ghost stores are connected with Passenham. A Deanshanger girl leaped into the mill stream one night and was crushed by the mill wheel, and some time later, at midnight on Deanshanger Feast, a scream was heard from the stream. The verger told a tale of how, one stormy night while ringing the bell, his candle blew out. He let go of the rope to light it again, but the bell kept ringing! Then there is the phosphorescent skeletal form of a huntsman with a broken neck, dragged in the stirrups of a phantom steed, which disappears among the gravestones. This one is known as Bobby Bannister's Ghost, after a man who was killed in a riding accident.

Old mill at Passenham

131

Pattishall 🐝

Pattishall and its neighbouring villages are set in a rural area on the borders of the Northamptonshire Heights and the Nene valley. The parish lies four miles north of Towcester on the Roman Watling Street. It comprises the villages of Pattishall, Astcote, Eastcote, Dalscote and Fosters Booth.

Pattishall, the largest village in the parish, is mentioned in the Domesday Book. The church of Holy Cross stands on a small limestone plateau and dates from Saxon times. Although a lot of the village has been developed in recent years, there are many attractive old stone houses in the narrow street which leads to the village green. The village still retains its post office by the green and a thriving primary school stands on the outskirts of Pattishall.

The village of Astcote had a thriving industry well over a hundred years ago. There were at one time three small factories involved with shoemaking. The raw materials were collected from Northampton and turned into handmade shoes and boots, often in the cottages. Many of the present day villagers have ancestors who were involved in the shoe trade, and the same family names have remained in the village. All industry gone, Astcote can now only boast a small general shop.

Eastcote is still basically a farming village, although the cows no longer walk down the main street on their way to be milked. Eastcote does have a small claim to fame, being mentioned in the *Times* newspaper on the 5th January, 1915. During the First World War, an internment camp was established here for German seamen. One of the inhabitants wrote a letter which was published in the newspaper, about life in the camp. He stated: 'The natives of our village are very nice. They bring us cigarettes, fruit and papers and stop to chat.' Many of the prisoners whiled away the time making model boats, and a complete model harbour was built by the brook. Among the older buildings are The Eastcote Arms public house and the Baptist chapel, built in 1838.

Dalscote, now a small hamlet, was once the site of a larger settlement. In the surrounding fields overlooking Northampton, stone rubble and post-medieval pottery have been found. Where once there was habitation, there are now crops on the rolling landscape.

The name Fosters Booth derives from Forester's Booth, and the present Peggotty's Restaurant used to be that inn. There is some decorative raised plaster-work on the south side of the building of a hunting scene. The ancient royal forests of Whittlewood used to lie to the south and the hunters could well have visited Fosters Booth to partake of refreshments.

Paulerspury 🐚

Paulerspury is situated along the A5, the old Roman Road. It is thought to be a Roman settlement with pear and plum orchards and fish ponds.

The village was named 'Paruelos-Puri' after the Parueli family who were lords of the manor in the 13–14th century. The fine old church is dedicated to St James and houses wooden monuments to a knight and his lady from the 14th century. These were beautifully exhibited at the Heritage Exhibition in London.

The Throckmortons were a famous family of Paulerspury. Bess Throckmorton married Sir Walter Raleigh. The Throckmortons were very active politically during the time of Henry VIII, Mary Tudor, Elizabeth I and Mary Queen of Scots.

The old flint house is the home of the Rolls Royce Foundation. Several times a year there is a gathering of vintage and veteran cars and contemporary Rolls Royces – enough to gladden the heart of the enthusiast!

Lace making was very popular in Paulerspury in the mid-19th century. At one time 130 lace workers were employed in this cottage industry. Paulerspury lace became famous and much sought after by fashionable Victorians. Queen Victoria in fact requested a piece of Paulerspury lace. This was made by Mrs Dunkley.

Paulerspury is now very fortunate to have many artists, craftsmen and craftswomen living in the village.

Pitsford 🐚

Pitsford lies five miles north of Northampton to the east of the A508 road. It was already an important place at the time of the Domesday Book where it receives two mentions. The original village was situated north of the church down towards the turnpike, but was completely destroyed by fire in 1619.

Pitsford, which now lies to the south of the church, has a population of about 500 and still retains many of its old stone buildings, a church, a public house, a school, farm buildings and cottages. Beside the High Street is a mound known as Longman's or Layman's Hill, which is thought to be a Saxon long barrow. In the early 19th century skeletons were found when the mound was cut during work to widen the road.

Today the village is best known for its reservoir, which was opened in 1956 by Queen Elizabeth the Queen Mother. It is not surprising that the valley between Pitsford and Brixworth was chosen for the reservoir as there were over 300 wells and springs registered in the village.

The oldest building in the village is All Saints church. Although extensively restored in 1866, it still retains its 13th century tower and Norman doorway. The bell tower contains a fine set of six bells which date from the 17th century and bellringing is still a favourite pastime in the village.

Closely linked with the church is the village school, opened by the Church of England in 1848. Many of the older villagers remember when May day was a very important occasion. A May Queen and an attendant May King were chosen, as well as a mysterious figure called 'Jack-in-the-Green.' The Jack was of cane construction made by a blind man in the village. It was about four feet high and had leather straps inside to fit over the shoulders of the boy chosen to carry it. It was covered by branches of laurel, barberry and other evergreens.

There were five mansions where the gentry lived and many of the village families were employed as servants, gardeners and grooms. The owners of these properties are remembered as village benefactors, giving treats to the children, caring for the sick and elderly and giving the village hall and sports field, both of which are still in regular use today.

Although the bakehouse no longer provides the bread for the village, the butcher's shop has been replaced by a mobile van and the two blacksmith's forges, the wheelwright's workshop, the undertaker's and the two coal merchants have all disappeared, Pitsford High Street is still a busy thoroughfare. The village store and post office presents a bustling scene and a few doors away the 18th century public house, The Griffin, is still very popular with locals and visitors alike.

Polebrook

The village of Polebrook, three miles to the south-east of Oundle, contains within its parish boundaries two other settlements, Armston and Kingsthorpe, and clearly derives the second part of its name from the brook which flows into the river Nene about three quarters of a mile to the west of the village.

A thriving community of 320 inhabitants enjoy the obvious beauty of this village with its many old houses, mainly built in local stone with roofs of thatch, Collyweston slates and tiles. Some imaginative projects have converted many of the older buildings and barns into very comfortable and attractive homes.

Its most beautiful building, dominating the centre of the village is the church of All Saints. Mainly Early English, with some Norman work remaining, both the exterior and interior are characterised by an impressive simplicity. Polebrook's most eminent Rector must have been Dr John Wilkins, brother-in-law of Oliver Cromwell and a founder-member of the Royal Society.

All the memorials in the south transept commemorate the Ferguson family, since Brigadier-General Ferguson and his wife, Margaret, great-grandparents of HRH The Duchess of York, lived at Polebrook Hall for more than half a century. A Roll of Honour lists the many American servicemen of the 351st Bombardment Group who were killed while flying from Polebrook Airbase during the Second World War. A memorial has also been erected on the site of the former airfield at the end of what was the main runway. It was at this base (whatever the claims of other places!) that Clark Gable served.

In the 'Square' in the village centre is clustered a particularly attractive collection of stone cottages, the Old Duke's Head, formerly a public house, forming one side of the group. Behind a small green near the war memorial stands another fine stone house with a pantiled roof and it was from this building when, many years ago it was a post office, that the first old age pensions, 'Lloyd George's ten shillings', were issued. Later, the post office moved to another well-set 18th century house, the Gables, in the main street. Its final destination, before the village became stampless, was in the converted Wesleyan chapel nearly opposite the school. This, and the school were the only Victorian buildings of any significance. One of the oldest houses, beyond the school, on the way out to Lutton, is the Manor, dating at least to the 16th century. Undoubtedly the grandest house, imposing behind its wrought iron gates in the main street, is Polebrook Hall.

The village is justly proud of its Church of England primary school which, above all, brings life to the village with its 75 pupils receiving a splendidly broad-based, sound education, involving subjects undreamed of by those who built its original rooms in 1865.

Potterspury

The village was originally called Pyrie or Estpirie (East Perey), derived from 'pyrige' meaning 'the place where pear trees grow'. Following the introduction of potteries in the 12th century the name was changed to Potters Perry or Potterspury. Several of these ancient potteries have been excavated in recent years.

The parish church is dedicated to St Nicholas and there has been a church on the site since at least 1087.

An Independent church was established in 1690 by the Rev Michael Harrison. The history of the Independents in the 18th century is largely bound up with the name John Heywood. He was an eccentric and remarkable man, described as tall and thin with a mean and slovenly appearance, mostly due to the neglect of his imprudent wife who remained outside the church for the first 28 years of their unsuitable marriage. However, he was held in high esteem by many including the Duke of Grafton, who allowed him to use his library.

The Dukes of Grafton resided at Wakefield Lodge from about 1748, when the 2nd Duke commissioned William Kent to design and build a house on the site of a hunting lodge in the Whittlebury Forest, about a mile south of Potterspury. Kent brought in Capability Brown to landscape the park, who for the first time used water in the landscape.

135

Following the death of the 7th Duke in 1918 the estate was broken up and sold.

The village at one time had at least five or six public houses but now only two remain. The Anchor has been demolished, The Reindeer is an antique shop, and The Red Lion and The Blue Ball are private houses. Four of these premises were on the Watling Street but now only The Talbot remains as a hostelry on this road. The Cock public house is in the High Street.

Within and close to the village were several farms which employed most of the men before the advent of the railways and their workshops at Wolverton. Many of the women and girls were employed in lacemaking. The census return for 1851 lists 135 lacemakers, some of whom were as young as five. A department for girls was added to the boys school in 1857, to be followed in 1870 by an infants class. Several of the farm-houses have become private dwellings with the land being used for the building of new houses. At one time there were several shops in the village including a butcher's and two bakers. The post office, which successive generations of the Osborne family ran for over 100 years, has now moved into the only village shop which, incidentally, was originally a farmhouse.

A brook runs through the village and at one time supplied power to a corn and grinding mill. This power was later supplemented by a steam engine and later still by an oil engine. The mill continued in use until the 1940s and after being put to various uses it was converted into dwellings in the 1980s.

Preston Capes

Preston Capes, a village of about 50 houses, stands amidst the Northamptonshire Heights in delightful countryside six miles from Daventry. The main street rises steeply to reach 594 ft above sea level.

The village, once known as Preston Magna, formed part of the Fawsley estate until 1932 when most of the properties were offered for sale. At that time most of the houses had thatched roofs, although now only two remain.

Included in the parish is the hamlet of Little Preston, once known as Preston Parva, a collection of 15 houses about half a mile away towards Maidford.

The buildings in and around the village have not changed much over the years. Fourteen houses in Preston Capes and seven in Little Preston have been built since the 1960s. The whole centre of the village is now designated a conservation area.

There is no mains drainage in the area at the moment, no mains gas, street lighting, public house or shop. A sub-post office opens for 20 hours a week. Although there are no shops the village is well served by tradesmen who deliver essential goods.

William the Conqueror awarded the area to a French Knight, Hugh de Capes (Hughes Capet) after 1066. He built a castle on the site of the Roman encampment, which is now occupied by the manor house. Traces of the castle walls can still be found there. Behind the row of houses and bungalows in Church Way there is believed to be a Saxon ditch in which a Saxon ring was found and nearby a Saxon axe.

After the manor house the next most important house is the School House, which was built around 1690. The most unusual properties are Archway Cottages, which were built in the 18th century as four cottages (now two) for workers from Fawsley House. They have a red brick connecting archway which when viewed from Fawsley Park looks like a castle.

The old school, near the church, now a private book room, was built in 1845, enlarged in 1871 and closed in 1965. Part of the old rectory, next to the church, dates from the 16th century and is built on the site of a priory founded in 1090. The church of St Peter and St Paul dates from the beginning of the 13th century, with periodic improvements and additions.

The pattern of farming to the south of the village has changed since the 1970s. Hedges have disappeared to accommodate large-scale arable farming. Increased mechanisation combined with this has radically reduced the number of people dependent on the land for their livelihood.

There are seven working farms of which two are arable and one fattens beef cattle, while the rest mix arable and livestock farming in a more traditional way. One also trains racehorses. There are now no dairy herds. There are three smallholdings with small flocks of sheep.

Pytchley

The lords of the manor of Pytchley in the 11th century owed a service to the King, as did many other landowners. Their particular service was to maintain hunting dogs with which to kill wolves and foxes in Northants and the surrounding counties. The 'service' was maintained until the reign of Charles II in the 17th century. It was common knowledge that Pytchley had been noted for its hunting packs 'before the Conquest'.

Pytchley's comparative closeness to London led to many of the hunting gentry buying or renting mansions here for hunting over the centuries. The Isham family held lands in Pytchley from the 14th century and in 1580 Sir Euseby Isham built the Hall, a large elegant mansion facing west to the church, sited across the present Isham Road.

Other rich families lived in the Hall and in the mid 18th century the famous pack of hounds was formally founded. It was maintained at the Hall until 1824, when due to the gambling debts of the owner George Payne, the Hall had to be demolished. The kennels moved permanently to Brixworth.

Pytchley church dates from Norman times and has been added to through the centuries. The large size of the church reflects the greater numbers living in Pytchley when the Hall and other large mansions and farms required huge staffs.

Villagers through the centuries, if not connected in some way with the Hunt, carved a living from agriculture. The village was largely self-supporting, with certain families tending to be blacksmiths, bakers, butchers, cobblers and carriers. In 1607 there were 'disorders' when the violent-tempered Sir Euseby carried out certain land enclosures, but other crimes in the village tended to be only on a petty scale.

When the Hall was demolished, much employment was lost. The 1851 census shows a new way of literally getting 'pin-money' – 63 lacemakers among the villagers, making coarse lace to famous Flemish and Belgian designs. The later machine-lace of Nottingham would kill this trade.

In the late 19th century the population was twice as large as today. In 1898 the Midland Railway Company was building the line from Kettering, and labourers and their families lived in Pytchley. A great rivalry existed between the families running the two chapels – the Methodists led by the shopkeeper Sewell family, and the Wesleyans led by the coalmerchant Woolleys. Village children benefited from the rival events on successive nights organised by the chapels – and by the church!

With the coming of motor transport, workers went as shift-workers at Corby's steelworks and at the Weetabix works. Work patterns rapidly changed. Pytchley has become the commuters' route between Kettering and Northampton, which has unfortunately led to traffic problems in the High Street and Isham Road.

Quinton

Quinton parish extends from Wootton Brook in the north to Salcey Forest in the south, but most of the dwellings surround the church and the village green. Archaeologists have investigated the remains of a moated medieval manor house and earlier sites of Roman and Saxon origins, but there are only a few old stone houses remaining. The houses to the north of the green were built by the council after the Second World War and the more modern houses in School Lane and Preston Deanery Road were built some 30 years later. The Old Bakehouse with its protruding semi-circular oven, where older residents can remember Sunday dinners being cooked, attracts the interest of passers-by.

The church, dedicated to St John the Baptist, is the focal point of the village. Built mainly in the 13th century on earlier foundations, it had its tower raised in the 15th century and the chancel and porch added three centuries later. Now, surrounded by a well-kept churchyard and framed by majestic lime trees, it is much-loved by residents and admired by visitors.

The rectory beside the church is now a private dwelling as the spiritual welfare of the parish is cared for by the rector of Wootton. It is rumoured that one incumbent of the rectory allowed his horse to live in the rectory lounge.

The school, which closed in 1937, was built in 1876 with bricks carried from Northampton station by the villagers. It is now the property of the village and is the venue for village activities.

The village is surrounded by arable land. Courteenhall Estate farm some land to the west, but most belongs to Quinton Green Farm which runs a large herd of dairy cattle on the land surrounding the farm buildings. A few residents are employed on the land but most commute to their places of employment. There is no village shop, but the tradesmen call regularly with milk, meat, vegetables and fish.

Ravensthorpe 🐑

To the north-east Ravensthorpe overlooks a shallow valley, which was flooded by the reservoir in 1896. This covers 183 acres and provides not only water for the village but an attractive leisure facility as well.

In the village is the home of Horace Batten, bootmaker. He is one of the few craftsmen left working in the village and he has followed in the footsteps of three generations in the business of top boot manufacture. Handmade beechwood lasts are used and when these 'last-makers' die out along with special leather workers such as the hand-sewers, Horace fears that this industry will die out with them. Sadly, when he retires the business will close.

The oldest building in the village is St Denys' church. Built of brown ironstone it dates back to between the 13th and 14th century. Inside, the absence of a lord of the manor has meant that the interior is free of memorials, which adds to its attractive simplicity.

Nearer the centre of the village is the green, where there are two large copper beech trees. The larger one was planted in 1897 for Queen Victoria's Diamond Jubilee, and the smaller in 1935 for King George V's Silver Jubilee. The trees are much prized and in good condition. The green is sometimes used for social activities – occasionally a travelling theatre group set up here and give an open air performance.

The Wool Festival was held in June 1982 as a social event and to raise money for village amenities. The main event was making the Althorp Coat – villagers tried to make a replica of the Throckmorton coat of 1811, duplicating the condition of sheep-shearing, wool-spinning, washing and drying the cloth, and cutting and sewing the coat in less than the original 13 hours and 20 minutes. The shearer took just four minutes to shear each of the 17 Jacob's sheep. From the spinner the wool was handed to weavers, carders, teasers and tailors – 30 in all. A large crowd gathered to see it made with only 12 minutes to spare. The coat is now permanently housed at Althorp House.

In the High Street is the Post Office Stores, housed in a most attractive whitewashed cottage. This was built in 1610 with mud walls and a local straw thatch, with the extension being added in 1875 to house the postmaster/mistress's family. It is valued not only for its facility but as a place to have a chat and catch up on the news!

Ringstead ✿

The name Ringstead may be derived from one of the ancient parish fields, the Anglo Saxon 'hring' meaning a circular place. The village was first documented in 1124.

The parish, of around 1,300 inhabitants, is located between Thrapston and Raunds, in East Northamptonshire.

Ringstead's oldest building is the mainly 13th century church of St Mary, in the Early English style with some Decorated portions. The Baptists have had a chapel in the village since 1714, although the present one was erected in 1785. In addition, there is a Methodist chapel (from 1857) on the site of the former blacksmith's shop.

There are also many private residences in the parish that have been built from the attractive local ironstone, in differing shades of brown, usually alternated with the lighter freestone; most of these date from the 17th and 18th centuries.

Modern amenities include several shops, a Church of England primary school, riding stables and a children's recreation ground.

The public houses are the Axe and Compass and The New Inn, with a working men's club opposite the village hall (erected in 1861). There are the usual darts and bar billiards, as well as the local version of table skittles using 'cheeses'. There is also an annual tug of war, on Boxing Day at the Axe and Compass, in aid of charity.

We are in footwear country, and shoemaking was carried out in the village hall and elsewhere. These days, the only shoemaking is in nearby Raunds, although, quite recently a small 'closing' business has started up in the village.

The ghost of unhappy Lydia Attley, a young girl rejected by her lover, who disappeared in 1850 after going to meet him at his orchard, haunted the area for 20 years. It would walk from the orchard to the church – and to a spot where the skeleton of a girl was found in a ditch in 1865. Her lover, Weekly Ball, was put on trial at Thrapston but the finding of the bones did not provide enough evidence to prove the Ringstead butcher was the murderer. He was acquitted but the local feeling was so strong against him that, almost immediately, he left the village.

Ringstead was also the birthplace of Alf Roberts, father of our current Prime Minister, Margaret Thatcher. Many generations of her ancestors, humble shoemakers and labourers, lived in Ringstead.

Roade

At first sight Roade village is neither beautiful nor ugly. It is in fact just an ordinary village, with pretty corners of thatched cottages looking onto green spaces, Victorian houses with walled gardens and large trees, and also estates of modern open-plan houses and bungalows, factory buildings and warehouses, which all seem to exist quite happily side by side.

The neighbourliness of the village has been enhanced since 1963, when a fund was formed to help the aged of the village. This scheme was thought up when a pensioner, living alone, was found ill and dying.

One of the features of Roade is the railway cutting, which is 65 ft at its deepest point and was dug out of almost solid rock. In 1838 when the first train travelled through Roade, it was the largest man-made cutting in the world. The station was opened in 1851, and from then on it progressed from goods to passenger trains, and was the main mode of transport until it closed in 1964.

As well as people going out of the village to work, there are also a considerable number coming into the village to work at Pianoforte Supplies, something of a misnomer, as they do not make parts for pianos anymore, but concentrate mostly on parts for the motor industry. This factory is owned by the family of the late Sir Cyril Cripps Kt, MBE, and was purchased by him in the early 1920s and built up until in the 1960s, when trade was booming, they employed about 2,000 people.

Sir Cyril did many things for Roade. He supported the football team, donated a first class pitch and pavilion for the cricket team, and did the same for the bowling team, bringing both sports to a county standard.

All this of course expanded Roade from a small sleepy village to a large

The village of Roade

141

bustling one, and houses and estates, including a large comprehensive school, have been built until a green belt was imposed around the village. New houses are being put up in all sorts of unlikely places!

The delightful church of St Mary is said to originally date back to the Norman Conquest, but like so many churches the origins are lost in the mists of antiquity. It has been restored several times, the last time being after the Second World War. The pride of the church is the six bells. Four of these are very ancient, but the two new ones were donated and dedicated by Sir Cyril and Lady Amy Cripps, in 1952 and 1979 respectively. The young bellringers are becoming quite well-known.

Rockingham 🐝

The village of Rockingham is situated on the border of Northamptonshire with Leicestershire, in the picturesque Welland Valley.

Rockingham was for centuries famous for its Forest and Castle. Once one of the largest in the Kingdom, the forest covered much of what is now Northamptonshire. Vast inroads have been made into the forest since those days, but even so large portions of it still remain.

The Castle was built by William the Conqueror on the site of an ancient fortress. It commands the valley of the river Welland. For 500 years the castle was a royal residence, used regularly by the early English Kings both as an administrative centre for the Midlands, and also as a hunting lodge.

During this period, many important events occurred at Rockingham, including one of the earliest recorded assemblies of State, the Council of Rockingham in 1095, and a great siege later in the 13th century, the marks of which can still be seen on the walls.

King John was a frequent visitor to the Castle, and on his last journey North in 1216, during which he lost most of his personal possessions in the Wash, he left behind an iron chest which can still be seen in the Castle.

In 1530 Edward Watson, a local landowner, obtained a lease of Rockingham from Henry VIII and set about restoring what remained of the Norman castle, converting it into a comfortable Tudor house. His grandson, Sir Lewis Watson, bought the freehold from James I in 1619, and, apart from a brief period when the Castle was occupied by the Roundheads during the Civil War, the Watsons have lived here ever since.

As the Castle grew in importance, so did the village – being designated a Borough in the 12th century and a 'Towne' by Royal Charter of Elizabeth I.

Much of the Tudor village was destroyed during the Civil War and the village was later reconstructed out of stone on the hill below the Castle.

This is essentially the village as it stands today, the earliest house being dated 1670.

Rockingham was a former market town, but the market has long since fallen into disuse, as has the fair which for a long time was held on 25th September. A portion of the old market cross is still standing, and is now surmounted by a memorial to the Watson family.

The village was modernised by Richard Watson in the 19th century, when several new houses were built and the older cottages enlarged. Further improvements were carried out in the 1950s.

The village has one old established store, which until recent years was also the Post Office. As a Post Office it transacted every kind of business and at one time housed a manual telephone exchange – a far cry from the present automatic STD exchange.

The old School, situated next to the village store, was erected by the Hon Richard Watson in 1844, who pioneered rural education in the neighbourhood. The school opened with 90 pupils from neighbouring villages. As the years passed the roll began to dwindle, until by 1946 it was left with only 9 children.

The authorities regretfully decided to close it and the building is now used as a Village Hall.

The church is dedicated to St Leonard – the patron saint of prisoners. The church is a low irregular structure consisting of a nave and chancel, with a memorial chapel to the Watson family. The tower and most of the body of the church were destroyed by the Cromwellian forces during the Civil War, but a small Chapel was built about 1650.

The Church remained in this state until 1843, when it was extensively restored by Richard Watson.

Twenty years later the Watson family, the rector and parishioners placed a new roof upon the nave and enlarged the church by the addition of the north aisle. In 1868, the church was beautified by raising the roof of the chancel, and adding two arches.

In recent years thousands of pounds have been spent on major repairs and restoration.

Rothersthorpe ✍

Rothersthorpe is an old, old village full of secrets. Situated on the prehistoric Jurassic Way, it has at its heart an ancient earthworks – The Berry.

Here the future Northamptonshire may have been born when in AD 918 the Saxon army of Edward the Elder, marching on Northampton from its base at Towcester, defeated the Danish forces to the south-west of the town, and annexed the area covered by the present day county. The post-enclosure (1810) farm of Danesfield could represent the approximate site of this encounter.

The village church of St Peter and St Paul again has very ancient origins. Little is known beyond the present building, which owes much to the monks of St James Abbey, Northampton. Older edifices must have stood on the site of the church, to which the base of a 7th century preaching cross and a Norman font bear eloquent witness.

But it must not be thought that Rothersthorpe lies mouldering in the past. A new school and village hall have been built to the highest standards.

1959 saw the coming to the parish of the M1 motorway, and the subsequent service area has given the name of the village a degree of national fame for the first time in its long history. This increase in the ease of communication has also brought in its wake the possibilities of development. The Parish Council has been extremely active and successful in obtaining a conservation area and in championing village views.

As with many small villages the last shop was forced to close in 1968 and the Baptist chapel a few years later. The Chequers, the name perhaps dating from the time when the monks from St James Abbey collected their rents with the aid of a chequered counting board, still continues to refresh both the local population and the casual traveller. The houses of the village dating from before 1860 are of Northamptonshire stone. The late 17th century manor house has within its grounds a very large dovecot.

Rushton

The ancient, scattered but neat, village of Rushton, was mentioned in the Domesday Book as Riston or Risetone.

Many 17th century buildings remain, although now changed to residential occupation. They are built mainly of the buff coloured oolite ironstone found locally and in more recent years quarried for the steelworks at nearby Corby. A good example of this pleasant mellowed stonework can be seen in the buildings constituting the High Street post office and general stores, with its stable, bakehouse and upper level granary still there, but adapted for present day use.

In High Street is the village pub, The Thornhill Arms, named after an early lord of the manor, and there is an excellent view of the parish church of All Saints, with the cricket field and pavilion just below.

Just beyond the junction of High Street and Manor Road stands the old forge which was used until just after the Second World War. The older part is now a workshop and garage for a modern residence, built on the site of the blacksmith's yard.

Rushton Hall has historical connections with the Tresham family — Thomas Tresham the builder, being the grandson of Sir Thomas Tresham, the last Lord Prior (in England) of the Knights Hospitallers of St John of Jerusalem. Francis Tresham was involved in the conspiracy leading to the

The Thornhill Arms at Rushton

ill-fated Gunpowder Plot, and relied on his uncle, Thomas the builder, for funds.

Another of Tresham's buildings well chronicled, is the Triangular Lodge, built on the north-west perimeter of the Hall grounds. It is easily reached by following the road to Desborough. During springtime, the Hall grounds are carpeted with snowdrops and in days past these were sent to London from Rushton station.

Before the present school was built, the north chapel (chantry) of All Saints was used for many years as the village school, with the schoolmaster remunerated in earlier times by the patronage of the lord of the manor residing at Rushton Hall.

The present village hall, which adjoins the village school playground, was the former Methodist church, money for which was raised by the efforts of villagers. It is now used for a variety of functions and was modernised and extended in 1983.

The annual village church fete is held in the High Street in June and is well supported by everyone.

Scaldwell

The village lies just off the A508 Northampton to Market Harborough road, behind Brixworth. Its green is surrounded by many trees and the 12th century church stands on a hillside behind it, with its beautiful, pinnacled sanctus bell tower.

In the churchyard are the remains of a preaching cross and legend has it that somewhere in the village is hidden the stained glass from the church windows, taken to save it from the Roundheads – but, unfortunately, never found.

There was once a healing well in the village and at least 20 other wells scattered around, because the name Scaldwell actually means 'shallow welling out of water'. The pond on the green was the original source of water for the village pump. This in turn fed a series of horse troughs, all of which have been buried – leaving only the blue brick pump housing exposed. The Town 'Well' House is the oldest in the village and at the time of the Dissolution of the Monasteries under Henry VIII, several people were arrested here for trying to conceal church plate and relics. The 'Town Well' charity remains to this day.

The artist George Clark – famous in print circles for his pictures of important houses – lived in the village and the author H. E. Bates stayed here on several occasions. He reputedly used Scaldwell as the setting for his novel *Love for Lydia*.

Like most small villages it supported its own mill – operational until 1916 – but unusually there was also a 'vellum factory' run by two eccentric brothers.

Up until the 1950s ironstone quarries were worked around Scaldwell and visitors would enter the village under the railway, reminiscent of a cable-car, carrying hanging buckets overhead. Now all that remains are the parapets of the bridges at the road sides. The railway has long gone, the tunnels filled and the ground levelled, so that anyone looking over the bridge would only see flat fields.

It is said that there was a 'Grey Lady', who walked the village heavily veiled. This was reputedly the ghost of Madeleine Bell, a Scottish murderess whose case was found 'Not Proven' under Scottish law for the murder of her fiance. There are several other reported ghosts in Scaldwell – but all friendly. They include a whistling groom and mysterious flames seen flickering inside a house.

Shutlanger

Shutlanger is a small village lying three miles east of Towcester, between the main A43 and A508 roads.

Life here now is very different to village life some 50 years ago. There seemed to be more village characters then – such as Bill the chimney sweep, who wore trousers made from blankets and was so fat that it must have been many years since he had seen his feet. With his brushes and rods strapped on his bike, he would set off ponderously, stopping to chat with everyone he met. After all, he was only an hour late!

Mr Hales was the baker, a man with a bushy white beard. On a Sunday children would walk to his shop with their mother's batter in a jug, ready to pour it round the joint which he was cooking for them.

Then there was the man who was 'carrying on' and villagers thought he should be taught a lesson. They decided to give him a 'luebelling' session. At a prearranged night they gathered at his house, carrying various utensils and sticks. A signal was given and it seemed as if every demon had risen from the land. There was a deafening row as they banged and crashed everything they had. When they thought he had 'got the message' they went quietly away. The man moved away from the village very soon after.

It is a sad thought that our children may not have the same memories of a village which lived and worked together.

Sibbertoft

Outwardly Sibbertoft has changed little over the years. It sits on top of the hills near the boundary of Leicestershire and Northamptonshire. Being over 600 ft above sea level, in winter snow often covers the village when the valleys below are quite clear. The surrounding rolling country-side is typical of the hunting Shires and the famous Pytchley Hunt meets in the village each year.

The river Welland rises in the village, in the cellar of the old rectory. It emerges north of the village and over the centuries has formed the lovely Welland valley. It finally reaches the North Sea at the Wash.

The church, dedicated to St Helen, records rectors back to 1220, but is certainly much older. Clerics have included the Rev Miles Berkeley, a 19th century botanist. He published several reference books and 'made notable discoveries regarding Vine Disease Fungi'. There was also James Sturgis, the Hunting Curate who conducted services wearing riding clothes and boots under his robes. His family were the last to live in the Mansion House, which was at the bottom of Westhorpe lane, then called Cattle End. The house had been knocked down by 1877, though why is not known.

The Civil War disturbed the peace of the area, especially in 1645 when the battle of Naseby was fought nearby. Most of the fighting took place a few miles to the south, though King Charles' standard was raised at Moot Hill to the east of Sibbertoft. Coombe Hill saw both the King's army marching up to the battle and bands of wounded survivors escaping northwards after the battle was lost.

By the 1890s, much of the land belonged to the Villiers family. The autocratic Lady Elizabeth Villiers lived at Sulby Hall and ruled the villagers with a rod of iron. Riding to church each Sunday, if she saw washing hanging outside the home of any employee, the offending family was dismissed. In 1897, her will stipulated that her funeral carriage be pulled by matching black horses, to be shot after the funeral.

Her niece, Miss Elizabeth Mansell, inherited the land and Sulby Hall – sadly, knocked down in the 1950s for the lead on its roof. In 1911, she built the reading room in memory of her two brothers, both killed in the army. This memorial became an important amenity which has given much pleasure to the village ever since.

During the Second World War, an airfield was built just outside the village on the Welford Road. Part of this was bought in the 1960s by the Coventry Gliding Club, so a major war left us with a leisure amenity. However, the airfield now raises the greatest threat to Sibbertoft, with the threat of extensive development.

Silverstone 🦢

The origins of Silverstone go a long way back into history: at one time it lay deep in the heart of the ancient Whittlewood Forest and its inhabitants made their living from charcoal-burning and other woodland crafts. The forest was rich in game and in the 12th century a royal hunting lodge was in use in the centre of the village by King John. Although the lodge is long gone, it was close to a series of fish-breeding ponds, the earthworks of which can still be seen to the west of a part of the village known as Little London. This is believed to be so called because refugees fleeing London at the time of the Black Death settled here.

But, as in most other parts of the county, the Black Death took its toll in and around Silverstone. A hamlet, Charlock, was decimated and abandoned: the remains of its field system, hollow-ways, ponds and house-platforms are still clearly visible as earthworks on a hill to the west of the present village. Another victim of the plague was Luffield Abbey, once a thriving monastic community, where everyone perished. The abbey fell into ruins and the last traces were finally obliterated in the Second World War when an aerodrome was built over the site. This aerodrome was converted into the world-famous Silverstone Racing Circuit and the monastery is remembered in the naming of Abbey Curve on the race-track.

For most of the time the village is a peaceful, rural place. It is well-provided with a range of services: four shops, one with a post office, a modern surgery and dispensary, church and chapel, and two pubs (there used to be at least seven!). Village children are lucky to be able to spend both their infant and junior school years in the two village schools.

The village still retains vestiges of its ancient links with the forest: in the centre there is a massive timber yard that specialises in English oak and supplies oak for many purposes including boat-building. Until recently there were also many small timber businesses, hurdle-makers and so forth, although retirements have seen many of these close in recent years. There are still remnants of Whittlewood Forest close to the village: Hazelborough Forest and Bucknell Wood, run by the Forestry Commission, are much used by local people.

A well-remembered unusual period in Silverstone's history was in the late 1940s when Cody's Circus had its winter quarters on a farm in the village, with elephants, lions, monkeys and ponies. A real character was Jocko, the chimp, who lived in the farmhouse with the circus' owners and used to receive and entertain their guests. If his owners were going out, they would equip him with a block of wood, a hammer and some nails and he would keep himself busy knocking in nails all the time that they were away!

Although it has no pretensions to being a 'picture-postcard' village,

Silverstone does have many old, attractive and interesting buildings, some of them listed, and of course there are many tales of the ghosts which haunt them. For example, there is a mysterious phantom woman's face which appears in a local farmhouse's upper window, and even an old chap in a cloth cap and carpet slippers who announces his presence with the smell of stale tobacco smoke! Luffield Abbey is supposed to have been haunted by a deer with a strangely human face and there are stories of headless horsemen being seen at night on the Old Riding in West End and other parts of the village. Finally, the ghost of a mistress of King John is believed to appear in the Compasses, a previous village pub now a private house, where she is reputed to have been foully murdered one night. But not many local people will own up to having seen any of these apparitions!

Southwick 🌿

Southwick is three miles north of Oundle, and lies in a valley. On the slope to the north is a spur of Rockingham Forest, and to the south is Short Wood, a Northants Wildlife Trust property renowned for its bluebells. The size of this small village nearly doubled in the 1950s, when 16 council/forestry houses were built.

When Southwick is approached via the Woodnewton road, the first thing to catch one's eye is the Hall, an interesting, rambling, hotch-potch of architectural styles dating from the 14th century. The house has only been owned by three different families and even they were connected. The Knyvetts from the 12th century to 1441, the Lynnes to the early 1800s, and the Caprons to the present day. There are many legends associated with the house, mainly from the Lynne occupation. Mary Queen of Scots' burial certificate is said to be walled up in the house.

The parish church, dedicated to St Mary the Virgin, is adjacent to the Hall. Originally built by the Knyvett family in about 1230 with the tower and spire added by Sir John Knyvett in about 1350, the church was extensively rebuilt by the Lynnes in the 18th century.

The local pub is the thatched Shuckburgh Arms, believed to be of 16th century origin. It was bought into the estate by Mr George Capron in about 1839 and was named after his cousin, the Rev J. Shuckburgh.

A village show has been running since the 1960s in conjunction with Glapthorne, each village hosting the show in alternate years. There has been a set of handbells in the village for about 200 years and on Christmas Eve, except during the war years, it has been customary for the bells to accompany carol singing around the village.

Spratton 🦢

Spratton is an ancient Saxon settlement. It is situated between the villages of Chapel Brampton and Creaton, and is seven miles from Northampton and 13 miles from Market Harborough.

There are three approaches to the village from the main road, known as Holdenby Road, Brixworth Road and Smith Street. These three roads join like the prongs of a fork and eventually lead into the village of Brixworth.

The village has from early times been essentially a farming community. There are four shops in Spratton, and two schools.

The lovely old church built of local stone, with a seating capacity of 400–500 stands on high ground, surrounded by a stone wall. Since Saxon-Norman times it has kept watch over the community, its tower, then spire rising aloft. For many years its bells have echoed across the valley.

The church was originally known as St Andrew's, then as St Luke's before reverting back to the name it is known as today, St Andrew's church. Mention must be made of what is a fine example of woodcraft, namely the carvings on the end of the choir-stalls. On them are represented a simple countryman playing his pipe, a choirboy, a venerable old bishop complete with beard, and an angel, whose wings are exquisitely carved. These are indeed the work of a master craftsman.

Stanion 🦢

Stanion is situated about three miles from Corby and six miles from Kettering, with a population of about 1,000. It is a village with many old and picturesque cottages and houses.

There is a 13th century church with a very tall steeple which can be seen from a great distance. In the church there is kept a bone about five feet long, which is supposed to be a rib from a cow that provided all the milk for the village. The cow, it is said, was killed by a witch and was buried in a field known as 'Cowthick'. All this happened many years ago of course!

A church service is held every Sunday and the Sunday school is well patronised. A Methodist church was built early this century and both services and a Sunday school are held there, along with a Women's Fellowship for ladies of all denominations.

A new school was built in 1967 and there are about 70 children in attendance from Stanion and the surrounding villages. There are two shops, including the post office, and two public houses – The Lord Nelson and the Cardigan Arms.

The village has a Parochial Church Council as well as a Parish Council and there are many thriving activities to suit all ages. Most of the surrounding land is arable and there are three farms in close proximity to the village.

Stoke Albany 🐿️

Stoke Albany has some of the best features of a Northamptonshire village. Around the tranquil beauty of the village green is set the old hall house, a medieval church, chestnut trees in the churchyard, the war memorial in front of them and meadows and cornfields on the hills beyond. The scene has hardly altered during the last 100 years, except the prunus trees on the green which were planted to commemorate the Queen's Coronation.

The village was mentioned in the Domesday Book, and in the 13th century William de Albini, lord of the manor, from whom the village takes its name, laid out a new settlement consisting of four parallel streets together with a new manor house.

All tradesmen once lived and worked in the surrounding area. In 1885 there was a stonemason, butcher, wheelwright, shoemaker, baker, blacksmith, carpenter, several farmers, and three public houses. Now unfortunately there is only one public house! Interestingly in 1777 the trades were even more varied with a skinner, cordwainer, miller, weaver, chandler, wool comber, wool stapler and shepherd. On the good side though the village now has a post office with a special postmistress, Mrs Margaret Bellamy, who was awarded the British Empire Medal for long service to the Post Office, in 1986.

Stoke Albany still has a village feast, which has been held since 1279 following St Botolph's Day, the 17th June. The feast is held on the green opposite the manor house with lots of stalls and games.

Stoke Albany has many old original buildings, some lying in the four parallel streets off Ashley Road. The oldest building in Stoke Albany is an old hall house, some of which dates from the 12th century, next to the church. The manor house situated in Ashley Road is a lovely stone house with stone mullioned windows and leaded lights. Thanks to conservation little of the outside has changed.

The old school, now the village hall, is on the green by the church, and was founded and built in 1871, on farmland once belonging to the old hall house. The infant and junior children attended here until 1966 when the school was closed.

The church is dedicated to St Botolph, a monk and patron saint of travellers. As a reminder of the days when tarmac paths and roads were not in evidence, over the porch is a wooden tablet requesting that men shall scrape their shoes and women take off their pattens before entering.

Stoke Bruerne 🐚

In 1902 a young pupil at the village school wrote a description of her home – 'It is a very pretty village situated in South Northamptonshire with a population of 400. The Grand Junction Canal runs straight through the village, it is specially interesting because of its locks and the tunnel, the boats have to be taken through the tunnel by means of a steam tug which goes from 5 am in the morning till 9 pm at night every two hours. The Towcester and Olney Railway runs through the parish and has a station about half a mile from the village. The line is now only open for luggage as passengers did not pay.

'The chief occupations of the people are agricultural labourers and working in the Brick-field and on the Grand Junction Canal. We have a full post and telegraph office in the village, we have one delivery of letters and two going out posts. There is one public house, The Boat Inn. There is one blacksmith's shop and two shoemaker's shops and five grocer's shops. We have two woods in the parish, The Plain Wood and Stoke Park woods. The only drawback in Stoke Bruerne is that we are so very short of clear pure water in summer.'

Today, the population of the village is 358. Although the farms are much the same, fewer people are employed on them. British Waterways employs a number of people, some on maintenance of the canal, some in their Waterways Museum and several in their souvenir shop. The biggest single employer is The Boat Inn, a free house, now extended beyond its bars to a tea room and a separate restaurant.

The village is extremely fortunate still to have the small school with its roll of 40 pupils. There are two teachers and help is given by the Rural Schools' Project. Sadly, the chapel has been closed and is now a Rural Life Museum.

Much of the property once owned by the Duke of Grafton has been sold. Mains water and main drainage came to the village in the 1950s. The brickyard no longer produces bricks and the railway line has been scrapped and the land sold to the farmers whose land it ran through.

The village, situated between the greatly expanded Northampton and Milton Keynes and only four miles from the M1 is now within very easy reach of London.

Stowe IX Churches 🐚

The hamlets of Church Stowe and Upper Stowe, together with half a dozen houses in between, combine to make the parish of Stowe IX Churches.

Not only is this community a happy one, it is a fortunate one, for the Stowes are set high, thus commanding views of a hilly landscape which

152

seems to move as the light varies. No towering mountains here, no rocky outcrops, nothing dramatic, just a deeply satisfying and gentle beauty.

Upper Stowe once boasted a pub – The Bird in Hand, but this has been a private house since the 1950s. Closed too, is the village school which flourished from 1841 until 1953; this is now St Michael's church rooms and used as a village hall. The small but beautiful church of St Michael stands on the brow of a steep hill. The Arnold Charity was set up in 1689 to help in the training of apprentices but is now used for a broader area of educational activity and youth work.

There is no bus service to the village, nor is there a shop, but Stowe does have a small post office, which was opened in 1945. In an attractive setting opposite the tiny Victorian church of St James in Upper Stowe an antique and craft centre with restaurant was opened in 1986, where visitors can watch local craftsmen at work in converted stables.

There are several theories as to how the name of Stowe IX Churches was derived. In medieval times the village was simply known as Stowe, meaning holy place. It was also known as Stowe-Ni-Churches at one time, and was perhaps changed by a clerical error. Some say that as Stowe is over 500 ft above sea level, nine churches could be seen. The ancient manor house stands next to the church, and it is possible that at one time the lord of the manor was the patron of nine parishes. An old legend tells of how the builders of the church unwittingly chose a site near to a fairy ring in the centre of England. Each time they started building, the fairies and goblins came at night and knocked down the stones. After the eighth attempt, a praying monk remained at the site throughout the night. This seemed to have been effective as at the ninth attempt the building was left standing and the workmen were able to complete their task.

Sudborough

Sudborough, nestling in a wooded hollow off the busy A6116 between Thrapston and Corby, still retains the olde worlde charm of earlier times.

The village is in the heart of the old Rockingham Forest, and there are still enough woods and new forests around to give it a secluded, private appearance. That is helped by the three roads into the village: the main entrance, off the A6116, features a severe bend forcing traffic to slow; the Newton Lane turning, further up the A6116 towards Corby, is a narrow, high-hedged road that looks particularly uninviting for traffic. And the other way in, the best, with a lovely aspect of the village from an overlooking hillside, is from Slipton, itself another sleepy village.

Most of the 150 residents will tell you that Sudborough is the prettiest and nicest village in the county; regulars at The Vane Arms will swear it is the friendliest pub selling the best beer in Northamptonshire! Whatever the pub regulars say, and however much some may mourn the passing of the old village brewery, All Saints' church is the chief glory of the village. Its setting, near Harper's Brook, and its dignified, mellow stonework, add an aura of agelessness to the village.

A booklet available in the church chronicles its varied and chequered history, and much of the village itself. It includes details of the crusading de Veres, the occasion when the parish was closed illegally, the time when Highland troops were defeated and one was buried in a place later known as The Soldier's Grave, and the much-recounted tale of one parishioner, Samuel Mayes, who met a tragic end in a poaching affray. A song, handed down over the years and still sung at village events, begins:

> 'Poor Samuel Mayes of Sudborough Town,
> A lad of well-known fame,
> Who took delight both day and night,
> To hunt the lofty game.'

Sulgrave 🦡

Sulgrave is a compact and attractive village located in a sparsely populated area of undulating and pleasant countryside and lies five miles north of Brackley, ten miles west of Towcester, and seven miles east of Banbury. The village marks a settlement of the early Britons, as discovered during archaeological excavations between 1960–80, on the site of the Saxon castle.

There are a number of important listed buildings in the village, in particular the 16th century Sulgrave Manor, ancestral home of the Washington family. Other important larger buildings include the Rectory Farm complex, the 18th century vicarage, the Thatched House Hotel and the Old Farmhouse, all of which form well-defined features in the village environment.

The church of St James the Less was built in the 14th century although the base of the tower is Saxon. A tomb in the south aisle is the resting place of Lawrence Washington and his family, ancestors of George Washington, the first President of the United States of America. The four panels of Elizabethan glass above the Washington pew show the mullets and bars which may have inspired the stars and stripes.

Many visitors still come to Sulgrave throughout the year including a large number of Americans who come to view the ancestral home of their first president. Although much of the village has undoubtedly changed over the last 100 years the intrinsic charm still remains. The population is estimated to be just under 400, many of them families who have lived in Sulgrave for hundreds of years.

The village school plays a very important part in the day to day life of Sulgrave and the Historical Society has started to involve more and more villagers in the setting up of a permanent exhibition showing aspects of village life over the centuries. The Old Brew House at the manor is being refurbished so that visitors to George Washington's ancestral home have the opportunity to see how Sulgrave has developed over the years to become the delightful place it is today.

Sutton Bassett

Sutton Bassett lies on one side of a ridge of land jutting into the valley of the River Welland. Off the road at the top of the hill leading out of this hamlet of 39 houses, there is a bridle path from which you have a magnificent view containing no less than 10 churches. On this path there is also a small cottage, now derelict, a water pumping station, and a post of the Royal Observer Corps (a reminder of grimmer days). On this site there used to be a windmill which was dismantled within living memory.

Reference in Domesday Book shows the land to have been owned by many people including The Countess Judith (niece of William the Conqueror), Robert de Buci, Richard Basset, Chief Justice of England, and the Bosworth family.

Originally Sutton Bassett was a hamlet in the parish of Weston, and its church – All Saints, a chapel of ease – was an extra church but without a graveyard. It is basically a Norman building of simple grace with a Norman window in the north wall of the chancel, a Norman doorway in the nave and two 13th century windows on the south side, and a 13th century bell-cote. On each half-pillar at the entrance to the chancel there is a carving of a face and opposite an animal of the 12th century.

Additionally Sutton Bassett had a Methodist Chapel erected from a cottage at the end of the 19th century as a memorial to the Sedgeley family. It is next to the Queen's Head public house, and although it is now once again a private house it can be recognised by its attractive fan windows.

The hamlet consists of a number of old grey stone houses with mullioned windows, of which the manor dates back to the 17th century. There are three farmhouses, stone and brick, and a variety of new houses.

The Queen's Head public house dates far back – it is known that in 1884 James Barron, platelayer, bought it for £260. It is basically a stone building with red brick additions, the bricks probably having come from brickworks, traces of which have been found in the field behind.

In the past every one found work in the village, on the farms, etc. the women doing a great deal of lace work in their homes. Nowadays, apart from the working farms, most people commute to Leicester, Market Harborough and even London. However, the population is very much alive, with many village interests.

Syresham 🐑

'Take your seats for Syresham for Syresham's the place,
Where they never never worry nor fall into disgrace,
Where all the boys are brothers and all the girls are sweet,
If you tumble down in Syresham, they'll set you on your feet.'

This chorus of an old Syresham song typifies the sturdy, independent, warm hearted spirit of a people once dependent on the forests of South Northamptonshire for their livelihood. Agriculture no longer employs many people. Most are self-employed or travel to nearby towns.

At one time there were as many as 17 shops in the village, but now only one general store/post office and a butcher remain. Long gone is the large country store of King's, which boasted a fleet of lorries, vans and motorcycles, serving all the surrounding villages. King's ales and stout were well known and much sought after, and half the village was employed on these premises. The highlight of the year was the annual outing to the sea when four coaches would set out at the crack of dawn.

The Jubilee Tree marks the entrance to the village from the A43. This was planted to celebrate Queen Victoria's Jubilee in 1897.

A plaque in the Wesleyan chapel commemorates the death of a Syresham shoemaker, John Kurde, in 1557. He was burned at the stake for his religious beliefs.

The village has always been a model of the most desirable kind of community, a tranquil, timeless, ideal where lives are played out in harmony with the soil and seasons, and with a contented social order. More recently the old, the sick, and the poor, have either been exiled by soaring house prices, or moved to council estates where they become isolated. One of the cornerstones of village life, that sense of families inhabiting the parish and sometimes the same house for generations, has already gone. Those who remain, together with the new villagers are forming a new community, and new organisations and new ideas are bringing the village together again. Old established organisations, the Women's Institute, Church, Chapel, Cricket and Football Clubs are working side by side with the Friendship Club, the Friends of the School, the Sports Club, the Bowls, and Evening Classes, and are testimony to the energy and enthusiasm of the community.

The old traditions remain – Mayday, maypole dancing, bonfires, carol singing and Feast Days, and now new ones are added – quizzes, knockouts, boot sales and so on. But the rural aspect remains. Syresham is justly proud of its school of 70 primary pupils, and the lively activities which are centred around it give a heart to the village.

Sywell 🌿

The centre of Sywell still retains its old world charm, with its small green surrounded by cottages, which outwardly have not changed since they were built in the mid 19th century by the Loyd family as a model village. Also on the green are the church and old school, recently converted to a village hall.

Just off the green is Sywell Hall, a fine Elizabethan house. For a time the Tresham family, of Guy Fawkes fame, lived here. It is believed that Mary Queen of Scots stayed here, and while here lost a ring. When the house was being renovated at the beginning of the 20th century a ring was found, believed to have been that lost all those years ago.

Another family to live at the Hall were the Pells, who started a charity in the village. Watkin Owen Pell joined the navy at 11 years old and lost a leg in battle when he was 12 years old. Despite this he had a distinguished naval career, rising to the rank of admiral.

Sywell has rather an unusual ghost. The story is concerned with a great Turf scandal. In 1884 *Running Rum* won the Derby, but was challenged as being a four year old and not a three year old. During the ensuing law suit the horse could not be produced. 'You will never see the horse again', the judge was told, 'but you may have a quarter of him if you like'. *Running Rum* was brought to Sywell at dead of night, butchered and buried in the grounds of Sywell House. People have told of hearing a phantom horse come up the yard and buckets rattling.

Although horses are still stabled at Sywell it is more likely to be the planes and helicopters from Sywell Aerodrome which disturb the peace today.

Many Second World War pilots remember Sywell as where they learnt to fly, often on a five week intensive course. This was not only British pilots but also those of the Free French Air Force. During the war Sywell was the centre for the repair of Wellington bombers. Planes or their parts were brought in on 'Queen Mary' lorries, to be put together and flown out to take part in the war again. Today much of the wartime building is an industrial and warehouse estate. The clubhouse forms the nucleus of Sywell Motel.

Besides having an industrial estate Sywell is known for its recreational facilities. Sywell Country Park, which includes the old Sywell reservoir, is a good example of nature conservation and provides opportunities for birdwatching and country walks.

Tansor 🌿

Tansor is an ancient village and there has been a settlement here since pre-Roman times. The Domesday Book recorded the village as Tanesovre.

The church of St Mary dates in part from Saxon times and rectors are recorded by name since the 13th century. Of particular interest are the carved misericords, which include carvings of the falcon and fetterlock, an emblem of the House of York.

On 17th September 1819 a farmer called John Cave conveyed a portion of land to trustees, the rents to be used to relieve poverty in Tansor. It was to be used for 'clothing, meat, blankets, coal or other necessaries at the discretion of the rector and churchwardens on Christmas Day forever.' The land is still let for agricultural use, though the income is now used for wider charitable purposes.

The 19th century saw the advent of the railway, with a line running through Tansor from Peterborough to Northampton. The source of employment remained, however, the land, with the church as a focal point of village life. It was the coming of the motor car in the 20th century which started the decline of the village sense of community, here as elsewhere. People ceased to walk to neighbouring villages and public footpaths and bridleways fell into disuse and are now impassable. Agriculture became mechanised and only a small number of people living in the village are involved now. The population of the village has fallen to under 200.

There are people still living in Tansor who have known two public houses in the village, the White Horse and the Black Horse. Both, now, are private residences. There were two bakehouses, one at the rear of The Old Post Office, where bake ovens can still be seen. In the 19th century this baker kept the White Horse. Milling was carried out at the windmill, still standing but without sails or any other working parts. Another bakehouse stood against Elm House, also in Main Street. A blacksmith's forge was situated at the thatched cottage next to Greystones.

Latterly there has been much alteration and upgrading of older properties but since Tansor has no mains sewerage and no street lighting, there is unlikely to be much development in the near future.

Thornby 🌿

Thornby is amongst the highest villages in Northamptonshire. Its streams feed into the west-flowing Avon and the east-flowing Nene. To the south there are magnificent views over Northampton and beyond. The village lies astride the A50, and lanes to the surrounding villages are hedged with trees, lining fields showing age-old strip cultivation. The church dates from 1275.

There is a history of territorial dispute between the local landed families; and the rents from Thornby Poors Lands, once a disputed tract to the north of the village, provide funds for the relief of 'the Poor of Thornby'. Thornby Hall is a magnificent Jacobean residence, to the east of the village, and is among the many places that Cromwell is said to have slept the night before the battle of Naseby in 1645. To the west, lies the Victorian Thornby Grange, visited during the late 1920s and early 1930s by the then Duke and Duchess of York, later King George VI and Queen Elizabeth, our present Queen Mother.

From the beginning of this century, little change occurred. In country renowned for its horses and hunting, Thornby had as many as 30 grooms. There were shops and two inns and a blacksmith's forge. The village had its own cricket and football teams. However, despite the arrival of an electricity supply in the 1950s, the village declined. The population reduced and the village school was closed, the few children travelling daily to schools in Guilsborough and Northampton. By 1970 only one inn remained, the population was well below 100 and there were numerous houses empty. The rector's duties were now undertaken by a priest-in-charge, who looked after three other parishes as well.

The first new houses to be built in the 20th century appeared in 1973. Others followed, unoccupied houses, barns and stables were adapted and converted. Thornby Hall was converted to a special school, further expanding the population. In 1985 a project was started for the conversion of the original village school building into a village hall.

Thorpe Mandeville 🐿

The earliest mention of the parish is to be found in the Domesday Book, where it is styled Torp. The manor was held by the Pinkneys and was passed to the family of Amundville in about 1243, from whom the name Thorpe Mandeville comes.

The Humphrey family, whose ancestors are buried in the church as far back as 1665, still take an active part in the community. From the churchyard can be seen the Ox-yard, which in the 13th century was the site of Thorpe Feast, usually taking place on the Sunday following the 6th July. A lofty avenue of elm trees at the western end of this wonderful field marked the area occupied by the original manor house.

The Ox-yard pond was a glorious meeting place for the children – for newt-catching in the summer, for finding pale autumn crocuses on the bank, for skating in the winter. There was a cricket pitch and green pavilion there, where teams from neighbouring villages came to play. Village children would swarm up the stone wall to play on the smooth grass at play time.

The old manor house was garrisoned by Oliver Cromwell in the Civil War and the mounds thrown up at this time were still visible in 1897 (as recorded by the Rev Algernon Guise Humphrey in the parish magazine). The 'new' manor house was built east of the church by Cromwell's niece.

The most ancient 'big house' in the village was the rectory – now the Court, which is about 400 years old and is a fine house with pastures for grazing. 'The Doctors Close' is so called because the Rev Nathaniel

Humphrey's living was held by a Doctor Deacle who farmed this plot, and also kept his calves in the little field in the corner by Bulls Lane. It was called Calves Close.

The Three Conies has a sun dial on its wall with the dates 1622 and 1847 inscribed. The inn has certainly refreshed villagers for many a year and has also been a meeting place for the Bicester Hounds. There have been colourful gatherings both here and at the manor house. Before 1850 the magistrates held their meetings at the Three Conies.

Behind the pub was a garden called the saw-yard and a large stone house belonging to the Humphrey family with a large dovecote. This no longer remains, but a row of cottages called Dove Cottages and Dove Close are reminders of what once was. Ivy Cottage, another lovely old building, was the home of the shoemaker. A subsequent owner had one of the church bells re-cast to celebrate the occasion of his daughters' marriage.

On the village green there once stood stocks, and the duck pond remained until 1988. The ducks, loath to leave the village, still wander the lanes and have to make do with puddles in Townsend Lane! 'Thorpe Feast' still takes place, in the form of a village street fair.

Tiffield

Tiffield is a village lying north of Towcester, two-thirds of a mile from the A43. At present it has 120 houses and there are just under 400 inhabitants in the parish.

Three silent witnesses of village life are the church of St John the Baptist, the village Church of England school and the Church Room. The church, extended in 1856 especially to accommodate the staff and boys of the new reform school near the village, seats a congregation and choir of 80 to 100 people and is just big enough nowadays for the Christmas carol service. The school, built in 1872 when large families and tight rows of desks were common, now has room for fewer pupils with modern tables and chairs.

At the turn of the century most of the population had work in the parish – on farms, at the wheelwright-cum-joiner-builder's, at the blacksmith's, the brickyard, in domestic service, 'up' at the reform/ approved school, or on the railway. The community supported a general store, a post office, a butcher's and a public house. Within 50 years increasing mechanisation of farming and the motor car together reduced greatly the work available. Only the farms and the wheelwright's survived as major employers; the former with fewer workers, the latter, the family firm of Eyden founded in the 17th century, turned to the other side of the business, sending young Frank Eyden to learn the building trade. He did well at his studies, and returned home with an enthusiasm for cricket – and a motorbike and side-car with which he provided for a time the only means of emergency transport in the village for getting someone quickly to hospital.

About 50 new houses were built and occupied in the years 1968 to 1973. The arrival in 1969 of many new young households coincided with the proposal to close the village school (which had been such a selling point for the houses). Battle was engaged. Villagers, Parish Council, Parochial Church Council and the Diocese saved the school which in 1973 needed an extra (mobile) classroom.

Private transport is essential for most villagers to get to their place of work. There are many professional and business people, of whom only a few operate in the village. One farm has begun a new enterprise, the production of sheep's milk and yoghurt.

With persistence and goodwill over the last twenty years, public-spirited villagers have provided many social events, clubs and organisations. Groups of villagers tidy the churchyard and other public areas, and walk the footpaths. By '83 we had planted many a tree, and went on to plant more. The Tiffield News, published every three months and delivered to every house since January 1982, gives information on village matters and group activities.

Fortunately the community can now absorb newcomers and survive the effects of shifts in age and interests on the membership of its organisations, which is just as well for people move in and out of Tiffield all the time. It is accepted that young households have to be mobile for reasons of employment and family needs. New children settle quickly into school where their teachers find time to make them aware of their village and its tradition.

Titchmarsh

The passer-by approaching Titchmarsh, especially from the Oundle-Thrapston road, is soon aware of the village's outstanding feature, the square and pinnacled 15th century tower of the church of St Mary the Virgin, crowning the ridge on which the village stands, between the A604 and the A605 (Huntingdon) road.

Apart from its spectacular tower, the church has many interesting features, including the ha-ha which marks the churchyard boundary on west and south sides. There is a fine ring of eight bells, used regularly by the local team and visiting ringers from far and wide.

The domestic architecture of Titchmarsh ranges from 17th and 18th century cottages, some thatched, through to 20th century barn conversions on two sites in the village.

It is a village with historic connections; John Dryden, the 17th century Poet Laureate, spent his boyhood here, and in 1668 Samuel Pepys came to Titchmarsh to the marriage of his friend John Creed to 'Betty' Pickering, only daughter of Sir Gilbert and Lady Elizabeth Pickering. In the church there are fine memorials to members of the Pickering and Creed families, two painted by Elizabeth Creed, (née Pickering) at an advanced age.

As an agricultural village, Titchmarsh had its heyday in the mid 19th century, when the whole population was engaged either in food production or in the 'service industries' of a self-sufficient community. Now although farming is still very important, many householders are employed outside the village. It remains nevertheless an integrated whole, with several active societies, a village store, two public houses, a thriving village hall, (the 'Club Room' dating from 1862), and the school, first opened in January 1843.

Twywell 🌿

This historical Northamptonshire village was mentioned in the Domesday Book, and was once an Iron Age settlement.

The village church, dedicated to St Nicholas, dates back to the 11th century, originally being built in the shape of a cross and on the site of an even older building. You will notice in the stonework large quantities of ironstone, ironstone quarrying being one of the main employments of villagers for many generations. Coal mines, furnaces and tramways were closed down many years ago, much of this land now being arable and pasture. Farming was the other major employment.

The three stones displayed in the splay of the window to the right of the altar were sent to the Rev H. Waller by General Gordon from Calvary in 1880. Dr David Livingstone was also a great friend of Rev Waller, and in the church are displayed pieces of the actual bark in which Dr Livingstone's body was carried by his two faithful native boys, Susi and Chuma. Susi and Chuma lived for a time in Twywell's rectory helping Rev Waller with the research of Dr Livingstone's work. They joined in village life, also attending this church.

Another interesting building is the round house which is the first house seen on entering the village from the main Kettering/Thrapston road. This was believed to be the old toll house when a toll or tax had to be paid before one had the privilege of travelling over the road. The house dates back to 1663.

The Manor House Farm dates from 1591 and some parts of an older house, which may have come from the old monastery which used to stand between Slipton and Sudborough at 'Money Holes', were used in the building of it.

Situated at the top of the village during the 18th century was the engineering firm of Blackwells, although nothing can be seen of this today. This firm was owned by two brothers who were farmer engineers. 'Blackwells Close' field is named after them. Some of the first winnowing machines were made here. Clocks were also made and one of these can be seen today in Islip church. One of the early grandfather clocks made here is still in use at Woodford.

Walgrave 🌿

The village is six miles from Kettering and nine miles from Northampton. There was a settlement here in Saxon times and it is recorded in the Domesday Book. There are now about 750 inhabitants, well served by a post office, butcher's shop and Co-op.

Like all villages, it has a variety of architectural styles with old cottages, Victorian terraces and new executive-style housing, and a fair few council houses. Hall Farm is the remains of a once much larger Elizabethan house, but retains the original carved oak staircase. The oldest house in the village is dated 1568.

To administer to spiritual needs, there is the parish church which is 650 years old, a Baptist church which is 200 years old, and a smaller Strict Baptist church also, but there is only one remaining public house out of five originals to administer to the flesh.

Parish church at Walgrave

Several notable incumbents of the parish church are recorded. John Williams, rector from 1614–1641, had the audacity to defy Archbishop Laud and is said to have retreated to Walgrave because it was as 'safe as a mousehole'. Dr Arthur Wingham is said to have married himself to his maid without the help of other clergy, and Dr Gifford was a relative of Thomas Hardy and married him to his first wife. A later rector, Thomas Badcock, had sewers installed in Walgrave long before Northampton had such luxuries.

It is said that many years ago one parishioner said to the rector, when asked to attend services 'Sir, I has to work sixty hours a week; I've got a wife and ten kids to look after and an acre of garden ground to tend. Sorry sir, I just ain't got the time to be religious.'

Walgrave is fortunate to have a primary school. The school – once an 'all-age' school – was built before the First World War. It now boasts its own swimming pool bought by the Parents' Association. The traditions of maypole and country dancing are still continued with a performance each year.

The leather industry has always been prominent. Oliver Cromwell is said to have had his footwear made in the village, and there are still houses with 'shops' attached, where families 'cobbled' until around 100 years ago when a large factory was built to make shoes. Unfortunately, this fell into decline a few years ago, but has been taken over by a firm making high-class quality leather goods and belts. The flag for the Queen's Award for Industry proudly flies from the mast.

Wappenham

The ancient village of Wappenham at the heart of England is small and friendly and boasts few claims to fame. Its present population is divided between older residents with ancestral ties to the village, and commuters working in London or the growing new city of Milton Keynes.

The villagers at one time supported five pubs. These are all long gone, as is the primary school. Most of the pubs have been converted into private homes. The school is used as a village hall and is becoming an increasingly important focal point of the village. The shop and post office continue to provide a much-appreciated service for the locals.

There has in recent years been some infill development, but nothing to change the character of the village. There is no street lighting in Wappenham, no gas and no railway (that, too, disappeared in the wake of progress).

Many of the houses in the village are large and attractively built of Helmdon stone or red brick, but none is so large as to suggest the presence of a resident squire at any time.

Back in the Middle Ages, Wappenham was a forest village subject to special laws and privileges and with direct connections to the king. It stood at the crossroads of England, with the Welsh Lane and Oxford Lane crossing at the top of the parish, Watling Street a few minutes ride away and important roads to Brackley, Buckingham and beyond, skirting its sides.

St Mary's church has an unusual one-handed clock, which is still in working order and is almost certainly Elizabethan. The three church bells were cast at Buckingham between 1590 and 1620.

The elegant red brick house alongside the church was the rectory, designed in 1832 by the renowned architect, Gilbert Scott. Scott also designed the village school, two houses and a granary and a cart hovel in the farmyard of Rectory Farm.

Life in Wappenham has gone on quietly for centuries, with just the odd moment of excitement! Despite his connections with the church, a certain Mr Theophilus Hart, who came into the village in 1642, was renowned for his extra-marital activities with the butcher's wife. The butcher was, to say the least, not amused. One day in 1686 – after a long chase over fields and hedges – the butcher caught and murdered Theophilus. At the time, the ardent lover was aged at least 65!

Warkton

Warkton is a small conservation village on the outskirts of Kettering. It has about 44 houses, 29 of which are owned by Boughton Estates Ltd. Only three new houses have been built since the 1920s. The old school has now become the village hall, but there are still three working farms, a village blacksmith and a post office. Villagers can get into nearby Kettering on the Friday bus.

The church of St Edmund is part Norman, with 15th century windows. The chancel was built in the 18th century by Ralph Montagu as a chapel for family tombs, two of which are by Roubiliac and one by Van Gelder.

The artist Sir Alfred East – who was very fond of painting the landscapes of his native Northamptonshire – once said that 'if Warkton were a hundred miles away they would go to see it'. It is part of the estate planned by Ralph Montagu, who developed it on the lines of Versailles, which he visited as English Ambassador. He was very impressed by the gardens, and his son, the 2nd Duke (known as Planter John), laid out 70 miles of elm-lined avenues linking half a dozen surrounding villages.

The 2nd Duke of Montagu was an extraordinary man, born in the year of the Armada, and many of his friends thought he had never grown up! He married Mary Churchill, daughter of the great Duke of Marlborough. He is remembered as a kind man and established one of the first homes for old and decrepit animals. The Montagu line died with Planter John and the estate passed to the Dukes of Buccleuch, who retain it to this day.

Warmington

Bounded on two sides by the main Peterborough/Kettering road, Warmington seems to be laid out like a spider's web. In the centre is the butcher's shop, the post office and general stores.

The first documentary evidence of the existence of the village came in a charter of AD 660. The village grew substantially during relatively prosperous times for agriculture, and the wealth generated led to the building of the present church being started in the 12th century. The church, dedicated to Mary the Virgin, is notable among county churches for its vaulted roof. Over the ensuing centuries there have been various additions to it.

The village continued to thrive until the great agricultural depression began around 1874 when there was much desertion of the land, several bankruptcies among farmers, and the village population began to decline. This decline was not really halted until the First World War when the government dictated what crops were to be grown.

Since the Second World War, in common with other villages, the scene has become less agricultural and Warmington is now more of a dormitory village for Peterborough. The mill is no longer a working one. There is no longer a shoemaker, blacksmith, wheelwright, baker, tailor or carrier. There is only one pub, The Red Lion, and one club, where there were once at least four pubs, so the interdependence of the people has vanished. Community spirit remains, however, kept alive by the various clubs and societies in the village.

Across the road is Eaglethorpe (once a village itself) and the river Nene. There is an old mill and many boats moor here from the Elton Boat Club. There are walks across the locks and for the energetic a footpath to Fotheringhay.

Watford

Watford is a small village lying to the west of Long Buckby, with which it shares part of the hamlet of Murcott. It was once much larger in extent as it is the site of two deserted villages. The small centre of the present village consists of various dwelling houses, a post office and a public house which at present is closed. This, the Henley Arms, is named after the manorial family whose large and lovely home, dating from the 16th century, has now been demolished and the land redeveloped.

All that remains of former agrarian glory is Watford Park, with its stately trees and roaming sheep and cattle – a very pleasant way to approach the village of Crick to the north.

The parish church of St Peter and St Paul is built chiefly in the Decorated style of the 14th century, as is the east window, though the tower dates from the 15th century. There is a Wesleyan chapel dated 1846 and two schools of the Victorian period – now the children travel by bus to schools in other villages.

Westwards is the Watford Gap through which passes the A5 or Watling Street, the M1 and the Grand Union Canal. This area contrasts markedly with the pretty, compact village centre as it contains the Watford Gap Service Station and a small industrial complex. Here there is a canalside pub and the site of the former Welton (or Crick) Station – the station houses still flanking the canal.

Weedon-Bec 🐦

Weedon-Bec, a village steeped in history, lies close to the Roman Watling Street, which crosses the river Nene in the region of the church of St Peter and St Paul. Weedon-Bec derives its name from its connections with the abbey of Bec Hellonin, dating from the 12th century, in France.

The village of today appears to be split into three sections. There is the old village with its thatched cottages, brick terraces and Northampton-shire stone walls; Upper Weedon, with views of the historic Royal Military Depot; and Road Weedon, which today supports several antique shops.

St Peter's church nestles between the Grand Union Canal and the railway line. To the south of this site, a chapel once stood dedicated to St Werburgh. This area of land was known as Ashyards and at different times over the ages, large stones have been retrieved from here, in all probability being ruins of St Werburgh's priory. St Werburgh is best remembered for the persuasive way in which she banished a flock of wild geese which were plaguing the cornfields of Weedon. The geese obeyed her and have never been seen over Weedon from that time!

One of Weedon's most familiar buildings must be the old school, which when it was founded and endowed in 1712, was known as the Free School. A native of Weedon, by the name of Nathaniel Billing, after the death of his wife, converted all his personal estate into money to provide 20 poor children of the village with the chance to be educated.

Alice Old was one of Weedon's oldest residents. Inscribed on her gravestone, which lies to the south of St Peter's church, is a list of six sovereigns throughout whose reigns she had lived, commencing with Elizabeth I and ending with William and Mary.

The Royal Military Depot was established here in 1803, when it was considered that as Weedon was situated in the heart of England, it would be a safe place for King George III and other members of the Royal Family to come to in the event of a French invasion. Also troops could be easily sent from here to any part of England. The barracks became redundant in 1965.

Weekley 🍃

The ancient village of Weekley lies just off the A43 main road which runs from Stamford in the north to Oxford in the south. It is much the same as it was 200 or more years ago. Originally the property of the Dukes of Montagu it has been owned by the Dukes of Buccleuch since 1767.

Boughton House, their Northamptonshire seat, can be seen spanning a 300 year old avenue from the main road half a mile north of the village.

On entering Weekley, the visitor leaves the A43, passing the post office-cum-tea shop (which provides a happy welcome to visitor and traveller alike). Close by, he will see The Old Vicarage – now a home for the elderly – designed by Sir Arthur Blomfield. On proceeding up Church Walk he will note the former village school which Nicholas Latham established in 1624. The building has also been used as the Estate Office. Opposite is the village hall which was built by the 3rd Duke of Buccleuch in the 18th century.

Close to the church is the Old Almshouse dating from the year 1611 – a really interesting and beautiful small house.

One of the entrances to Boughton Park, the scene of many activities, including local cricket matches, is close by.

An old statue called 'Stone Moses' once adorned the park but was transported many years ago to a field near the main road, where he now stands, wrapped in his stony thoughts.

The church is a little gem, in the main of the Perpendicular period; there are the monuments of the Montagu family at Boughton and the registers date back to the 16th century – an interesting entry is written in one of the later registers of a journey of Queen Victoria through the village in 1844.

All who come to the church are inspired by its beautiful setting and calm atmosphere. Also there is a timelessness about Weekley which is a tonic to visitors in this age of hustle and bustle.

Weldon 🍃

Once known as Weldon-in-the-Woods, the village has been the home of some notable people, amongst whom were the family of Basset. Baron Basset was one of the earliest possessors of the manor of Great Weldon and this family held the manor for many years.

In 1478, it was sold to Henry Colet, Alderman of London. It then passed into the hands of his son, John Colet, Dean of St Paul's and celebrated founder of St Paul's church. His mother Dame Christina also lived here for her lifetime. During the reign of Elizabeth I the manor passed into the hands of Sir Christopher Hatton.

George Jeffreys, born in 1610, was an organist of repute. He was a strong supporter of the Royalist cause. He became a member of the King's Musick, and in 1643 was appointed organist to King Charles I. After the siege of Oxford, Jeffreys returned to his home at Cumberford Place, Weldon. He served as steward to his patron Sir Christopher Hatton, and also spent much time composing music. He died at Weldon in July 1685.

One villager remembers attending the village school before the First World War: 'Built in 1817 it was a homely place. Large coal fires burned in each room during the winter. Boys, girls and infants each had their own separate entrance and lobby in which to hang coats. We sat in long backless desks. In my first year, we were given trays of sand and a kind of wooden skewer, with which to practise writing our letters. Later, we had a piece of thick cardboard on which we wrote with chalk. Bead frames were used for counting. Our main hand work was to lace together two pieces of leather with coloured laces. On Friday afternoon as a treat we were allowed to draw with coloured chalk on coarse paper. Later, when we went into the 'big room', we had to learn our tables, also learn and recite poetry.

'As this was a Church of England school, we had to be able to recite the Catechism, collects, psalms and chapters from the Bible. We attended needlework class once a week. Here we had to make calico underclothes, and knit socks. We were well taught in history, geography and map drawing, including maps of the main rivers and railways. We also had to know trades etc of towns through which these passed. The year before leaving part of Friday afternoons was given over to Hygiene, when we had to draw various parts of teeth and learn the care of them amongst other things. Perhaps our school life seems old-fashioned today, but we were well taught.'

Welford ✺

Even before the Domesday Book was produced in 1086, Welford was established. By 1274 there was a weekly Friday market, and the annual fair was held on the Feast of the Annunciation of the Blessed Virgin Mary, August 15th, and the two following days.

The church was once a chapel of ease of the nearby Sulby Abbey and the underground tunnel which supposedly joined the two is marked by strange 'echoing' sounds across the fields in its path. In 1968 great excitement was aroused when two brothers, Jack and Jim Vaughan, digging holes for posts for new fencing in a farmer's field, unearthed a small black object. They threw it on one side, but eventually took it home, cleaned it up and realised it was a piece of Church plate. Subsequently it was presented before a court who decided it was a 15th century chalice and declared it Treasure Trove. It is now in the British Museum and is known as the Welford Chalice.

In the stage coach days, Welford (being halfway between Leicester and Northampton) emerged as an important resting place, there being seven inns or coaching houses along the length of the present High Street. The canal and the railway both played their part in the development of the village, with the population fluctuating until we come to today, when again roads have become so important. The canal is also again popular – The Black Prince Canal Boat Hire having a depot at the end of the Welford Arm.

A school was established very early in the 18th century, which still caters for the infants and juniors of Welford and Sibbertoft. From 1951 until 1958 it was also the educational 'home' of some 60 to 70 Polish children. They were living in the Polish Camp situated on the old wartime airfield at Sulby. As the authorities realised that these children would never return to Poland their own airfield school was closed and they were sent to Welford school. They arrived being only able to give their names and their ages in English. So thereby hangs many a tale in the days that followed their first arrival – tales of care and patience, of misunderstanding and frustration, but eventually of a happy and integrated school until 1958 when the Polish Camp was closed.

Welton ᘓ

Welton is a charming residential hill-top village on the western edge of the county, close to the Warwickshire border. Its name is derived from the springs and wells in the locality.

The church, dedicated to St Martin, is situated up the steep winding hill, sheltered by the still rising hill to the west and north. Inside, the building is light and airy. The ancient tub-shaped font, reputed to be Saxon, is said to have been dragged from East Anglia in one piece. In 1899, inspired by the saintly Canon Lidel, five villagers carved the beautiful pulpit and the alms box, representing an open hand.

In the churchyard most of the gravestones have been thrown down and are now grassed over, soon to be lost for ever. One still standing marks the grave of a six year old boy found starved to death in 1806: its touching little verse at the base has now crumbled.

Welton Place was built in the 18th century, on a site selected by Joseph Clarke and his brother Richard. In the 19th century rare trees were planted on the hill behind the house and round the magnificent lake. Some of the cedars are still there, with the preservation order on them. The little garden flower clarkia is accredited to the Clarke family.

The estate was surrounded by lovely stone walls, some still standing – one with an archway leading to the church opposite. Welton Place was in the Clarke family for well over a century and was known to villagers as

'The Big House' and, of course, the head of the Clarke family was the squire of the village.

The mansion was let to Major and Mrs Garrard, who were the Crown Jewellers, and the family was often visited by members of the Royal Family. Later the building was converted into flats but, sadly, in 1974 it was demolished in favour of large detached houses which are still being built alongside the lake. On the land skeletons, Roman urns, copper, glass and many Roman coins were found.

Today some of the older houses are still in existence in the village, and over the years these have been added to by more modern dwellings of different periods and styles. Welton is a thriving community with many new families due to additional housing. Luckily there is still a primary school, with a children's adventure playground, a residential home for the elderly and two farms, all providing some local employment.

West Haddon 🦢

At the beginning of the 20th century West Haddon was very much a rural farming community with several public houses, various shops and tradesmen of all kinds, which made it more or less self-contained.

From the 1920s the nature of the village gradually changed, most noticeably in the 1930s when people left agricultural and horticultural work to take up jobs with the large manufacturing firms in Rugby, Coventry, Birmingham and Northampton. Excellent bus services were provided and travelling was comparatively easy. There were quite a few hardy folk who cycled back and forth to both Rugby and Northampton well into the 1930s. With the subsequent development and wider owner-ship of the motor car providing mobility, the village has become some-thing of a dormitory. The result of this has been expansion, and the village has seen the building of a considerable number of houses of all types.

Entrance to All Saints church is through a porch built in 1682 at the cost of the churchwardens of the time. This porch protects the door into the south aisle, which with its studs and ironwork has been there since the early 14th century. The church contains one of the rarest fonts in England. Near the south wall in the churchyard is an altar tomb of a distinguished vicar of West Haddon – Griggory Palmer. He was born in the village in January 1608 and was vicar from 1641 to 1693. The inscription on his tomb includes the words – 'He ended his life on the 11th day of June 1693 he being 85 years 5 months and odd days old'.

At the western end of the village are six almshouses, built in a block by a local benefactor in 1846. They were for six aged couples. He gave the adjoining three fields to be rented out so that the income from them would pay for repairs, any surplus being divided among the poor of the parish each Christmas time. The benefactor's sister added a striking clock which was mounted on the building at a cost of £50 in 1857. The clock was known locally as 'Chloe' and chimed the hours away day and night until a few years ago. It has now fallen silent, but it is still there to remind those around of its better days.

Legend has it that in a West Haddon field there was an eminence called Oster Hill, and under it were buried several officers of ancient times who fell in battle. At their interment a spear was stuck in the ground and to erect a monument the earth was raised level with the head of the spear. Also, according to legend, Oster Hill is the ancient tumulus of Ostorius Seapula, the celebrated Roman Governor under Emperor Claudius. It is evident he died in Britain but neither the exact place of his death nor his burial are recorded in history.

Weston-by-Welland 🌿

Weston-by-Welland lies below the north side of a ridge of land jutting into the valley of the river Welland. A visitor who wishes to enjoy a magnificent view, should walk a few yards up the bridle path which runs off the road at the top of the hill overlooking the village. From there he will see not only far into Northamptonshire, Leicestershire and Rutland, but also the village below, clustered around the church.

There are a mixture of buildings, some several hundred years old, some modern. Looking at the slow-flowing river, whose floods used to deposit rich silt every year on the fields, and at the rich grazing land feeding up the best beef in England, it is easy to guess why men have lived so long in these parts. Within a mile to the east of Weston, archaeologists have uncovered a Roman settlement, and below it evidence of human dwellings several hundred years earlier.

The first church was built in the 13th century. It was dedicated to St Mary and was rebuilt in 1866 in exact facsimile of the old building at the expense of the vicar, the Rev Samuel Danby, with the assistance of some of the better-off landowners. It is worthwhile using binoculars to view the carved heads on the battlements of the tower. Within it are five bells, the earliest dating from the 16th century. In the churchyard there are a number of interesting dark grey slate gravestones.

The vicars lived in a large house opposite the church. The Danby family followed son after father in the living, right into the 20th century. Weston does not now have a resident vicar and the house is a private dwelling.

In front of the church used to stand the village pond and to the east of it a mullion-windowed house. When it was demolished in 1966 a mural painting was discovered on plaster under the wallpaper. This dated from the 16th century and depicted a royal figure and her court.

On the east side of the church was a village green with a school beyond it, now a white private house. In 1873 this was replaced by a fine red stone and brick school and schoolmaster's house. By 1960 the numbers of children had fallen and so this school too closed and is now a private house.

The Wheel and Compass pub was in earlier times called the 'Carpenters Arms'. Originally a two storey stone building, it had a third storey added in the mid 19th century, it is thought, to cater for the Irish labourers who had come to build the railway. The advent of the railway changed the lives of the villagers. People became more mobile and more goods could be brought into the village. The station was about one mile from Weston and remains of the track can still be seen to the north of the village.

Whilton & Whilton Locks

The church clock at Whilton is Elizabethan and is peculiar in that the dial has only four minutes marked to each five minute interval. As this dial has not been altered since first installed it may indicate that the inhabitants of Whilton have always been able to tolerate a little wayward behaviour!

This tolerance may have been rather strained, however, by the terms of the will of one of their more eccentric rectors – Langton Freeman. In his will of 1783 he gave the following instructions. 'For four or five days after my decease and till my body grows offensive I would not be removed out of the place or bed I shall die on and then I would be carried and laid on the same bed decently and privately in the summerhouse in the garden ... and to be wrapped in a strong double winding sheet and ... to be interred as near as may be to the description we receive of our Saviour's burial. The door and windows to be locked ... the summer-house be planted round with evergreen plants and fenced with iron or oak panels and painted dark blue'. The summerhouse has disappeared and no one knows what later became of the Rev Langton Freeman. Perhaps his spirit still haunts the garden of what is now known as the Manor House.

Whilton has a long history of adapting to change resulting from its geographical position. Almost the centre of the country, it has two Roman roads passing through the parish and gained its first importance as a Roman settlement and staging post on the Watling Street running from London to Holyhead. This road remains a major trunk road but now there is the M1 running parallel, and with its more modern service area adjacent. The Grand Union Canal, constructed in the 1780s, also runs parallel as does the London to Birmingham railway built in the 1860s.

Nowadays, although all trace of the original manor has been lost, Whilton still possesses a number of pleasant older houses, a cob cottage and a picturesque church. The mill ceased to function in living memory. One of the smaller stone houses of 1689 is said to contain floorboards made from the doors of the old prison in Northampton. It was sold in the

Depression in 1932 for a sow and a litter of pigs! Practically all the older houses seem at one time or another to have served as shops, or tradesmen's dwellings. In 1777 the main occupations related to the wool trade – wool combing, spinning, weaving and framework knitting, and shoemaking. In the 19th and early 20th century it was almost a self-contained community with butcher, slaughterhouse, bakehouse, alehouses, wheelwrights, blacksmith, carpenter and undertakers, carriers, dressmakers and lacemaker, not to mention the school.

The school began in 1768 in a farm and buildings left by Jonathan Emery an ancestor of a family still farming in the village. £500 and 11 acres of land went with the bequest and a later benefactor Mrs John Worsfold in 1815 gave money which purchased 15 acres of land: – 'to instruct the poor children of the parish in reading, writing, casting of accounts, the church catechism and the principles of the Christian religion'. These wills seem a distinct improvement on that of Langton Freeman. Sadly the school which at one time had 69 pupils closed in 1955 with only 14 children attending. Now we have over 50 children in the village, those of school age being taken by bus to other villages. The schoolhouse has reverted to being a private dwelling but the school room has become the Village Hall and some at least of its original intentions continue.

Whilton Locks is a thriving community with cottage industries such as potters, a garden centre, numerous smallholdings and a marina.

Whilton Locks gains its name from the flight of locks on the Grand Union Canal. In days gone by Whilton Locks boasted a pub, The Spotted Cow, a blacksmith, a grocery and lime kilns. One bargee, John Woodward, used to keep donkeys as well as horses to pull barges. Apparently, he never swore and was known as 'the beautiful man and his donkeys'.

But by far Whilton Locks' best claim to fame is that it is thought to be the site of the birthplace of St Patrick of Ireland. During the Roman occupation, in the fields where Whilton Lodge now stands, was once a Roman settlement, known as 'Bannaventa' and it is here that the infant Patrick is said to have been born, subsequently going to Cornwall and then to Ireland. Excavations have revealed Samian ware and coins at Bannaventa but unfortunately the site has now been ploughed.

Whittlebury ꙮ

Four miles from Towcester and seven miles from Buckingham stands Whittlebury, on the A413. Travelling from Silverstone, Whittlebury is seen to dominate the ridge of a hill. It is a small village steeped in history, with a mixed friendly population of approximately 500.

Several Iron Age and Roman sites lay within part of Whittlewood Forest, which skirted the village. Following her last battle against the

Romans, Queen Boadicea is reputed to have been buried in Whittlewood Forest.

Much to his surprise one villager, enlarging his garden path, came across a shallow grave containing a Roman skeleton. As it was obvious that a Christian burial had taken place, the Rev Peter Townsend, in May 1983, reburied the remains in St Mary's churchyard.

Excavations in a stone-pit in 1850 discovered the remains of buildings. One contained at least twelve rooms and a bath suite. The mosaic pavement was a striking design of red and white. The second building lay to the north of the site and had two mosaic floors.

Stag's Head House, built in 1834, is situated on the corner of High Street and Church Way; a house once loved by housewives, for this was the bakery. On Sunday these ladies would take their joints of beef etc there to be roasted, whilst they went to church. Imagine the aroma at that corner! At that time this small village could boast of two butchers, two public houses, two shops, a post office, a bakery, a smithy and a doctor's surgery.

The church stands in a good position along Church Way. The tower is of the 13th century and the first priest was recorded in 1232. In the early 19th century Lord Southampton had the church chancel repaired, new pews provided and built on the vestry.

Two houses beyond the school stands Whittlebury Methodist chapel, dated 1763. John Wesley preached on 20 occasions at Whittlebury. According to his journal he first preached 'To a truly loving and simple people. I preached at the side of the new preaching house. I suppose most of the town were present.' The pulpit is the original one from which John Wesley preached.

Whittlebury Lodge, a stately looking building set in extensive grounds with lake and deer park, was built for Lord Southampton in the mid 1800s and most of the villagers were employed as domestics, gardeners, gamekeepers etc.

When the Lee family owned the Lodge village activities such as church fetes and flower shows took place there. The cricket field by the side of the house was the envy of people for miles around. The now famous Edrich brothers, in their early days, were often seen playing with the locals. In the winter rich and poor alike enjoyed skating on the lake and a close community spirit always existed. The Lodge and grounds is now converted into 31 homes.

Wicken 🐿

A typical Northamptonshire village, first mentioned in the Domesday Book. Between 1218 and 1282 it was divided into two parishes, named Wyke Dyve and Wyke Hamon, the brook running through the village being the boundary line.

There were two churches, St James's in Wyke Hamon and St John's in Wyke Dyve. The present St John's replaced a cedar wood church with a thatched roof. This was in Water Slade Lane and is shown on a map of 1616. The work on St John's church was completed in 1770. The two parishes had been re-united in 1587 and called Wicken. Every year since then, on Ascension Day, this has been celebrated, and there has never been a break in this tradition.

In the early 1800s Wicken Park was bought by Sir John Mordaunt, who sold it to Lord Penryhn in 1860. It is now a private school.

As well as the manor, there are four Tudor houses in the parish of Wicken. One was built by Sir John Mordaunt at Wicken Park, one is at Cross Tree Road, and one is next to the blacksmith's shop, probably built by the family farming Sparrow Lodge Farm. The one opposite the post office was firstly a hospital, then a prison, and for 150 years was the village bakehouse.

The village has changed a great deal, with new houses built and such places as the post office, bakehouse and the old forge becoming dwelling houses, but Wicken still retains the old-world atmosphere of a country village.

Gateway to Wicken church

Wilbarston 🦢

The village was once part of the Rockingham estate. It is surrounded by farmland, truly green and pleasant; mostly worked by local farmers, although some land has been retained by Rockingham Estates, as the castle stands but five miles away. It nestles in the picturesque Welland valley in an area formerly covered by Rockingham Forest.

The 12th century church of All Saints is worthy of a visit to see the unusual painted ceiling and beautifully carved oak screen. Close by is the 17th century Old House, where the ghosts of Sir George and a nun are reputed to have appeared after the removal of certain gravestones. Since the Bishop of Peterborough used the house as a robing room in 1973, the ghosts have not been seen! This house was formerly the rectory when Wilbarston had its own curate.

The Church of England village school founded in 1845 continues to thrive, now taking children from several villages in the Welland valley. The boundary wall between the school and The Old House is an ancient dovecote.

Another interesting feature is the number of springs under the village keeping the many wells constantly supplied. These were in use up to the introduction of piped water in 1957. Some pumps and wells are still operational.

Some years ago the village had three pubs and many shops which catered for everyone's needs, but now there is only one village store, which is also a post office. The one remaining pub has been greatly improved and refurbished. Of the two former bakehouses, only one remains (now a private house).

Wilbarston has always been a caring village. Indeed in 1791 Robert Swan gave 11s a year to the poor and 3s 4d for an annual sermon. This was later known as 'Swan's Charity', with £2 being donated for the purchase of 'red flannel', given alternate years to elderly ladies and gentlemen of the parish. Later, every four years, elderly residents were chosen to receive a pair of towels. Today, existing charities have been amalgamated to form Wilbarston Relief in Need Charity. In addition to this, the WI now runs a Community Care Scheme.

The modern community hall caused comment in *Punch* when the winning entry in the 'Name the village hall' competition, provided the name 'The Village Hall'!

The Parish Council at Wilbarston is believed to be the first in the area to introduce its own quarterly news-sheet for circulation to every household. Known as the Wilbarston Chronicle, it contains information regarding bus times, new houses and roads, news from the Parish Council Meetings and reports from every club and group in the village. It is a veritable fount of local news with humorous as well as serious articles. It is produced and edited by the villagers.

The year ends with a British Legion Dance and at the stroke of midnight, youngsters carry on a recently instituted custom of beating 'The Drum' round the village, returning to the Fox Inn where it is now housed. Older than this tradition, the drum was made in Victoria's reign and was formerly played in the village jazz band. In addition to this proud possession is a set of handbells which was donated many, many years ago by the people of the village. These are now in the care of the Parish Council.

Wilby ✤

Wilby is a village of about 700 inhabitants, situated two miles from Wellingborough on the A4500.

The village has developed ribbon fashion on either side of the road, with council housing and a private development at the bottom of the hill, leading uphill to small terraced properties, then on to the older part of the village. Here there are stone-built properties, two farmhouses and two public houses. The larger houses include Wilby House, an attractive Georgian dwelling, commanding splendid views over the adjoining fields.

The church stands in an elevated position in Church Lane. The architecture dates from Early English to a fine and most attractive 16th century tower and spire, with an octagonal lantern with four flying buttresses. The tower houses a light ring of six bells. The school stands next to the church, and the original building dates from 1854, but it has been extended.

There is only one farm left now in the village, and the one shop in the village is also the post office. The two public houses almost opposite one another are the Horse-Shoe, which at some time had been the black-smith's shop, and the George Inn, a larger building of dressed stone. There is also a working men's club.

Wilby Park was the site of the Wilby Lido, which in the 1930s to 1950s had an outdoor swimming pool and changing rooms. They were demolished in the 1960s, and the site developed as a mobile homes park.

There is a legend about the Wilby witch, whose name was Kate, and she lived with her husband Tom, a woodman. On more than one occasion when Tom sat down to eat his mid-day meal, he found his food had been stolen. This began to worry him, as he found no trace of man or beast, until he began to suspect his own black cat. One day he saw the cat slinking away from his belongings, so he decided to take action. The next day he lay in wait and caught his cat stealing his food, so quick as lightning he took up his axe and chopped off one of his cat's paws. When he got home that evening, he found his wife Kate in a dreadful state – one of her hands was missing, chopped off at the wrist!

Wilby as a community has suffered from being built alongside a very busy main road. For many years the villagers had to endure the noise and danger of an intolerable load of traffic thundering through the village. In November 1981, the new A45 was opened and the present road down-graded. There is now a weight limit on vehicles travelling through, but it is still a busy road.

Winwick

Winwick is a very pleasant village, with the lofty tower of its medieval church looking down upon neat and tidy houses and gardens, spreading out to the south-east. It would be difficult to find a village more truly rural in the whole of the county. It has no shop, no public house, no village hall, no school, no public rooms or post office. Residents in need of the services these absent offices would provide must travel elsewhere.

There was a school from 1846 to the late 1940s. A tablet on the building which was formerly the school reads – 'Erected by the Rev J. A. Jeremie Rector 1946'. The building now forms part of a private residence.

The church, dedicated to St Michael and All Angels, dates from the 13th century, but considerable restoration was carried out during the 19th century. The church possesses a fine old barrel organ which dates from the 1840s. The registers date back to 1567. For some years during the 17th century there were more marriages in Winwick church than there were bachelors and spinsters in the parish! It seems to have been a kind of Gretna Green for runaway couples in Northamptonshire.

Near the church is a charming 16th century mansion which of recent years has been subject to alterations and modification and today forms four separate residences. From the distant past until the 1960s the manor house with its land and nearby farm had been the mainstay of the village; in fact a number of the houses were erected in the 1920s to accommodate staff and workers employed by the manor house and its farm. In the 1930s the farm was one of the most modern and up-to-date in the county and was much admired as such.

According to information posted in the Church porch – 'Sir Thomas Malory author of *Le Morte d'Arthur* was Lord of the Manor at Winwick. *Le Morte d'Arthur* was printed by Caxton (the first English printer) in 1470. It is the forerunner of the poem by Tennyson, *The Idylls of the King*, and other books and films about the Knights of the Round Table.'

Wollaston

When Wollaston first developed it grew along a 'line'. This started at Cobbs Lane and continued past the 'clusters' of Bell End at one end and Rotten Row/St Michael's Lane at the other end of the High Street, and continued towards Strixton. The name of Wollaston comes from Wulflaf's Town, Wulflaf being an early Saxon.

The oldest part of the village is Beacon Hill, which is an ancient castle earthwork which belonged to Bury Manor, and which used to be called Mill Hill. It was surrounded by a great ditch which, when investigated, was found to date back to the 12th century.

In 1260, Wollaston was granted a charter by Henry III to hold an annual fair. This was probably held at Michaelmas (September/October) and was held in St Michael's Lane, which is no doubt how it derived its name.

The first school was opened in Wollaston in 1842. This was held in the building adjacent to The Cuckoo, opposite Bell End, and was a private school, in that it was run by the curate, Rev J. J. Scott, out of his own funds. The school was not government controlled until 1873. The building was then bought by the Keep family, and the school was held in the parochial rooms in College Street (then called Backway).

The lovely mottled red/orange bricks around Wollaston no doubt came from the two brickyards in Wollaston itself (one along the Grendon Road, near Cringle Farm, and the other where the industrial estate now exists). If you look closely, you can see that the patterns of the courses are different from the way houses are built today; some have a chequerboard effect, some look striped. Another interesting feature is the way bricks are laid according to the lie of the land; if the land sloped, the wall sloped too. This is particularly noticeable when walls have been recently repaired. The repair will be level whilst the rest of the wall will be at an angle.

The High Street was at one time cobbled and this is sometimes visible when the road starts to wear at the edge. The smithy (or forge) was located opposite the Methodist church and part of it can still be seen.

Woodford

Woodford is situated on the A604 between Kettering and Thrapston, with a population of about 1,200.

The lovely church of St Mary the Virgin stands majestically by the river Nene. Inserted in one of the pillars on the north side of the nave is a glass case containing the remains of a human heart, found during restoration work to the column in 1867. There are many theories about whose heart it is and one story is that it belonged to a gallant knight killed on the Crusades, whose heart was returned to the village by his friends. It was possibly the heart of one of the Traillys, lord of the manor 700 years ago.

There is only one chapel now – the Baptist chapel that was formed in the early 1820s and today has a strong following. There was also a Methodist chapel but that closed in the 1970s.

Like all small villages at the turn of the century Woodford was self-sufficient in trade and industry. One of the major industries was mining.

There was ironstone mining, limestone pits and furnaces. All of these industries employed a number of men from Woodford, Twywell, Slipton and Islip. The work was hard, but there were happenings on the lighter side. One of these was the way the men earned a little extra cash. Horses were used down the pits and the men grew mushrooms on the manure. Twice a week the mushrooms were taken to Covent Garden and sold. The money was then divided between the men.

Later in the 1930s and 1940s Woodford had two bakehouses and two fish and chip shops, one of which had a bad fire when the pans set on fire. There was also an undertaker who made coffins in the shed in the yard of his house.

Cobbling was also a busy trade. One or two people mended shoes in their own homes, but Mr Cyril Wilson had a shop on the green where he not only mended shoes but made them as well. He used to make the boots for the men working in the furnaces. There was also a blacksmith's, which has now been converted into a private home for the elderly.

In 1887 Wallis and Linnell, Clothiers opened a factory in Newtown Street and later Ideal Clothiers of Wellingborough did likewise. Both factories employed men and women, from Woodford and surrounding villages. In 1925 Wallis and Linnels formed their own ladies football team. They played a charity match with Kettering on Peterborough Football Ground. Woodford won 1 – 0. Miss Dorothy Clipstone took a penalty and kicked the ball so hard she broke the netting!

Woodford is not the bustling village it once was. The mines have long gone and the factories closed a few years ago. However, Wallis and Linnels' factory is used for another industry and the old infants school is used for a closing room. All the small individual trades have gone and people have taken their custom to nearby towns, but there are still three very good shops which all sell a good range of merchandise.

Woodford Halse

Woodford, Hinton and Farndon are all mentioned in the Domesday Book as separate villages but nowadays they rejoice in the grand title of Woodford-cum-Membris for parochial business or Woodford Halse, and one cannot tell where Hinton ends and Woodford Halse begins. Yet it was not always so, for there is a manor house in both parts and no doubt life went quietly on until the 19th century when the railway came.

It must have seemed unbelievable to the sleepy inhabitants – land, and indeed whole farms, were bought up by the railway, bridges were built, railway banks and cuttings were made, itinerant workers, many rough and uncouth, arrived living in squalid camps and working like slaves until the line was completed. Then houses, shops and churches had to be built for the railway workers. Woodford has four churches – Church of England, Moravian, Roman Catholic and Methodist, for this had become a prosperous place with the trains rattling through day and night and everyone in the village relying on them for their livelihood.

The railway brought visitors too. The Gorse, now a thriving social club, was built as a hunting box where gentlemen could stay and keep their horses when hunting with the well known Midlands packs of hounds.

Two World Wars came and went with the loss of many lives but Woodford continued to prosper until the time of Dr Beeching in the 1960s. The station and the Great Central Line were axed, and a deathly silence descended on Woodford. The village was a ghost of its former self. It was a dark period in the history of Woodford, but places that have existed since Norman times are not easily destroyed and like a phoenix rising from the ashes, Woodford gradually began to rise again.

The railway will never be forgotten by Woodford men. There is a Railway Club where they gather to reminisce or watch slides of the good old days of steam. Station Court is a block of flats for the elderly with a resident warden, and there is a small amount of light industrial units situated at Great Central Way. New houses are being built, for with the new M40 situated near Banbury, Woodford will be as easily accessible from Birmingham, Coventry and London as it was in the age of the train, and prosperity is gradually creeping back.

The old blends in with the new, the stone houses with their lovely mullioned windows and the brick of the newly built ones. The river Cherwell, which is still in its infancy here, bubbles happily along and forgets that the railway altered its course. New young trees have been planted on the railway bank and bulbs have been planted by the WI and other organisations throughout the village.

Yardley Gobion

The village of Yardley Gobion lies near the southern tip of the county of Northamptonshire; to the east it is flanked by the Grand Union Canal and the river Tove whilst to the west there are open fields to the A5.

Until 1947 the village was virtually only the High Street, Moor End Road, Chestnut Road and Grafton Road, with a sympathetic mixture of stone or brick, thatched or slated houses. The council estate (built in 1947) was followed by two private estates in the late 1960s which, with the limited infill development since then, has expanded the village to about 450 dwellings and a population of around 1,400. Apart from farming there is little or no employment in the village.

The Anglican church, St Leonard's, is relatively modern, having been built in 1864 by the Duke of Grafton, who added a clock over the porch in 1889. However, a church dedicated to St Leonard existed in former times on the site of what is now 1 High Street, with the churchyard on the land adjoining the High Street/Grafton Road bend. Between times and for those who eschewed High Church, a United Reformed chapel was built in 1826 overlooking Chestnut Green; regular services are still held. Within St Leonard's there is a lectern dedicated to eight Canadian airmen whose aircraft crashed on the outskirts of the village (between the High Street and the new bypass) in 1944.

No. 1 High Street was formerly The Pack Horse pub before its conversion to residential use. The older villagers can remember when there were four pubs and five shops; today, despite the vastly increased population, there is only one pub (The Coffee Pot) and three shops. The village also had two blacksmiths (one at 7 High Street and the other at The Coffee Pot), but these have also gone with the changing times.

In the early 1900s there were two bakehouses in the village, at what are now 21 High Street and 16 Moor End Road. There were also several wells but none are currently in use. The last public well (on Elm Green) originally supplied the village pump, which was also given by the Duke of Grafton in 1889. This well was capped with concrete and grassed over when the County Council levelled the green (and took away the remains of the old tree after which it was named) in the early 1970s.

When Orchard Close (a small housing development off the High Street) was being built in 1968, post-medieval pottery kilns were found on the site together with large quantities of 18th century slate. Further finds of kilns show that from the 14th century Yardley Gobion had a substantial pottery industry. In 1973 two more kilns were found off the Grafton Road north of the village and in 1978 yet more kilns were found in the Moor End Road near 'Highcroft'; all were dated as late 14th or early 15th century.

On the outskirts but forming part of the village is Moor End, first mentioned in 1304. In 1347, Thomas de Ferrers was given licence by Edward III to build a castle, tower, moat and bridge. However, in 1363 the land reverted to the Crown before the castle was completed in 1369. The castle (and its Manor) were last recorded in 1541 although the site is still marked on OS maps and Moor End Manor Farm still flourishes. During the Civil War, Moor End was taken from the Crown by the Parliamentary Party but was reclaimed by the Crown during the Restoration of Charles II. In turn, Charles II gave it to his son, the 1st Duke of Grafton, and it remained with his heirs until the breakup of the Grafton Estate in 1919–1920.

Near Potterspury Lodge School but within the parish of Yardley Gobion (just beyond Moor End) is the famous Queen's Oak; here, Elizabeth Woodville (or Wideville as it was then spelt) first met King Edward IV whom she later married on 1st May 1464 at Grafton Regis, about one and a half miles north of Yardley Gobion. Their children were the ill-fated 'Princes in the Tower'.

Yardley Hastings ⚜️

The woods of Yardley Hastings are situated in the ancient Hundred of Wymersley, mentioned in the Domesday Book. Names dating back to 1325 slip off the tongue of the old folk – Roundhae, Colliers Herne, Ferne Hills, Rollpytt, Spotloe, Church Slade, Grymsee and Allness, 613 acres of coppice planted with great trees.

The undergrowth was used for faggots for fuel, hedging, hurdle-making, sheep crib-making and thatching spars. Farmers had the right to cut undergrowth for their own use. Oak was sawn into planks, poorer quality for fencing posts and rails, bark for tanning. Ash trees made wagons, cartframes, wheels, horse collars, handles for scythes and crooks.

The 6th Marquess of Northampton ordered the felling of the remaining mature oaks and leased 850 acres to the Forestry Commission. The Ministry of Supply requisitioned 537 acres of Yardley Chase for the storing of ammunition, a legacy from the First World War. The forest was gradually converted to High Forest with many species of pine – Scots, Corsican, Norway spruce, Western red cedar, Silver fir inter-mingled with beech, poplar, birch and elm.

Several dramatic events took place within the secluded woods. In 1840, three young men planned a poaching trip after a day's harvesting and a drinking session in the Rose and Crown public house. They carried guns and shot a hare but were surprised by John Dunkley, a keeper, who accosted them. A shot was fired and the keeper lay dying. The men crossed fields and hid the weapon near the Old Iron Tollgate on Wilmer Hill. Later they were arrested and deported to Australia.

One day the foresters had a terrible scare when the highly dangerous war weapons and gelignite exploded, breaking the brickwork surrounding the arsenal but leaving the roof intact.

The whole village of Yardley Hastings was alarmed when a German parachutist was discovered and captured by Len Smith and Percy Keggin in October 1940. His parachute and wireless transmitter were found at Hollowell planting. When handed over to the police, he had £100 in English money and a false identity card.

The village remembers the famous oaks of Yardley. Cowper's Oak (burnt and gone), where the poet was inspired to write 'Thou was a bauble once, a cup and ball', and the Gog and Magog of William the Conqueror's reign, struck by lightning so that only a shell remains.

Yarwell 🐟

Yarwell is an ancient and historical small village on the eastern edge of Northamptonshire. It is approached from the east over the Swallow brook, which is the parish boundary. The village itself lies about half a mile above the bank of the river Nene and the grey stone houses may be seen nestling around the square-towered church. The view of this section of the river is much appreciated by local people and visitors alike.

As part of Rockingham Forest, there are some remnants of the original woodland, which yield a wealth of wild flowers. There are many interesting walks, which are much appreciated by local people who have had to fight hard to protect their heritage against the ravages of the bulldozer. The underlying ground contains sought-after building stone and there was a plan to turn a disused quarry into an international motor cycle rallying track, or a rubbish dump for the towns close by.

All around there is evidence of old limestone quarries and the village had many stonemasons among its residents, especially in the latter part of the 19th century. The name Ireson is still well known locally and Mr W Ireson, the last of the old stonemasons, died in 1971 aged 91. Most of the houses are built of the local stone and roofed with Collyweston slates. The last of the small thatched houses have either been pulled down or altered and extended.

The Methodist chapel opened in 1840 and is still flourishing, although many around have been closed. The church school opened in 1874 and was used until 1961 when it was decided to bus the children to the larger villages or towns. The closing of the school affected life in the village as there are very few children around in the daytime and the May Day festivities are no longer held. The increase in motor traffic has successfully driven away the old street games, but the children do have use of a four acre playing field and a very useful village hall.

Central to the old village is the 13th century church dedicated to St Mary Magdalene. Yarwell has always been linked to nearby Nassington ecclesiastically, with a vicar at Nassington and a curate for Yarwell, but the two were linked together in 1920.

In the chancel can be seen a handsome black marble tombstone to Sir Humphrey Bellamy, merchant, dated 1715. The local folk legend has it that Humphrey was a poor boy on his way to London to join his uncle and make his fortune. He was taken ill on the way and the kind people of Yarwell took him in and looked after him. When he was better and able to continue his journey he vowed that he would never forget their kindness.

He did make his fortune and his body was brought back to the little church to be buried. He left money to provide bread for the poor, to be put on his tombstone on St Thomas's Day. In common with Dick Whittington Sir Humphrey's uncle was also a fishmonger. The money

Old cottages in Yelvertoft

was amalgamated with other charities and modern research tends to discount this story, but the village likes to believe it is true.

The village still retains its friendly spirit, perhaps because it is small. Although the number of houses has grown to 100, the population is still under 250. It is lucky to still have a post office and general store and there is one remaining public house, the Angel.

Yelvertoft

Yelvertoft is not a conventionally pretty village, but the cottages which line the main street have a charm of their own. Some of them are right on the pavement, others stand back, while 19th century cottages butt up against Georgian farmhouses. The four main lanes run at right angles to the main street, and their names are reminders of long-past farmers – Ward's, Tarry's, Swinnerton's and Ashwell's.

The brooks which run along the lanes seem innocent enough, but whenever there is sufficiently heavy rain the village is liable to flooding. It is still an agricultural community and you are quite likely to meet cows, sheep or the odd pig in the village streets.

Life in the 1920s and 1930s seems in retrospect so much more peaceful. In the early years of the century the wharf on the Grand Union Canal was still busy and the horse and trap remained the only means of land transport for a long time after that. There were two bakers, a blacksmith, a grocer, a butcher and three inns. A traveller would come from Northampton with other items and it was also possible to order goods through the carrier from Rugby. The manor owned little land around the village and there was therefore no 'squire' in the village.

Yelvertoft is a friendly village, still with its two village greens. The church is along the main street towards West Haddon, at the opposite end of the village to the Victorian school and the village hall.

In 1887 the village celebrated Queen Victoria's Golden Jubilee. When all the bills were paid for the day of revelry and sports, enough money was left over to buy three lime trees. Rev Jenkins planted one on the green in the centre of the village, Rev Parkins of the Congregational church planted one on the green opposite the reading room, and Mr Elkins, a local gentleman, planted one beside the school. They stand today as links with the villagers of the past.

St. Mary's
Duddington

Bettina Smith

Index